Stairwell 7

The City

&

Society

a series of books edited by **GERALD D. SUTTLES**
University of Chicago

Stairwell

Family Life in the Welfare State

7

Neil C. Sandberg

S SAGE PUBLICATIONS   Beverly Hills   London

For information address:

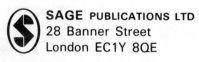

SAGE PUBLICATIONS, INC.
275 South Beverly Drive
Beverly Hills, California 90212

SAGE PUBLICATIONS LTD
28 Banner Street
London EC1Y 8QE

Printed in the United States of America

Library of Congress Cataloging in Publication Data

Sandberg, Neil C
    Stairwell 7 : family life in the welfare state.

    (The City and society ; v. 3)
    Includes bibliographical references.
    1. Columbia, Md.—Social conditions.
2. Columbia, Md.—Poor—Case studies. 3. Welfare recipients—Maryland—Columbia—Case studies.
4. Public welfare—Maryland—Columbia. I. Title.
II. Series.
HN80.C69S25   362.8'2   78-6481
ISBN 0-8039-0969-1
ISBN 0-8039-0970-5 pbk.

FIRST PRINTING

CONTENTS

TO MARY AND CURT

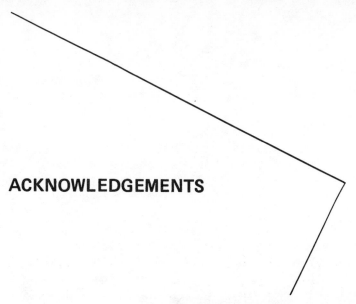

ACKNOWLEDGEMENTS

A number of prominent social scientists were extremely helpful in the development of this book. I am particularly grateful to Margaret Mead and Herbert Gans for their important suggestions on the treatment of the data.

The insights and understanding of my editor, Gerald Suttles, were invaluable. I am also indebted to Nathan Glazer for his helpful comments on the analysis of the data and to Daniel Elazar for his thoughtful and perceptive preface. The American Jewish Committee deserves special appreciation for the research sabbatical and logistical support that made the project possible. I am, of course, solely responsible for the conclusions presented in this volume.

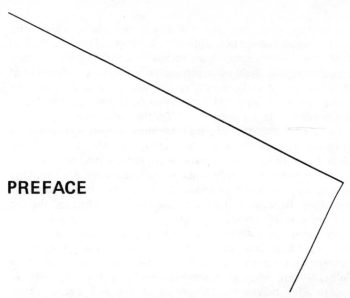

PREFACE

Neil Sandberg has written a compelling, enlightening, and sad book. It is compelling in that the people whose lives are documented within it represent a certain kind of cross-section of American society down on their luck who both reinforce certain stereotypes and break many myths about that segment of American society which utilizes the country's welfare system. It is enlightening because it not only gives us insight into their lives and thoughts but does so by confronting so many of those myths. It is sad because the people in *Stairwell 7* are living illustrations of the limits of the welfare state.

In his analysis of cases, Sandberg describes a higher class of welfare client than those at the bottom of the heap. After all, they were screened and placed in a project designed for people who were potentially capable of being restored to independence and, indeed, one family, the Corbins, was so restored. Yet it is clear from the book that the other families are not likely to make it out of the morass in which they find themselves. Therein lies the sadness. Nor are they likely to adjust to dependency in their own minds, however habituated to it they become in fact.

Every society has had such people within it. But only with the advent of mass society, with the breakdown of community and the concentration of such people in such great numbers that they become essentially isolated from the rest of the social fabric, have we had the problem which Sandberg portrays.

Indeed, this book deals with families one step removed from older forms of community, at least in their own recollection. It deals with a project that was designed to remedy the deficiencies caused by the breakdown of those forms by the creation of new ones, and it documents how the new forms have failed to emerge, much less take root, under the conditions prevailing in Underhill. The reader will not be surprised to learn of that failure. It could hardly be otherwise given the circumstances: the heterogeneity of the people involved at one level and their homogeneity on another; the diversity of ethnic, racial and regional backgrounds, yet the sameness of their inability to cope with the contemporary world. On the one hand they came to Underhill with their hostilities, latent or manifest. On the other, they came alone without the strength of those among their families, friends and neighbors who have been able to cope, to assist them in their own efforts. In all likelihood, the older forms of community have disappeared from the American scene "for good," at least for most Americans, but this reader is left with the clear impression that, even if they cannot be recreated, no substitute for them is in the offing. Thus the welfare state will continue to try to fill the gap and will do so imperfectly and at high cost.

Perhaps more than most Americans, the people of Underhill and those like them are the products and victims of mass society. At every turn, Americans have chosen to defeat the possibilities for community on behalf of the "goods" of mass society, whether its material rewards or the personal freedom it seems to offer individuals. The people of *Stairwell 7* stand as reminders to all of us that liberty has its price, equality its problems, and that even in matters humanitarian there is no such thing as a free lunch.

Daniel J. Elazar
Bar-Ilan and
Temple Universities

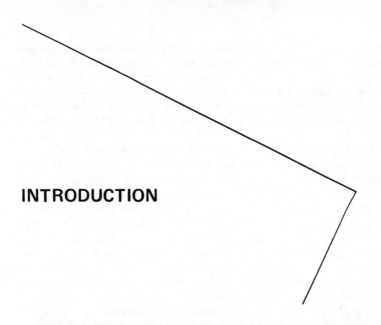

INTRODUCTION

Since the publication of Oscar Lewis' *in situ* case studies of the poor, the examination and explanation of poverty has become a central preoccupation of sociologists and public policy makers. The books published on the topic must number in the hundreds and the articles are practically uncountable. Yet in my reading of this literature, there have been very few efforts which genuinely seek to retrace Lewis' steps and provide a rich, descriptive account of family life among the poor. Despite its heavy debt to Lewis' work, the sociology of poverty is overwhelmingly a "theoretical literature" in which competing ideas are juxtaposed to one another in the absence of much descriptive data, especially the sort of data that Lewis himself sought to draw upon to understand "the culture of poverty." A mountain of theoretical conjecture dominates a molehill of empirical findings.

There are, of course, some exeptions[1] but, by and large, debate has settled down to a sterile face-off between structural and cultural interpretations of poverty. Both approaches tend to caricature the poor themselves and the situation they face. Typically each interpretation moves to the polar extreme of one or another determinism; cultural determinism or structural determinism. Such a debate fits easily within existing political ideologies but neither polemic provides a very adequate sociology of poverty.

A fair reading of Lewis' work moves us in a very different direction. In his descriptive work Lewis did not seek to "explain poverty" but to demonstrate that under the most fateful conditions the poor were able to contrive a style of life of their own rather than the one dictated to them by circum-

1. Such as Howells, *Hard Living on Clay Street*.

stances. Circumstances might inflict poverty, but they could not restrain the inventive powers of the poor themselves. What Lewis saw was a chronic unwillingness of the poor to accept public definitions of their circumstances and a persistent tendency to innovate with the materials left them. The importance of voluntarism and individual inventiveness in Lewis' work has been lost in that of his followers, or for that matter, from the work of his critics.

Neil Sandberg brings these issues back to life and puts them into the foreground. He does so by adopting the research strategy of the close-grained case study. A few families, intimately known, speaking in their own language provide the bulk of the work. After reading these accounts one cannot fail to recognize the variability in how people respond to poverty, how they seek to escape it or contend with it; how they are frustrated by the American welfare state and, at the same time attempt to manipulate the welfare state; how they disclaim their poverty and at the same time employ their poverty to lay claim to a special status; and how they keep searching for a collective definition of their poverty while also making of themselves an exception. What one is struck by is not the determinism of culture or situation, but persistent improvisation. Indeed the general pattern is not one of group solidarity or cultural consensus, but of extensive exploration. People explore their past to find either an explanation for their poverty or a reason for why they are treated as the disreputable poor. They explore the welfare system for signs of weakness or the hope of launching new careers. They explore local relations in the hope of finding friends and, if not friends, then somebody they can "use." They are neither structural puppets nor cultural incorrigibles. Essentially they are improvisors; people who keep trying to find a niche for themselves on a narrow ledge.

Appropriately Sandberg has selected for study not the fatally poor that Lewis focused his attention on, but the near poor who make up such a large proportion of those who must improvise. In their "layer cake" image of social structure sociologists have found a neat, compelling and seemingly permanent way of describing total societies. In this image the poor are always poor. But in the real world people move in and out of poverty, and in the course of their journey they often move a considerable distance—in both directions. Real life, then, is far more mixed than we would be led to think by a "stratification theory" which alone gives people permanent statuses. This movement adds to the ambivalence felt by the poor and the mixture of strategies they may adopt in coping with poverty. It is especially difficult to talk about the "community of the poor" as if it were a persistent entity. Where racial or ethnic boundaries coincide with poverty, some kind of community may be formed; but shared poverty alone seems to encourage improvisation rather than a uniform culture or political unity. Thus it is not too surprising that the near poor in America scatter their political preferences and their claims for economic membership. Put simply, so many of them are transients that class solidarity alone is uncompelling.

What Sandberg emphasizes is that the most uniform experience of the poor is their encounter with the American welfare state. That experience is in large part a chronic confusion. It could hardly be otherwise. The U.S. welfare system has grown to monstrous proportions, making it a welfare state comparable in expenditures to the more admired ones of Northern Europe. Yet it remains an extremely fragmented set of units—not really a system—but a multiplicity of programs for different poor people, or at least, for people who have come to poverty from different directions. Learning how to manipulate or use the welfare bureaucracy is often beyond the talents of dedicated social workers and frequently escapes the abilities of the poor. Eligibility standards are so complicated that they are simply indeterminate. It is impossible to tell if someone is cheating or if he is cheating, whether he is doing so for a "good" or a "bad" reason. As Sandberg documents, the major impact of the U.S. welfare system is demoralization. It demoralizes those who attempt to help the poor, because they must learn to gouge the system for "good causes." It demoralizes the poor themselves because they must become parties to a ruse to "finagle" things in favor of themselves—even when they are the most deserving of the poor.

It is this last observation of Sandberg and his informants which seems to me most provocative. The most uniform experience of poverty is the encounter with the welfare bureaucracy; with its complexity, with its necessity for personal compromise and self-corruption. To the extent that they make up a social class, it is their encounter with the welfare bureaucracy that gives the poor a common outlook on the wider society. What they gain from this encounter is a sense of their own self-corruption and the corruption of the wider society. As Sandberg points out, a more unified system of social welfare might not be more generous, but it might embody a more defensible normative order: a normative order more defensible to both the poor and the non-poor alike.

Gerald D. Suttles
University of Chicago

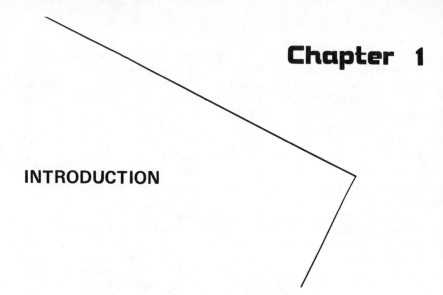

Chapter 1

INTRODUCTION

This is a story of six poor and near-poor families and the efforts of the modern welfare state to aid them. The families are black and white, young and old, the handicapped and the victims of floods who need emergency housing. Federal laws give them preferential access to housing at lower than market rentals, and they are brought together in a publicly assisted housing project in conformity with the integration strategies of social planners.

These families are among the millions of people who have left the sheltered enclaves of their ethnic and regional groups in search of a better life. As they encounter difficulties in their new situations, they are no longer able to call on the private support systems of family, friends, and community. They seek the help of government agencies set up primarily to assist the completely destitute, and find that the welfare state is poorly equipped to deal with their needs. Beyond their ineligibility for many assistance programs, they are confronted with a fragmented welfare system whose bureaucracy is often unsympathetic and hostile.

Attractive apartments were made available to the six families in the Underhill housing project in Columbia, Maryland, a new town between Baltimore and Washington, D.C. Underhill was constructed under the 236 subsidy program of the Department of Housing and Urban Development (HUD) for low and moderate income families. It is owned by a group of private investors, including a subsidiary of Columbia's development corporation that also provides the management and maintenance services. Because many of the families have problems, the project's management is called upon by HUD to be responsive to their needs and to facilitate the delivery of social services.

The project is located in a wooded cul de sac near expensive private homes and not far from a shopping center. Its 108 units are distributed in six buildings with 18 separate stairwell entrances. There are six apartments in each stairwell, two on each of three floors. The manager occupies one of the units and another is used as the project office.

The six families live in Stairwell 7; three are black, three are white, and five have children living with them. Two of the families are headed by females; one family is an elderly couple, one of whom is completely handicapped. Their economic and income patterns vary, with some employed in or near Columbia and others commuting long distances to work. All the families are receiving or have received assistance from the welfare state through such programs as Aid to Families with Dependent Children (AFDC), food stamps, Medicaid, Social Security, unemployment insurance and veterans' pensions.

The manager of Underhill is Archie Conover, a young, socially motivated man whose idealism might be characterized as utopian. His personality and actions reflect the profound influences on his life of the racism he observed as a white youngster growing up in a southern city. They are also a reaction to the frustrations he experienced as a divinity student and circuit riding preacher in the rural South. He and his wife are obsessed with overcoming racial prejudice, a commitment given substance when they take several black foster children into their home.

Archie is given an opportunity to create the better world he believes in when he is offered the job of managing Underhill. He is inspired by the developer's promises to make the town a place for all people, a community that will encourage and facilitate human growth and development. This ideal is embodied in the "people tree," a symbolic Columbia sculpture that shows the linkages and interdependence of all people.

The possibility of fulfilling Archie's dream is reinforced by HUD guidelines which call for racial, socioeconomic, and age mixing in publicly assisted projects. This is the goal of many social planners who seek to encourage upward mobility by creating new community arrangements for those of differing backgrounds. Archie says, "I wanted to meet housing needs as much as possible, but I also wanted a broad mix of people of different colors, religions, ages and cultures."

He expands his concept of creating a sense of community by adding, "It was also the idea of being three generations here, not related, not necessarily even of the same race, but we were all part of the family of man. My hope was that we could all be a family, either within the same household or within easy distance of each other. There was a time when grandparents took care of grandkids and so there wasn't a need for day care. Children took care of their parents and there wasn't a need for nursing homes. Everybody helped each other within a family structure, but our mobile society has changed all that. It's rare nowadays for three generations of a family to live in the same town, let alone next door to each other or in the same house."

As manager of Underhill, Archie has virtually absolute control over which families are accepted as residents. His influence is also manifested in the power he has to affect their lives. He can agree to a delay in payment

Stairwell 7

Top Level

Hunt Family

Clara	— mother
Karen	— teenage daughter
Gary	— teenage son
Elizabeth	— teenage daughter
Julia	— youngest child

Corbin Family

Joe	— father
Sally	— mother
John	— teenage son

Middle Level

Bonnoli Family

Wally	— father
May	— mother
Joseph,	
Louise,	
John,	
Betty	— small children

Turnfinder Family

Elmer	— father
Nancy	— mother
Walter	— small child
E.J.	— infant son
Aunt Matty	

Lower Level

Smith Family

Verna	— mother
Albin	— teenage son
James	— teenage son
Ellen,	
Barbara,	
Anna,	
Shirley,	
Gloria	— younger daughters

Harris Family

Ada	— wife
Clarence	— invalid husband

of the rent, to a move to a more desirable location in the project, or to allow a boyfriend to move in with a family headed by a single female. But his ability to facilitate social assistance is limited by insufficient resources, by inadequate backup from management, and by the difficulties he encounters in dealing with a complex and inefficient welfare state bureaucracy.

He says, "Within the first couple of months, I was faced with families who moved in without enough beds or kitchen utensils, with families that didn't have enough food to last until their next check got here, and with women who were pregnant and wanted an abortion. There were women who had left their husbands and were now being harassed by them. They wanted to know what kind of police protection or legal help they could get. Some of them needed to figure out how to get a job or how to get the kids cared for, some had to have counseling for emotional disturbances, and others merely needed a shoulder to cry on. There was just about every problem you could think of, and they were all coming at me at once."

The project represents an improvement in the lives of some of the families in Stairwell 7, but for others it is a constant reminder of failure.

There are those who are pleased to be living in better housing, large apartments with air conditioning and handsome physical surroundings, at low to moderate rentals. Others are demoralized because they are forced to dwell in close proximity to people whose ways of living they find different and sometimes repugnant. Some have personal problems and habits that offend their neighbors, and many suffer from physical illness and psychological stress, conditions that help keep them poor. All have varying degrees of difficulty in adjusting to a new place and to different kinds of people.

Ada and Clarence Harris are an elderly black couple living marginally on Social Security and a veteran's pension. A former professional in the social service field, Clarence is now a bedridden, arthritic cripple. Ada is afraid of her neighbors and repelled by their life styles.

She says, "There's nothin wrong with Underhill; they have built these nice apartments that are very comfortable. Since it is housing, it was built for people who are poor and for people a little better off. And they kind of graded it for retireds and some who they know they're not goin to have but so much money." She adds, "I guess you have to be compassionate and accept those who were too poor to have been taught how to live and how to treat people. Still, it's hard to live near em. You either move, or you just stay and put up with it."

Ada complains of the roaches brought by the unclean living habits of the Smiths next door and the Turnfinders above. Her distress is heightened to the point of hysteria by the noise levels of the Turnfinders and her fear of one of the Smith boys. She says, "Once, I wasn't afraid of much because my husband watched over me. Now I have to watch over myself and over him, so I have to be careful."

Verna Smith is a dignified deaf woman with seven children who receives welfare benefits from the Aid to Families with Dependent Children program. She perceives Underhill as a good place to raise her children and as a significant step up from their previous conditions in the slums of Washington and in a black ghetto project in another part of Maryland. Verna is very fearful and keeps her doors and windows locked. She says, "Livin down here with just the kids and myself, sometimes I get frightened." For her two oldest children, Albin and James, the improved physical surroundings of Underhill cannot overcome the deeply rooted trauma of earlier experiences, including the brutality and rejection of their father. Their hostility and anger are expressed in various kinds of antisocial behavior that ultimately lead to their incarceration in jail.

Living above them are May and Wally Bonnoli and their four small children. They are a young white couple whose economic failure has resulted in substantially reduced circumstances. This contributes to enormous social and psychological tensions between them and with their neighbors.

The Bonnolis complain constantly about the noise of others, and this leads to serious interpersonal problems in the stairwell. Wally says, "I don't wanna listen to horns blowin and beepin, and fire engines, or loud music of boom, boom, boom playin and kids runnin through the buildin. I wanna sit down and I wanna relax. I got hobbies, plenty of em that I love, but I got a champagne taste and a beer pocket and I can't afford it. So the only thing that I look forward to every day is to come home and just say the hell with everything."

May is much more positive about Underhill, and sees it as a place to recover from adverse circumstances, to save some money, to get ahead. She says, "I don't feel that Underhill's a step down; I think for us it's a step back up."

Next to the Bonnolis are Nancy and Elmer Turnfinder, their two small children, and their Aunt Matty. Their West Virginia, hill-country life style is reminiscent of Erskine Caldwell's *Tobacco Road*. Although Underhill represents a substantial improvement in their situation, they miss family friends, and the ways of living of their regional culture. Their deeply rooted racial biases and dirty apartment bring them into constant conflict with their neighbors.

Nancy says, "This is a beautiful place. The only thing wrong with it is the damn niggers." Elmer comments, "I sure say you should belong to your own people. Cause God Almighty didn't put em on this earth for mixin." And Aunt Matty adds, "I don't think they oughta make places like Underhill for mixin." They don't get along. In the first place, the colored people wasn't ready for integration. Any darn fool knows that. They weren't ready to be just pushed right up with the white people. And the white people weren't ready to take that either. It should of been done by educatin them first and been done gradually. Back home they have a little place up on a hill called "Africa." They lived there for years and years, and that's where they stay."

The family does not take advantage of the amenities in the town. Nancy says, "You gotta pay to swim in the damn pool. You just go to a little old creek and swim all you want." Aunt Matty notes, "I tried the pool and that done it. There's nothin you smell but that damn chlorine. Last Sunday, we went down to the Potomac River, and we were dirty as pigs from that water. They got pretty beaches near here, but there's nothin like smellin dirty river water. You can't beat it."

Clara Hunt and her four children live on the top floor. Gary, the eldest, is a fairly well adjusted teenager who moves more or less freely in an inte-grated world. His sister, Karen, has been part of a group of teenage blacks who are virulently antiwhite and create a variety of problems in the schools and community. They have a teenager sister, Elizabeth, and a younger sister, Julia, who is afflicted with asthma. Although they see the project as an improvement from the ghetto slums, Clara and Karen are experiencing some difficulty in adjusting to an interracial and mixed socioeconomic environment. This is manifested in their lack of acceptance by middle class blacks. The situation is exacerbated by the tragic problems of Karen, who has experienced drugs, violence, and rejection.

Clara says, "Some people, when they make it, they forget there are other people back there experiencin this right now, and they put all this behind em. We call em black bourgeoisie; they're sort of separate. They're livin the white man's town now, not joinin any black nothin. They don't wanna think about those times or lend a hand or try to help somebody else get up to the point where they are."

She adds, "Blacks are more powerful now than they were; my parents' generation was not powerful. They had a few fights for the cause, equal rights, but not as many as you have now. They were quiet and didn't go out and riot. I think the riots did a lot. It was a bad thing, but I think it really brought about a change." Clara is worried about Karen and comments, "I think it's healthy that she's proud of her heritage, but I don't think it's right that she should hate all white people."

Karen says, "My friends in school is bad because they start fights all the time and don't go to class. They start racial fights all the time." Then she notes, "I wouldn't know how to cope with bein friends with a white person because I never had a white friend." She describes the social separation of the town by saying, "In Columbia, you're considered poor if you live in this kind of housing. It's like there's a lower class group and a higher class group. I've never really tried to associate with the higher class blacks because they've never tried to associate with me."

In the apartment adjacent to the Hunts are Joe and Sally Corbin and their teenage son, who are in the project as recipients of flood relief assistance provided by HUD. A more or less typical "middle American" family from a small town background in Howard County, they are ridiculed by their friends for living in an interracial environment and for benefiting from public assistance. This is compounded by the impact of the differing behavior patterns of their neighbors and their own humiliation in having to accept government aid. Life in Underhill represents a temporary setback, a situation from which they eagerly seek escape. For them, as well as for many others in Stairwell 7, conditions are often very stressful.

Joe describes life in the stairwell by saying, "There was a couple of people in our section that would be out in the street late, usin all kinds of language and everything else. When you'd go down in the mornin, there'd be trash all over the staircase, paper, beer cans, just filthy. We had company on a weekend; my wife's sister come and her mother. They said, 'Go downstairs and look at that filthy stairway.' There was spit all over the mailboxes and clods of bubble gum right in front of the door. It was so awful they said they didn't feel like they even wanted to come in and see nobody. You know, like it made them half sick." When the Corbins leave Underhill, Joe comments, "It was strange to me, like I was in a different world; it was a nightmare. But bein in my own house now, it's like livin again."

The daily problems faced by Underhill residents help show how people see things in terms of their own needs. Ada Harris is disturbed by the heavy walking of the Turnfinders, and they object to the high volume of the Corbin's TV. The Bonnolis complain repeatedly about the noise level of the Hunts, but Clara, Ada, and Joe complain about the loudness of the Bonnolis. Ultimately, Clara takes the Bonnolis to court to stop their harassment.

Most of the residents object to the dirty habits of the Turnfinders, which contribute to an infestation of roaches in the stairwell. Ada also complains about the Smith household, but Verna reports with pride that people compliment her on the cleanliness of her apartment.

Everyone is afraid of crime; indeed, this is reported to be the primary concern of project dwellers throughout the country. May and Ada are worried about the drug traffic in which one of the Smith boys is allegedly involved. Joe is afraid to walk the streets at night because of the stories he has heard of teenage violence, and Ada is even terrified of going to the mailbox. The Turnfinders, Ada, and Verna are anxious about someone breaking into their apartments. The irony is that one of Verna's boys is arrested and charged with armed robbery in another part of Columbia.

The social structure of the stairwell is further explained by the differing perceptions of the role of management. All of the residents except the Turnfinders see Archie as a helpful and supportive person. Yet Ada says to him, "Why did you put those people up over me and those people next to me knowin the problems I've got?" And May says, "Archie has limited time, but I have to give him a pat on the back. There's times when he doesn't get around when he should because he's really pressed."

Analysis of the people in Stairwell 7 calls for an assessment of the project and its place in the larger setting of Columbia, as well as of the network of contacts with public and private institutions. Underlying this analysis are the expectations of those who come to Columbia, expectations that are usually not met. This is powerfully stated by a fifteen-year-old girl in one of the other stairwells in Underhill, who says, "A lot of people come to Columbia with the idea that this is paradise. That's the point of view you get from the brochures and stuff. People come with the idea that Columbia has no racial problems, no money problems, no drugs, no fear, just jobs and leisure for everybody. But Columbia's like any other place, only worse."

She adds, "Still, they come and expect that all their problems are going to be solved and they can start over. Life will be great and people will be nice; they're expecting everything and they don't get anything. Their whole wall comes crashing down around them, and their little dream bubble bursts. There's nothing they can do about it and they're gonna be disappointed."

Intensive evaluation of specific families and their social relations helps us to understand more fully the realities of human life and the impact of both culture and personality. The study of the families in the stairwell, in the context of the project and the town, points up the complexity of relationships that is sometimes missed by sociological and psychological research. At times, the description of events takes on a Rashomon-like quality, with diverse interpretations of the same situations. Responses to the problems of noise, vermin, and crime show how differing perceptions emerge from a particular event. At the same time, the study underscores factors that are overlapping and mutually reinforcing. We learn about situations as perceived by the actors as the events unfold and are checked against each other. Sometimes the data are accurate about actual facts, and at other times they are more indicative of the personality and attitudes of the individual who relates them. These are not only life histories, but illustrations of the relationships between a known personality and a known culture using annotated verbatim material.

COLUMBIA

Columbia was created as an entirely new community in the softly rolling terrain of Howard County in Maryland. The idea of building better living environments through new towns goes back to the British Garden Cities Movement started by Ebenezer Howard and his colleagues in Great Britain, who sought to achieve efficient land use and attractive design as settings for more humane and satisfying interpersonal relations. They believed it was possible to combine in one community a place for slum dwellers and other classes to live, work, and play, a notion characterized as utopian by skeptical observers.

Many of the early residents of Howard County were tobacco growers, and agriculture is still a significant part of the economy. Industrialization has become increasingly important in this century, contributing in a major way to the opening up of job opportunities and the development of the county. The creation of Columbia by Howard Research and Development Corportion (a joint venture of the Rouse Company and Connecticut General Insurance) dramatically accelerated county growth. The first residents moved there in 1967, and by the summer of 1973, the community had some 26,000 people. The recession slowed down the growth rate, however, and it is uncertain when the goal of full development with a population of 100,000 will be achieved.

There will ultimately be seven villages surrounding the town center, each with several neighborhoods of 3,500 to 4,000 people. Near each village center are an elementary school, park and playground, swimming pool, small community building, and usually a convenience store. Each village provides some shopping and services as well as cultural and recreational opportunities, but many of the major facilities are in the town center. In addition to these and other amenities, thousands of acres of permanent open space are projected throughout the entire town.

Columbia is a relatively young, highly educated community with a very large proportion of residents who hold advanced degrees. It has an unusual degree of racial and socioeconomic diversity, and the estimated 18 to 19 percent black population is high for a suburban community.

As a result of migration, floods, and the redevelopment of dilapidated areas, federally subsidized housing programs have helped several hundred low income families move into several projects in Columbia. Here they find a better physical environment and improved amenities in an essentially middle and upper middle class town. They also find an insufficient social environment, which sometimes exacerbates the problems they bring with them and the new ones they encounter. The problem is that some families are incapable of making the relocation experience a positive one, incurring heavy costs in terms of personal and social disruptions.

The literature advertises Columbia as a place that will have housing for all who work there and want to live there. It is described as a place with a job opportunity for every resident, a dwelling for every job situation. The developer says, "We want a truly balanced, complete city where as many people would come to work in the morning as would leave to go somewhere else; a place where the corporate janitor and the corporate executive both live; where they would have churches, schools, lumberyards and cemeteries—the maze of activities that are the full life of the city." But Columbia has not produced sufficient housing for those who work in the town and who cannot compete in the housing market.

The development of subsidized housing depends in part on the cooperation and support of the county, which is asked to provide additional services. There is a need for different kinds of policing, education, health care and welfare aid, with accompanying financial requirements too huge for the county to handle. Some capital comes from federal grants, but there is also a local cost beyond the capacity of a rural county's ability to respond. This is one of the important reasons places such as Howard County have sought to prevent or limit the amount of low and moderate income housing under their jurisdiction.

Government programs continue to encourage the movement of families with serious problems to places where little or no help is available. This is the situation of the Department of Social Services in Howard County, a state-supervised agency funded by federal, state, and county funds. With a budget of little more than a million dollars, the department must administer and deliver a broad variety of services including foster care, Aid to Families with Dependent Children (AFDC), Emergency Assistance, General Public Assistance, Old Age Assistance (OAS), Aid to the Blind and Disabled, and food stamps. The agency is understaffed at a time when case loads are doubling and an unworkable ratio of cases per worker is set by a state legislature worried about the economics of inflation. Moreover, the level of education and professional training of some of the workers is limited. Delivery of social services is affected by these objective factors as well as by the personal attitudes of some of the staff. Workers dealing with fraud cases sometimes tend to look at everyone as potentially dishonest, a perception that can influence the way in which they resond to their clients.

The fact that the basic services are provided by Howard County is sometimes a problem to the people of Columbia because they do not have their own system of governance. The real governing unit is the County Council and its executive. In Columbia itself, the most important force is the Columbia Association (C.A.), a private corporation set up by the developer to serve the community and manage certain aspects of its affairs. The developer created a mechanism that would assure his control of decision making, probably as much to protect his financial investment as because of his personal interest in the life of the community as an expression of his social ideology. Many residents feel this is unhealthy and that the community should have been allowed to struggle at the beginning, forming its own types of organizations and institutions rather than having the developer create them.

The C.A. secures its financial resources through liens on property. Home owners, businesses, and industry share the cost of conducting C.A. programs through their assessments. Further income is derived by charging residents for various services and activities. There is an amenity package of several lakes, 27 neighborhood centers, a range of recreational facilities, and many acres of open space. Minibus transportation, preschool programs, cultural events, and a zoo are also available.

A variety of citizens' groups, including elected village advisory boards and neighborhood associations, provide input for the system, but the real power is in the hands of the developer. In order to effect change, the residents must petition and pressure the C.A. because it controls the money and makes all the budget decisions for community operations. But there is a real problem of citizen participation because the residents have very limited means for gaining access to the resources of the C.A.

One of the myths of Columbia as a utopian community is the notion of total racial integration. Despite the fact that they are contrary to the Columbia concept, various black structures have developed. There are discussion groups on black identify, black theater groups, the teaching of Black Muslim philosophy, and social interactions that involve black people to the exclusion of others. All tend to work against the development corporation's goal of reaching integration by having residential areas with more or less the same racial profile. In the various processes of self-selection, people often sort themselves out along racial lines.

Because Columbia was planned and structured as an integrated community, no consideration was given to the possibility that certain kinds of people would want their own "turf." There was no facility with which blacks could identify, so some black teenagers took control of the community centers. Much of the tension stems from a small group of poor and low income black youngsters who live in federally assisted and low income housing. Together with other poor blacks from rural Howard County and nearby Baltimore and Washington, they are among the youth of differing racial backgrounds who contribute to violence in Columbia.

Clara deplores the separation of the races and says, "You see a group of white kids on this corner, and you go a couple blocks up the street and you see a group of black kids. They've sort of divided themselves like in the teen centers. The Columbia Association don't wanna admit it, but there is a black teen center and a white teen center. The kids have did this to themselves; they've divided theirselves."

The potential for interracial conflict is described by a teenage girl from another stairwell. She says, "Last year, we had like a few days where you could feel it in the air. The tension was thick and you could cut it with a knife. All the guys were with their knives, and the girls would hold their purses in front of em. It was just a few days in there where there was threats of riot all over the place, and some kids decided they weren't gonna come. And some kids from other schools decided they were gonna come just to see all the action, the fighting and everything. But it never came off."

Unfortunately, neither the county government, the developer, nor the Columbia Association have the skills to ameliorate tension situations stemming from interpersonal and intergroup conflicts, nor have they made available the needed resources. At the time of this study, the County Human Relations Commission had no professional staff, and today it is still unable to deal effectively with the complex problems of the community.

Columbia has been seeking economic and racial integration, but has not done what is necessary to make them work. But most developers do not even want to try integration and usually take the easy way out by avoiding, delaying, and even placing obstacles in the path of housing low income people and minorities. Thus James Rouse and his colleagues must be given considerable credit for having the courage and the motivation to innovate and to take risks with their own resources.

THE LOSS OF COMMUNITY

The U.S. is a preponderantly urban nation with a disproportionate concentration of the poor in the central cities and in certain rural areas. Over the past half century, the technological revolution in agriculture has contributed to a huge migration of millions of people to major metropolitan areas. This process is still taking place as marginal farmers and the unemployed seek greater economic opportunity in urban places, with the result that poverty has become more and more an urban problem.

New social policies have been developed to protect the families and individuals who are victims of this process. But instead of helping, they often contribute to human distress and to a breakdown of traditional ways of handling it. The "bricks and mortar" philosophy of planners and federal bureaucrats resulted in urban renewal and redevelopment programs that destroyed cohesive neighborhoods and dispersed individuals ill equipped to make it on their own. The interventions of the welfare state further encouraged the weakening of such social structures as the family, the ethnic group, and the neighborhood.

Research on the rise and impact of modern urban phenomena has often centered on the neighborhood. Industrialization, the adjustment of immigrants, ethnic succession, and the socialization of various groups have been well documented. There is also considerable literature on the inability of local government to provide adequate services, a condition leading to reduced life quality. This has been exacerbated by the outflow of jobs compelling established populations to seek work elsewhere.

Many of these individuals are low income workers who live in fear of layoffs, retrenchment, and plant relocation—terrifyingly impersonal events that come with no advance warning and offer no opportunity for individual influence or control. They are victims of an unpredictable and undirectable environment that presses in on them from every side.

Although they are a step above abject poverty on the economic ladder, such people are beset by economic problems and status anxieties. Their upward movement has been slow and uneven, with occasional gains endangered by the slowdown in the economy or drained off by inflation. These are people with serious problems with which they are often unable to cope. Their position is marginal and unstable as they stand at the periphery of an increasingly middle class American society.

Projects like Underhill bring together such marginal people—people who are neither clearly destitute nor nonfunctional, but who are not firmly linked to communal welfare efforts or to the modern urban economy. The community, the media, and the caretakers press them to emulate the middle class, but they do not have the personal or social resources to accomplish this. Their options are limited by federal programs and guidelines while meaningful alternatives are lacking.

The residents of Stairwell 7 seem neither to share a common subculture nor to reject the prevailing standards of the wider society. They are not part of the culture of poverty, a way of life that is considered by some to be intergenerational and to transcend economic deprivation. Their life styles are oriented toward the major social and cultural values of society, and their behavior tends to reflect this orientation.

Although all of the families in the stairwell have some ethnic or regional cultural practices to which they are attached and which often bring them into conflict, they are not too different from many better off families from the same ethnic or regional groups. To a great extent, they are the casualties of our society—those who have suffered health, marital, or economic failure. All have been self-supporting in the past, and some look forward to being self-supporting in the future. In this respect they are not that different from other families living in private housing.

The residents of Underhill have been encouraged to move from a close knit and complex network of relationships to one that is far less cohesive. It is difficult for them to develop ties and friendships that are meaningful, and their new social networks are less bound to locality, a factor that works against the development of a sense of community.

Community has been defined as including a territorial area, a complex of institutions within an area, and a feeling of belonging. It is more than a set of social identifications and interactions and living and working together; it represents a state of mind on the part of its members and involves interdependence and loyalty. This commitment to a collective purpose and common destiny is largely missing in Underhill.

The residents have not had sufficient time to develop neighborhood cohesiveness, nor do they have the benefits of family or ethnic ties to help them deal with adverse conditions. Even though they are encouraged to develop the social structures required for self-sufficiency and self-respect, the process is hindered by government bureaucrats whose welfare politics often represent a commitment to institutional survival rather than to service to the client.

The people in a particular locality cannot ignore one another, and those who regularly occupy the same place must either develop a moral order or come into conflict. The moral order worked out in Underhill is based on a common territorial enclave which forces its residents to develop human and personal relationships. But the project is not a cultural island with its own distinct traditions, nor are the social practices of its residents very different from those of the wider society. The people involved tend to be rather conventional, seeking to develop orderly relations even though they come from different racial, ethnic, geographical, and age groups.

The need for community is expressed in a variety of ways by the residents of Stairwell 7. They continue to maintain contact with family and friends outside the project and the town. May is very close to her family and there are frequent interactions. Elmer is in touch with his mother and sister; Ada gets help from her children; and Verna maintains relationships with her mother and the godparents of her son. They are not cut off from their previous environments, a factor that may have some bearing on their ability to adjust to present circumstances.

Nancy discusses her regional ties and says, "I'd like to move back to West Virginia where the houses are cheap. I don't like Maryland; I didn't even like it when I got married. We're all three from West Virginia, and you better believe we miss it. I miss the whole place; I just liked it there."

Aunt Matty comments, "When I first came to Baltimore after my husband died, I just stayed here because you could get one job after another. It was durin the Depression and it was always seasonal work, but I could get it. I've often wanted to go back home, but I'm stuck here now. Till recently, there just wasn't any place to work there."

Wally has a very strong commitment to his family and ethnic culture. His deep feelings emerge as he talks about his father. He says, "We try not to call on each other, but when he asks, I'm there. In an Italian family, we're close."

Clara feels cut off from her Baltimore inner city environment. She says, "I was lost when I first moved here, so I inquired about the bus service and schedules. The bus used to go into the city on Saturday, but it doesn't anymore. That's where I used to shop, in town on Saturday when I was off. I'd gather the children up, and we'd get on the bus in the mornin, go spend Saturday in the city shoppin and visit my mother."

Joe puts it another way, contrasting the people in Underhill with his former neighbors: "We was in a small village before where there was a small church, and we wasn't used to that type of people, that type of language and their carryin on. If somethin come up in our neighborhood, we'd sit down and talk about it. We didn't have cussin, carryin on, hootin, hollerin and complainin."

And a widow in a nearby stairwell says, quite graphically, "I don't visit nobody here. When I visit, I visit in Fenton City; I don't visit in Columbia. Only ones I visit is my family. I'm only livin in Columbia cause I had no other choice; there was no other homes for me to go to. I didn't move here cause I wanted to; I moved here cause I had to. The place I lived in was condemned, and I had no other choice."

Underhill is a territorial enclave that has been assigned to a group of people on the basis of income, age, and race. The residents are unsure of their position because they receive conflicting signals from the surrounding community. On the one hand, they are urged to utilize the town's amenities, to send their children to school with the other children, and to participate in the political process. At the same time, they are socially ostracized and unable to take advantage of some of the amenities because of lack of income, fear of rejection and, sometimes, different life styles.

The values and aspirations of the people of Underhill are not very different from the rest of the community, yet they are singled out and recognized as a low status group. Ada is shunned by some members of her church and by women in the street. The Corbins are ridiculed by their friends for "taking welfare." Wally is seen as a failure by his family, and Karen is rejected by middle class black youngsters. A community value system sets Underhill tenants apart as an inferior lot, low on the totem pole of esteem.

Within the project, there is a lack of mutual trust, and social relations are often restricted to those which are safest. People tend to stay within the household, and friendship patterns are usually established on the basis of race, age, and sex. These are the most comfortable relationships, based as they are on mutual needs and expectations as well as on similar cultural patterns and values.

The stairwell is permeated with feelings that range from coolness to outright hostility. These are sometimes evident in blatant racial antagonism, such as the antiblack attitudes of the Turnfinders and the antiwhite attitudes of Karen. Racial feelings also emerge in more subtle forms, such as when Wally talks about the planned mixing of races and May describes Verna as being afraid to complain because she's black.

Joe characterizes the situation this way: "When I was livin up there in Underhill, fellow employees workin with me had it in their mind that it was strictly for colored people. They knew I was there under HUD and no rent, but they didn't think any white person should be in there atall. When you moved in there, they just thought you was there under welfare or you was too lazy to work or out for a handout. They used to kid me about it."

At the same time, there is intimate communication across group lines as economic interactions and symbiotic relationships develop in the ecological processes of stairwell life. Verna babysits for May in exchange for an occasional ride to the shopping center. Karen's inability to talk with her mother leads to an association with May that transcends racial feelings. The contact between Ada Harris and Sally Corbin is particularly empathetic because Sally's father was a cripple, as is Clarence Harris. In all of these situations, face to face relations emerge in the context of larger social configurations.

The principal structural influences in Underhill come from outside the project. They include HUD guidelines and regulations, the goals and ideals of the developers of Columbia, the management corporation that provides maintenance, the county and state institutions that offer social help or that frustrate its delivery, the private helping organizations, and the system of governance of the Columbia Association. Underhill is also affected by informal structures, including family and friends who do not see it as a desirable place to live. The project has difficulty in developing a moral order because the power of these outside forces prevent its functioning as a more or less distinct cultural and geographical unit.

Some of the residents feel they have to work with each other for the common good, and organize a Tenants Council to improve their situation. Its philosophical underpinning is explained by May, who says, "Living within a neighborhood like this, we're a unit within ourselves. We've all got common problems or we wouldn't be here. Outside of Underhill, everybody has a right to live by the life style they like. But you can't survive in a community like this, as close as everybody has to be here, if you want to be by yourself. It's not for the individual seeking a solitary life; there's no way. In Underhill, you all have to work together to try to get things done. Whether it's to buck management on some kind of proposal they've got, whether it's to buck the government, you've got to provide a united force."

Others, like Joe Corbin and Elmer Turnfinder, want to be left alone; for them, it is enough that Underhill offers adequate shelter at a low rental. This view is expressed by a woman in another stairwell, who says, "I haven't taken participation in nothin here. I stay right here in this buildin. I don't go to no kinda organizations and I don't go to no kinda meetins."

May and Clara are the only ones who devote much time to the Tenants Council, but they fade out of the picture as their own problems preoccupy them. This suggests that poor and near-poor people may be too tired or busy with survival needs to become involved on a consistent basis. Clara takes an evening job in the hope that she can save enough for a down payment on a home. Wally works long hours in his construction job, Elmer works in the evenings, and Aunt Matty comes home late from her job in Baltimore. Joe has his regular job during the day and spends evenings and weekends rebuilding his flood ravaged house. Ada is always occupied in caring for her crippled husband, and Verna's seven children are as much as she can handle. Participation is also limited by the fact that all the residents want to own homes and see their stay in Underhill as temporary.

Archie describes the failure to organize an effective Tenants Council this way: "It's one person trying to speak for a community of 107 families, and I haven't had any influence. I've urged them to organize in written form and have people who could verbalize the need. This could carry a lot more weight because it would be coming from them directly. They nod like they hear me, but either they don't believe it, they're afraid to try it or they're not willing to devote the time to trying."

He adds, "HUD management guidelines say that you are to be receptive to some sort of tenant organization and, if it doesn't happen naturally, that you will encourage it. What HUD doesn't do is tell you how. I'm beginning to find out they never tell you how because nobody knows how."

The attempt to develop a sense of community in Underhill proves ineffective because it does not have the advantages of long term stability. The residents are relatively powerless and unable to influence decisions on Columbia, let alone the institutions of the welfare state which tell them how to live and what they can and cannot do. Despite Archie's efforts to bring them into the decision making of the town, few take up the option, and even when they do it makes little difference in the outcome. Their failure stems from the uncertainty of their structures and the fact that they have not settled in as a community.

THE FRAGMENTED WELFARE STATE

The welfare system was developed primarily to handle complete destitution, and is poorly articulated to deal with many of the problems of the families in Stairwell 7. In its desire to be helpful, government has created a multiplicity of new programs that are overlapping and conflicting. These programs embody rules and regulations that seek to monitor the conduct of recipients and impose the preconceptions of the caretakers. These and other factors reduce the clients' options and bring into question the legitimacy of the welfare state.

But the welfare state is much larger than the welfare system for the poor; government provides large scale assistance to the more affluent segments of our society. Through government guaranteed loans to Lockheed, direct financial benefits are provided to stockholders and workers. Other government assistance programs aid business through tax credits, accelerated depreciation write-offs, and oil depreciation allowances. Loans are guaranteed to companies through the Small Business Administration; the government also finances construction loans and research grants for hospitals. Veterans receive assistance through the G.I. Bill, and homeowners benefit from tax deductions for mortgage interest and through low interest FHA loans.

The present welfare systems grew, not as a concerted national drive against poverty, but rather through incremental, ad hoc decisions dealing with the disjointed facets of poverty and other societal needs. The Depression made it clear that conscious action by governmental authority was needed to rescue the country from a period of crisis. Government has since been responsible for the direction of the economy and for the partial redistribution of income through a multiplicity of programs.

By the 1960s, the U.S. had developed social policy commitments to civil rights, housing, health care, and income support in a variety of piecemeal programs that went beyond merely helping the indigent. Government had committed itself to redressing many economic and social inequalities and had created a substantial welfare state. A normative social commitment was made that is probably largely irreversible.

Federal intervention represented a departure from the early English tradition that relief is a local issue. Our early welfare system was based on the English Poor Laws of the seventeenth and eighteenth centuries, when people lived in an agricultural society with little mobility and where problems were handled largely at the local level. There are now tens of millions of people living in poverty caused by technological, industrial, and economic changes, but we are still using a system designed largely to provide assistance for needy mothers, the blind, and the aged. The problems of the poor now transcend local boundaries, however. Migration and urbanization have shifted the burden to new states and communities, which end up with a disproportionate share of a national responsibility. The process has been exacerbated by the exporting states, which have encouraged the exodus by their low welfare benefits and harsh administration.

Since the 1930s, government has intervened more and more because of the inability of the private sector and state and local governments to deal with the complexities of urbanization and industrial society. Johnson's Great Society was an extension of the New Deal, as were Truman's Fair Deal and Kennedy's New Frontier. These programs rested on the assumption that the federal government was a significant and necessary fctor in effecting social change and in determining the rewards of life in our society.

Public investments contributed to the development of jobs and income, but left unmet social needs in such areas as health, education, and care of the aged. While these services could be bought on the open market, most low and middle income families could not afford them. Thus the govenment developed a services strategy as an important adjunct to its income strategy. It also recognized a need to assist the minorities and the poor who could not help themselves and who had been victimized for generations.

The result was that government became the fastest growing sector in the economy: public expenditures nearly quadrupled and the share of the gross national product for which they accounted rose from 27.2 percent in 1954 to 35.6 percent in 1974. A significant portion of these expenditures were for social programs involving cost sharing for federal programs. This added to the fiscal burden of the cities and led to increased political resistance to raising property taxes, which are a chief source of revenue for local governments. The desire to make social help available to all who needed it came into conflict with the desire to control expenditures for welfare.

The early Johnson years were a golden age of American capitalist democracy, as per capita income and consumption expanded while we maintained stable prices and relatively full employment. Keynesians and others felt that fiscal and monetary policy interventions were eliminating persistent unemployment and chronic inflation. But the war in Vietnam soon destroyed the Keynesian consensus, because massive unemployment and double digit inflation appeared simultaneously.

Critics who opposed welfare state actions did so in the belief that they destroyed personal incentives and liberty, burdened society with bureaucratic rules and regulations, and led to inefficient and politicized economic decisions. They suggested that America's complex and inequitable tax laws contributed to inflation, economic instability, and taxpayer distrust and frustration. Our welfare system was seen as socially and economically disastrous because it degraded people, wasted billions of dollars, and offered the recipients little or no encouragement to be self-sufficient.

The budget process became a principal arena in which advocates and critics of the welfare state argued social reform. The debate now focuses on the principle of government intervention as a means of providing adequate social minimums for all. Conservatives feel that self-directing forces within decentralized markets will eventually lead to the absorption of unemployment. Liberals, however, say that the market has been discredited as a vehicle for assuring equitable distribution of resources and benefits. Those of Marxist orientation point to defects in the institutional structure of the economy as the source of recurring crises, and argue for the total replacement of capitalist institutions by a socialist economic system.

Liberals are seeking the further redirection of budget priorities to meeting the needs of disadvantaged groups and minorities victimized by prejudice and discrimination. In calling for expansion of the welfare state, they say that adequate resources have never been provided to achieve the desired outcomes of fairness and equity. They seek rapid economic growth in order to swing the budget from deficit to surplus, thus generating new revenues for social reform. This has led to ideological battles concerning deficit spending, income redistribution, and basic choices of priorities.

Opponents of welfare state interventions suggest that conditions of the poor have improved in absolute terms, but not enough to meet the rise in expectations. They call for lowering our aspirations because we have limited resources and there are certain things we don't know how to do. These perceptions are often grounded in the philosophical thrust for individual rights, as opposed to collective or community rights. The principle advanced is that individuals ought to be treated equally in their efforts to achieve success through their natural abilities and personal efforts. This viewpoint questions the ability of more participatory and redistributive policies to enhance human welfare.

At the same time, there has been a movement beyond the concept of rising expectations to one of rising entitlements. Today, people expect a job and a rising standard of living, and government is unable to deny that expectation. This has led to increased expenditures in the areas of health, welfare, and social services—and to larger budget deficits. The problem is that no one wants to pay for the inflation that results, while government finds it politically difficult to impose the costs on any particular group.

Successive generations of politicians have instituted efforts to cope with a wide variety of social ills. These efforts range from economic recession programs to those dealing with cancer-producing ingredients in foods. In each generation, there is a new set of challenges that result in new programs and new agencies to administer them. The agencies seek to perpetuate themselves and to protect and enlarge their activities. This is accomplished through alliances with other agencies also concerned with self-preservation, with congressional committees that create and sustain the programs, and with special interest groups that benefit from them. The consequence is a blurring of structures and functions that is stimulated by competition among agencies seeking to preempt territory.

The welfare state has become a morass of 50 state laws, all different, and hundreds of state and federal regulations with varying local interpretations. This is compounded by a multiplicity of jurisdictions established to provide public services that are supported by tax levies and service charges. Although multistate regional compacts and authorities have been formed, the maze of state institutions providing services is confusing and difficult to coordinate. This fragmented system has contributed to a parochialism among state and local governments that leads to competitiveness and the erection of barriers.

Burgeoning government programs have led to huge increases in the amount of money spent and the number of people served, but there has been little gain in the dignity and independence of clients. Virtually all parts of society agree that the welfare system is not working and must be radically overhauled. The fear of becoming a welfare state is reinforced by exposures of fraud and inefficiency, and many people now believe that government interventions do more harm than good. No one really understands the welfare system, and there is no consensus on what is necessary to reform it.

Simplified federal administration by a single agency has long been a classic reform goal. Reform economists pressing for measures such as the negative income tax believe that direct cash payments should be simply and quickly made to eligible families. The problem is that this makes it very difficult to separate the employable from the unemployable poor. Congress has been insisting that families with different employment possibilities be administered separately in order to develop work incentives. Consequently, the fragmented local-state-federal administration has been challenged by new kinds of fragmented federal proposals. Efforts to convert welfare into an incentive system lead to further program extensions, so that welfare reforms are characterized by conflicts in the reform plans themselves.

Intervention has been difficult because our political and bureaucratic mechanisms are poorly developed and because agreement on what is to be changed and at what cost to whom is difficult to achieve. The success of programs is often determined by those who manage them, and many institutions are not adequately structured and staffed to carry out innovative tasks. Because efforts to achieve fundamental reform have proven unworkable, welfare has become a political albatross and its conflicts have been patched over in the struggle between Congress, the Executive Branch, and special interest groups. In the meantime, people demand more of government but trust it less.

Most public assistance programs are funded and regulated by all three levels of government, although some are handled only by the states and local communities. Old Age Assistance, Medicare, and food stamp distribution are administered by the federal government, which also sets up minimal standards for public assistance programs such as AFDC and Aid to the Blind. States have to meet federal standards to get funds that are granted on a matching basis up to fixed maximums. Beyond this, state and local governments have great latitude in how the programs apply within the various categories of aid. Methods of determining eligibility are complex and inequitable, and put an impossible load on the welfare caseworker, making him an investigator, policeman, and clerk instead of a counselor for his clients. The system is devoted to catching chiselers rather than to helping the needy.

Current programs are directed almost entirely to unemployables so that large numbers of people who require help are excluded. Millions of men and women who are in need but who are neither aged, handicapped, nor parents of minor children are neglected. Those low income people who work at full or part time jobs but who do not earn enough to escape from poverty do not benefit. Because they are ineligible for many government assistance programs, such people are often less well off financially than the welfare poor. These are people who move in and out of the welfare sector as their limited incomes place them just beyond eligibility for assistance.

A number of the families in Underhill are confronted by this situation. They are people who happen to have a lower income than the majority and who need certain kinds of help. Their unstable position requires the support of the welfare state on a more or less temporary basis. Although they take advantage of public aid to the extent that it is avilable, they want to be independent and upwardly mobile. At the same time, they experience culture shock due to recency of residence in the project, lack of urban and occupational skills, and loss of aid provided by family, friends, and neighborhood. They are marginal people, victims of migration and of rapid social change who fall between the interstices of the social system.

The people in Stairwell 7 face a variety of problems that call for the help of government. Ada and her husband have a low income because of age and illness; they survive through Social Security benefits, a veteran's pension, and other public and private aid. Joe and his family require temporary shelter because of flood damage to their home. Clara does not earn enough to fully support her family. And Verna receives total welfare assistance as her attempt to become self-sufficient is thwarted by the welfare bureaucracy.

In describing her job experience, Verna observes, "I was workin for about four months, and at first I was assemblin things. Then I started makin mops and later we were doin different kinds of boxes. The problem was I made like about 12 dollars a week, and they took that out of my assistance grant.

I don't think they should have done that because it wasn't enough to take out." She decides this is an intolerable situation and says, "Well, I might as well stay at home."

Wally's downward mobility and dependency are characteristic of some of the project dwellers. He says, poignantly, "For the time bein we've got to live this way; we've got to live on a low income. We can't afford luxuries that other people have. I had a good education which I've still got, but I can't put much of it to use. We've seen some good times; we made good money; we're tryin to bring up our children right. What happened, happened, whether it's fate or destiny or God's will, who knows?"

A number of Stairwell residents discuss the problem of qualifying for government programs. May says, "We were on food stamps on month-for-month eligibility. So as soon as Wally started making five or ten dollars over the level, they cut us off. This I didn't think was fair. I think they should have tried to continue us for a month, maybe two months, until we could build up enough surplus that we really could be on our own. It's the same with Medical Assistance; as soon as you're making it, they don't give you a month or two to get caught up and really be on your own. They completely cut out all assistance immediately. I know cause it happened to us and to other families; it's a common gripe. They need the funds and the facilities for other people, but still I know several families that because they've cut them off so quick, a month later they've had to reapply and be certified for it again."

Clara has had a similar experience: "Once I applied for food stamps, but they said I was 50 or 60 dollars over the ceilin which they allow for my size family. I'm the sole source of income for my family, and I think this is ridiculous. Julia gets free lunch at school because of her illness. I think that's how she qualified, because accordin to that pay scale they have on there when you apply for it, I didn't think I was gonna make that either."

Elmer points up the frustrations of a number of these families in discussing his inability to get medical assistance and other kinds of aid. He says, "I don't get any help from the government or anybody; I work for everything. But why should I work and help to pay for keepin somebody else who's more able to work than I was? That's the only thing I got agin it. There's some of these people runnin around in this neighborhood who's livin right off'n welfare that's able to work as well as I am."

A young woman from another stairwell states the issue clearly by noting, "I've seen so many people that was better off than me that had these food stamps and medical cards and the right to go to a dentist and not pay a dime. And I thought, well my husband goes out and busts his tail every day for me and five kids. We're really sweatin it to make a livin, and we aren't qualified. He makes too much money. Yet we're in a government project the same as other people, and they have these benefits. We don't qualify for it; that's the only thing that puzzles me."

Poor families who need help for a variety of problems find that the various government services come from different agencies in different places with different rules. This requires frequent appointments and constant referrals, so many give up rather than fight their way through the maze. The complexity of this system makes it necessary for Archie to go to numerous agencies and fill out mountains of paperwork to get something done for one family.

Archie describes the lack of coordination in the delivery of services by observing, "Despite the large number of public and private agencies offering services, there isn't a single agency that has enough staff or a big enough budget to meet the needs of Underhill. If you combine the difficulty of transporting people from here to the agencies and their inability to come here, there's a real problem. But there are services that sometimes aren't even used by people here, and it's because of the missing links." He adds, "Everybody has been doing his own thing, and it's much better to have a centralized way of doing it."

Ada, who has the problem of getting adequate health care for her husband, comments, "I had wanted him to have therapy so badly, but when he was in the nursin home, they didn't seem to be equipped for it. The social worker told em that he was supposed to have all these things, but when I dared to ask about it once, they didn't seem to like it at all. I've never asked for it here, so I don't know if I could get it or not."

Verna is forced to go outside the public sector to get help for an emotional problem brought on by her tragic circumstances. She notes, "The Department of Social Services said since I wasn't havin any problems, that I didn't need a social worker. But if I did, I could call them. I told the manager I needed some help, so he got in touch with the Children's Aid and Family Service Agency and they sent someone to see me. She comes to visit me approximately once a week, and like if I have any problems with the kids or anything, she'll try and help me solve them. Most of the time she's helpful, but if I can't get in touch with her, I'll talk with my manager and he'll try to help me."

And Clara describes the insensitivity of the welfare bureaucracy this way: "Overall, I think the social service here is good but, when you're black, this depends on who you come in contact with. Some social workers, I don't know whether it's part of their job or whether they do it not realizin they're doin it, but sometimes they can make you feel pretty bad, like you're beggin or somethin. I think a lotta people that need help sometimes dread goin to them for help, thinkin they're gonna put them through the third degree or somethin like that. Sometimes it really hurts."

The rules and regulations that planners impose on the beneficiaries of government programs add another problem to an already burdened group. Public agencies set up guidelines that create new difficulties for the poor and near-poor and force them to act illegally. This is pointed up in the decision of government to check and recertify the incomes of Underhill residents every year instead of every two years. It means that those whose incomes have gone up will have their rents raised.

May complains that this is unfair because the two year limit is needed to give people time to put some money away. She observes, "Some wives work until recertification and then quit their jobs. We just got our letter for recertification, and in a way it'll benefit us. My husband's making less money than he was last year at this time because he had to take a cut in salary. Our rent won't go up, and starting next weekend I have a job, so that we'll both be working. And he also gets a raise next week. We have to get our recertification in before that which maybe sounds underhanded, but somehow you've got to get ahead."

There are also rules that create tensions among the residents, especially the one intended to keep pets out of the project. While Clara believes that some of the restrictions are needed, she is upset by others. She says, "Some of the rules we got here are good, but some I think are ridiculous. I don't see why we shouldn't be able to have a small freezer, one of these electric freezers that you can plug in. You can hava a television, and how much current does a freezer use more than a television or a record player? I'm sure they must have some reason for not wantin you to have one, but I don't understand it."

May also complains about this: "The one rule I don't understand and can't abide by, they won't let you have a freezer. And boy, for a family my size or a family like Verna's size with all those kids downstairs, this would be a real saving. It would be worth the initial outlay to have a freezer and be able to stock up stuff when they've got sales. That's my top priority if I can ever have anything."

Elmer is upset about the prohibition on shopping carts in the project, as well as about the limitation on parking places available to each family. But he is particularly incensed at the rule involving the number of residents permitted in each apartment. He complains about Archie's intrusion into his privacy, saying, "If your wife's gonna have a baby, you gotta tell him ahead of time. I figure that's none of his business. What is that to him?"

The special rules imposed on the residents of Stairwell 7 affect them in a way that challenges the legitimacy of the welfare state. Government programs aimed at upgrading their lives provide few subsidies and benefits. Their personal options are reduced, their services are inadequate, and they owe a lot of money in installment debts on cars and furniture. A government that appears to be unresponsive and indifferent heightens their sense of alienation.

Everything these people have valued seems to be disappearing as stable neighborhoods are destroyed, jobs become more difficult to obtain, social behavior is affected by a new permissiveness, and the concept of merit is changed to meet the needs of others. They see a terrible unfairness in their situations and an increasing lack of control over what happens to them.

While some are enjoying a higher standard of living, they are frustrated by higher taxes for increased government spending. Moreover, the gaps between America's economic classes have widened, and they feel resentment against those on the adjacent rungs—the very poor who are getting help and the middle class who are making it on their own.

The residents of Underhill are among the more mobile families who have moved to outlying areas seeking economic opportunities and improved physical environments. Some have been displaced by highways and urban redevelopment projects, while others have been lured by government financed housing projects offering the promise of decent shelter at a price they can afford to pay. Most have left friends, family, churches, and clubs that gave them social and psychological support. Few of these institutions have been replaced, so newcomers frequently find themselves lacking the support systems they need to adjust to new circumstances. Many are unable to cope with their problems because the move creates anxiety, tension, and stress within the family unit.

These are individuals who feel almost as powerless in relation to modern society as do the poorest residents of the ghetto. They often represent failures in the competitive American system who have not been economically upgraded and have not shared in the material and psychic rewards of our culture. This is a group that by and large has been left out of the expanding complex of government assistance programs. Their stories help illustrate the marginal position they occupy in our society because a fragmented welfare state seems incapable of helping them secure a better way of life.

Chapter 2

ARCHIE CONOVER
Helping and Watching the Poor

When I became manager of Underhill just before it opened, there were like a dozen priorities and each one had to come first. I just worked around the clock to try to get as much done as I could, but it was absolutely impossible because I was not given a clear picture of what the job was. In fact, I think I had a clearer view of my role than the people who hired me. But I don't think that's so unusual because my employers had never dealt with the management of subsidized housing and none of them were particularly people oriented.

They had a very different concept of the job than I did. We were at a point for a couple of days where I didn't expect to be hired because I didn't think I could do the job they wanted done. Besides, they were offering me an extremely small amount of money; they had in mind a 9 to 5 job for $3,500 plus an apartment. I explained to them that I saw the job as being a very full time thing with lots of it going on in the evenings and weekends. With the amount of money they were willing to pay me, I'd have to moonlight, which would take me out of the development when I was most needed. I told them I wouldn't take it for less than $10,000, and we settled on $8,000 and the apartment.

I was very honest with them that I knew nothing about management and budgeting and very little about maintenance. It seemed to me they planned on handling an awful lot of that and teaching me as they went along. What they were looking at in me was my background in associating with people, particularly people of different races and ages. I think they were on the right track in looking for somebody like me, but they were wrong in not giving me some training immediately.

I walked in here with a desk, a phone, and 1,600 applications and cards of inquiry for 108 units, some of them ready for occupancy in 25 days. This county needs 2,000 units alone for people living in substandard housing and overcrowded conditions. There are only about 100 units available for rent supplement people in the entire county, and Underhill provides only 22 of them because of HUD's 20 percent limit.

I actually interviewed over 400 families of all incomes and backgrounds, and told them what I wanted to see happen. I was looking for people to share transportation and babysitting and to try to fulfill each others needs. I said we would be a very mixed community, and that there was going to be an interdependence of different kinds of people who might not have lived together before. Some people liked the concept, but some never came back for a second interview and others were definitely very turned off. I now know that some pretended to be excited or to at least accept the idea because they needed housing. They saw a nutty guy who had this dream and said, "We'll go along with this until we get our name on the lease and then we can do what we want to."

Certain kinds of people were screened out because I didn't think they would fit into this concept of community. I screened out whites who to me had very serious problems accepting blacks. I screened out blacks for the same reason in reverse. Even though some of them said they didn't have these problems, I sensed the undertones. I could have been wrong but all I had to go on was my own judgment.

I also screened out people at the $5,000 and $6,000 income levels who worked in Baltimore but wanted to be part of Columbia. Their dream was very unrealistic because there was no way for some of them to be able to afford to live here and travel to and from the city. I could understand why they wanted to get out of the bad conditions where they were living, but I saw them as a potential problem, as not being able to meet the rent, breaking the lease, and causing us turnover and cost.

Sometimes I took risks like with this young couple—he was barely 18 and she was under 17. I interviewed them the night they were married and they were expecting a child. Everything about them, their age, their income, the fact that they were just married and that they were married because they were having a child, everything said they weren't stable, don't rent to them. But there was something very trustworthy about them, something that I couldn't define, something intangible that I felt. It was a marginal case that worked out; they're on time with their rent and they haven't caused any problems. They haven't been particularly active within the community, but any time they've been called on to specifically do something, they've always been willing.

We were trying to give first priority to people living or working in this county because Columbia had originally said it wanted to have people living and working here. We were also doing a lot of lobbying to get rent supplement and leased housing approved by the county, and we knew one of the things that would help get it approved was to say that Underhill was heavily filled by local people. They would react to this better than they would to saying we had filled it up with people from the city ghettos. We knew we were dealing with a fear that subsidized housing was going to bring the urban poor into this lovely county, and they didn't want that. We did bring in some poor from the city, but the majority are county people, some of them going back generations and others who were working here and needed to live in the area. Among them were some poor from small cities and rural areas in the county.

In the beginning, I made a very conscious decision not to rent to fair market people, to those who could afford the full rent, unless they had something in particular to offer to the community of Underhill. I did that for two reasons. With conventional housing so near us, I felt our kids would go to school together, families would shop and play together, and there would be a mix within the larger community. And because the need for housing at the subsidized level was so great, I didn't feel comfortable in giving housing to people who could afford to live elsewhere.

We needed more people at a sounder, more suitable economic level to balance the project even though we had them around us—people whose incomes would go up to the fair market level. Still, we're not even at ten percent yet, and I'm now at a point where I certainly would give serious consideration to a fair market family who wanted to rent here if I had the space.

The company allowed me to experiment, to innovate, and to try new things, although I was told my goals were too high and I wanted to move too fast. But I couldn't hear it because I was so sure that I was right. Still, the development organization generally supported the idea of Underhill and wanted it to work. One of the basic goals of the new town was that there be a place for all people, and Underhill helped to provide what they were looking for.

The biggest problem at the start was where to begin. With the huge amount of applications and cards of inquiry, there was a constant stream of people once the office opened. We were even afraid to put a sign out that identified the office because we couldn't handle the traffic. The phone never stopped ringing, and there was this deluge of individuals who needed our limited housing. The fact that there was so little time before they started moving in was certainly a big problem. I worked an average of 14 hours a day, seven days a week, seeing people, trying to determine whose need was greatest, trying to think out where to put them so that we didn't have a black stairwell, or a white stairwell, an old stairwell, or a crippled stairwell.

And then, as the people began moving in, they needed orientation to know what Underhill and Columbia were all about. Some of them needed food stamps and had no idea where to get them. There were all kinds of physical and human things that had to be handled, and there was just me to do it. It was a constant problem of knowing that there was more to be done than could possibly be done.

Within just the first couple of months, I was faced with families who moved in without enough beds or kitchen utensils, with families that didn't have enough food to last until their next check got here, and with women who were pregnant and wanted an abortion. There were women who had left their husbands and were being harassed by them. They wanted to know what kind of police protection or legal help they could get. Some of them needed to figure out how to get a job or how to get the kids cared for, some had to have counseling for emotional disturbances, and others merely needed a shoulder to cry on. There was just about every problem you could think of, and they were all coming at me at once. I really don't know how I dealt with it; I think it's because I was dumb enough to think I could. Maybe it was my innocence that got me through it.

I was never pressured from above; in fact, I was always lauded and told I was doing a good job. It was my own assessment of the needs I saw that was pushing me. As I look back on it, there are all kinds of things I'd do differently. I would have been much more demanding of help from above and much more demanding of having somebody in here on a regular basis to help with human relations things. I didn't know any better, and so I did the best I could.

After a year or so, I had an office routine, and things I had been forced to handle in the beginning were being handled by clerical help or by maintenance. I had also leaned the ropes about where to get social help, like for a family that didn't have food for the weekend. I knew who to put them in touch with or who should get in touch with them. I guess I was more social worker than landlord, but I tried to be both.

At the outset, I felt the very first thing to get done was to create as much of a balance as I could in the way of blacks and whites, young and old, the lowest level income and the highest level income, and so forth. My mandate for the balance came from several places. The HUD guidelines state that management will create a balanced community, although they never describe what that is. Then the County Housing Task Force had asked the people who hired me to try to create a balanced community. Actually, my own personal conviction of wanting to create and live in this kind of situation was the strongest factor. Still, there was that nebulous definition that didn't exist of what is a balanced community.

The HUD guidelines ask that priority be given to those over 62, to the physically handicapped, to people on active military duty, to those displaced by natural disaster, categories like this. Of course, these people could be any color and at various income levels; I certainly didn't have any kind of quota system. I just kind of in the back of my mind had an idea of what I'd like the community to look like and feel like when it got filled.

The 236 Housing Program does call for an income mix and it gives you limits and percentages. You can have no more than 20 percent of the development at the lowest or rent supplement level and no more than 20 percent at the highest or fair market level. It doesn't say that you have to have 20 percent of each, but you can have up to that. There are families in between the top and the bottom that pay differing rentals according to their incomes. The management firm is given a great deal of leeway in the 236 program, and the manager has an awful lot of discretion. This has been kind of hard for management and HUD to deal with because in most programs heretofore, there's been pretty well defined ways of doing things. The local HUD offices have trouble realizing that the manager does have that much authority.

Still, they do examine our records now and then to see what kind of a mix we have. Anytime someone's been here from HUD, they've always looked at percentges of black and white, how many rent supplement and fair market people, and so forth. They've always questioned that, but I never heard any comments at all whether what we have is good, bad or indifferent.

I wanted to meet housing needs as much as possible, but I also wanted a broad mix of people of different colors, religions, ages, and cultures. I did do that, and even with turnover, I'm very conscious of who's going where. There were some mistakes, and I see some places in the mix that are unbalanced and need to be balanced, and I've tried to do that.

And then I wanted to help create a sense of community within that crazy mix of people. I thought with the whole community new that it could be done quickly, but I was terribly naive. It really took longer than I thought because of the trauma of everybody adjusting to everything and me still adjusting to a new world. My wife, Cathy, and a social worker friend said to me, "You set out to do the impossible and you've accomplished 50 percent of it, so you can't say you've failed." That kind of made it look different.

As I look back on my dream, it was exceptionally idealistic and unrealistic. But it was still worth while to have had it because I think that by trying to accomplish things that were totally impossible some of them got done. I wanted Underhill to prove that Columbia could really work, that all kinds of people, of all ages, races, incomes, and life styles could live and work together and like it.

It was also the idea of being three generations here, not related, not necessarily even of the same race, but we were all part of the family of man. My hope was that we could all be a family, either within the same household or within easy distance of each other. There was a time when grandparents took care of grandkids and so there wasn't a need for day care. Children took care of their parents and there wasn't a need for nursing homes. Everybody helped each other within a family structure, but our mobile society has changed all that. It's rare nowadays for three generations of a family to live in the same town let alone next door to each other or in the same house.

I knew that not every person who moved in wanted that or could live with that. But that's what I was looking for, and I wanted it to happen immediately. Cathy's got this sign on the door that describes me. It says, "Oh Lord, give me patience, but I want it right now."

For as long as I can remember, I've never been able to accept stereotypes. I recall when I was ten years old working in a food store in Tennessee. Black construction workers would come in at lunchtime, and I called them "mister" and said "yes, sir" and "no, sir" to them. I was continually told by management that you didn't say that to colored people. I don't ever remember hearing the term "nigger" at work or at home; they were colored. I asked my boss why I couldn't call them mister, and I kept doing it.

I had the only kind of interracial contact that any child growing up in the South in the forties and fifties was ever allowed to have. Things were so structured that there was no way at all for this to happen except when the black was a servant. We never had anybody in our home to clean, but dad had black women and men who cleaned the place he worked at. I knew most of them pretty well, and I was very fond of them.

There was a black woman who cooked in a restaurant where our family sometimes ate. I knew her well for a number of years and really loved her. Once when I was about 13, I saw her getting off a bus and we recognized each other. I ran to her and hugged and kissed her. We stood and talked for a while and we were both very happy to see each other. By the time I got home, mother had four or five phone calls that her son had hugged and kissed a black woman in the middle of a downtown street. She was upset about it, but I think she also understood that I cared for that woman, whoever she was, and that she'd been somebody who meant something to me. I could never accept the fact that black people were any different or that they deserved any less respect; too many people are alike. So when I read the HUD guidelines that said one of the major objectives was to create a balanced community, that excited me. It still does.

I was born in Chattanooga, Tennessee, on the outskirts of the town. My parents lived in an apartment over a grocery store, but when I was less than a year old, we moved to a house that was rented and we lived there until I went away to college. I don't have a lot of memories of childhood. I'm afraid it's because childhood was not at all happy, and the memories that I have are pretty miserable. I was always regretful of being an only child and angry with my parents because of it. It might not have been as bad if there had been a lot of children in the neighborhood, but there were very few.

There was a railroad track within 200 feet of our house, and everybody on our side was in their late fifties on up to 80. It was a whole community of little old ladies that I cut their grass and went to the store for and sat on the porch and had tea with. I am still most comfortable with senior citizens because that's what I was raised with.

There were two or three guys in elementary and junior high school that were fairly good friends, but I couldn't bring them home because mother didn't like them. Mother never liked anybody that I brought home. They were never good enough for me. They were too dirty or too loud or too boisterous. I was never allowed to get dirty or to play football or anything like that because it was too dangerous.

I didn't have many friends in elementary school, but I did get good grades. Still, I had a terrible time learning to read. I remember crying because I couldn't read and trying to sneak out of school to go home. I don't know when I learned to read, but in the eighth grade we had some tests, and I was reading on the college level.

Junior high school was certainly the highlight of my young years. I never have figured out why, but I was Mr. Big Shot, with the exception of sports. I didn't know how to throw or catch any kind of a ball, and that was a real problem because boys are supposed to be able to do that. And I was so big that I would've been valuable in football because I have been over 200 pounds and over 6 feet since I was 12.

But I was in the National Junior Honor Society; I was president of the student body; I was in a choral group; I was in a debating group; I did lots of drama. There was nothing that went on in school, with the exception of sports, that I wasn't a part of. I've always been able to meet people easily, but it's been a front. Nobody knew how scared and how insecure I was because I never let it show. I was very good at hiding it, and I hid it by being the life of the party.

If my parents were pleased by my activities, they sure didn't show it. I begged them to come when I was debating or when I was in a drama, but I never could get either one of them there. When I graduated, I was voted the Boy Who Had Done Most for Hale Junior High. That was like being voted Mr. Hale, and it was one of the big moments of my life because it was from the students. There were awards I had won from the faculty and that was nice, but for your peers to vote you into something is much more valuable.

Life changed drastically for me in high school. There were only 400 or 500 kids in junior high and everything was great. When I got to high school, it was 1,800 students and I was totally lost. It seemed to me like the biggest emphasis that faculty, students, and parents had was sports. I didn't know enough about a football game to watch one, let alone play in one, so I felt totally alienated. I tried for the first few months. I got involved with the drama group, and I was part of a group that ran a book store for school supplies. I do think I tried, but I thought I'd never make it. So in the middle of my first year, in the tenth grade, I took a job back at the supermarket where I'd been before and kept it throughout high school. The only social life I had was the Methodist Church in what was called East Chattanooga, withing walking distance from home. That was a very safe group.

When I look back on it, I thought I had a pretty good relationship with mother, a close loving relationship. But now I see it as totally possessive. Mother had an absolutely horrible, horrible childhood and adolescence, and I was her one thing that nobody was going to harm or take away from her.

Daddy was a spoiled brat baby of seven and still is. He's very weak and mother's continued that. He couldn't even get dressed if mother didn't lay out his clothes for him. It's awfully hard to respect somebody who's that weak, particularly when there's never been an obvious show of any kind of concern for me.

I always thought we were poor, but now I realize that in the early forties daddy was making about $150 a week and we weren't poor at all. It was just that he used it all drinking and gambling and there was nothing left. We could have lived in a better neighborhood, and I could have had a lot of things that I thought we couldn't afford if it hadn't been for his throwing money away. In recent years, I've seen what a strong dominant force mother is, and with daddy as weak as he was, he was put exactly where she wanted him. She ran the whole show; she ran both of our lives and his drinking and gambling was probably an escape from her.

I've never known a great deal about daddy's background and his family, but we do know that all Conovers in this area sprang from a couple of brothers that came to North Carolina from Britain in the late seventeenth century. There's a woman that does geneologies, and she gave daddy a whole lot of information on the Conovers. It's spelled different ways, but we're still all related.

Mother's maiden name was Harrison, which sounds Irish to me. Her mother was half Cherokee, but not the Cherokees that Jackson sent to Oklahoma. They were the ones that hid out in the Smokies and wouldn't go. So I'm descended from the Cherokees that are now in Cherokee, North Carolina, on the reservation.

Mother was born in a little town near Knoxville. She was four when her father died, and her mother put all the kids in an orphanage. Mother was very pretty and lots of people wanted to adopt her, but she wanted to stay with her sisters and her brother. As they got older and left, she was finally adopted. This was when she was 12, and there were four years in what seemed like a very good relationship with her adopted parents. But then her adopted mother died, and a few days after that she came home from school to find the things she owned on the front porch and the house locked. There was a note that her adopted father had remarried and was going to be gone several months, so this was twice she'd been deserted.

I met my grandmother a couple of times when she was very sick. She was a very beautiful woman, very Indian looking. It was during the war and you couldn't get chocolate but daddy could because of some friends he had. We'd drive from Chattanooga to Knoxville in a borrowed car to take grandmother boxes of Hershey's chocolate. Although my grandmother had been selfish and unkind, mother still seemed to place so much value on the relationship. I never pieced this together until the late sixties, when we had four foster kids, and I couldn't help but relate this to their feelings of fantasy for a real mother. Whether it was somebody they knew or didn't know, a real mother was the greatest person in the world. A lot of what I saw in them I had seen in mother without recognizing it. Probably the years with our foster kids helped me understand mother better than anything else that's ever happened to me. We're now at a situation where we remember each other's birthdays and talk to each other by phone three or four times a year. They visited here on my birthday last year, but we have nothing in common. They can only talk about the past. They know nothing of what's going on in the world or even what's going on in the backyard.

I don't know when it started or why, but I had always wanted to be a doctor. I had planned on going to the University of Tennessee and then on to med school. Mother and daddy seemed to accept all this, and so I was assuming somewhere there was money for me to go. It was not until it came time to start thinking about registering that they leveled with me. There wasn't any money, and there was no way for me to go. So I worked a year between high school and college in a foundry.

From early elementary school on through, church had been a great big part of my life. My parents sent me but they didn't take me. This was in the Bible Belt South with its very fundamental Christian philosophy, with the Bible translated exceptionally literally.

There were three of us who, in a revival, said we had heard the call and God said we were supposed to be ministers. I don't know who went first and who led the other two; it was a hysteria kind of thing. I've never known and probably never will know whether I was clever enough to do that to get a college education. I certainly had convinced myself consciously that it was all very sincere, but as I look back on it now, I've often wondered if I fooled myself and all those people to get them to send me to school. Because that's how I went to college; the Methodist Church sent me to a small Methodist school in the South. It was a totally white campus and a totally white community.

I majored in psychology, and for three and a half of my four years, I was what's called a circuit rider. At first, I had three rural churches about 30 miles from campus. And then I had one church for about a year and a half consisting of three small congregations that were dying and banded together to build a new church. Those were experiences that I'm very glad I had. I'd never lived among rural people, and these were very rural backward people.

I guess I enjoyed the circuit rider experience because people needed me; they needed somebody. There was a certain feeling of importance that was good for my ego, but I knew that I was very inadequate for the job. I was still very insecure then and really basically quite shy, but I covered it up. I played the role of being very gregarious and outgoing and talking to a crowd of people, and nobody knew how scared I was. Sometimes I'd even forget to be scared by playing this role so well. I liked meeting the kind of people that I'd never known before; they were good people. But I disliked the job more and more when I began to realize that I didn't believe in what I was preaching, that it was all becoming pure hogwash. I was reading scripture and basing a sermon on that scripture, but none of it had any meaning to me. Toward the last year or so, it got to be a real battle to get the sermons ready and to get them delivered without stopping in the middle of one and saying, "All this is pure bullshit." I've often wondered what would've happened if I'd ever done that.

It was simply that suddenly I had begun to think for myself and to question, and the answers didn't come out right. The first thing was the Old Testament religion professor who insisted that the whale didn't swallow Jonah, that it was just a story, an allegory. I went to the president of the college to have the guy fired, because I felt if the president really knew what he was teaching us, he'd have to fire him. Many of the faculty were ordained Methodist ministers, and the president who was there during my four years became a Bishop. Now these were respected men of the cloth, and they were trying to teach me that all the things I had been taught all my life weren't true. So I decided I was going to have to figure all this out for myself. And the more I questioned, the less I believed.

I went from a Bible Belt, gospel preaching belief in God, to really hating the church, hating it with a passion for tricking me all these years. That's leveled off now, and I guess the only label for me is an agnostic who's tolerant of the church. I do believe there's some kind of power, something bigger than we are, but more and more I think that it's within us and only works when we interact. It's not really something supernatural at all. When people get together to try to figure something out, if there are four of us working on it, the sum power of those people is greater than the four. That's where it is.

Cathy and I were married in my senior year in college, but our relationship started long before that. In fact, my father used to walk her mother home from the movies years ago, when they were single. We have pictures of us together at several birthday parties as preschoolers, but we don't remember any of that.

Cathy was five and a half when she became ill with polio, and she wasn't expected to live. She was not well enough or strong enough to go to school, but she was very determined. When school came around the next year, the doctors and her parents felt that putting her in a public school would not be good for her. So of several alternatives, they decided a Lutheran school was the best one, financially and because of its location.

Her parents were exceptionally wise, and they tried to make sure that she was treated no differently than any other child. They withstood all kinds of friends and family who said, "You've been cruel to that child." And then there must have been a lot of gutsy determination in a very young child that added to the wisdom of her parents and kept her from ever thinking of herself as handicapped.

She used to have trouble getting the paper and the milk in the morning, because with two crutches, she didn't have her hands free. One day she threw one of the crutches in the fireplace and said, "Don't get me another one. I'll have to learn to walk with one, and that'll give me a hand free." In her senior year in high school, she won a very coveted award that always went to a star basketball or football player for being the best team person. She won it because she was such a good sport; it's something she still cherishes.

The day before we were to begin high school, Cathy came to our church to speak to the Methodist Youth Fellowship. She was then a district leader of M.Y.F., and she later went on to the state, the region, and as high as you can go in the organization. I was very taken with her lovely effervescent personality. I was also fascinated by the fact that, although she walked with a crutch, she did not act nor seem different, as a lot of physically handicapped people do. It seemed to me she was able to do anything she wanted to.

After the meeting, the other kids went into church and I sat out on the steps with her waiting for her father to pick her up. He was well over an hour late that night, so we had a good while to sit down and talk. We found out that we were going to the same high school the next day and were both pretty frightened by it.

The next day I didn't get a locker because the system fouled up somewhere. I ran into Cathy in the hall and asked if I could use her locker, and ended up sharing one with her for the first semester. Over the high school years, we were very good friends. We went places together and did things, but usually it was groups of us. It was kind of the misfits that formed their own little group. I didn't fit into things, and there were a lot of things Cathy felt she didn't fit into. Two or three others were part of the group, and we kind of did things together. I never really considered it dating, but Cathy argues with me over that.

Cathy went on to college, and I worked. Any time she was in town, she usually called, and I went over and had supper at their house. Then I went away to college after a year. I had these three rural churches and hundreds of kids who needed some activities because there was nothing for them to do. They all had their farm chores and work, but they had nothing in the way of recreation and no facilities of any kind.

I knew I couldn't do it alone, so I wrote the Methodist Conference office and asked for a youth worker. In the summer, they employed people to do just this kind of thing. They said they weren't sure who they could get for me because I had not given them proper notice, but that they'd do their best. Then I got a phone message to meet a train in town at a certain time, that my youth worker was going to be on that train. I wasn't even sure how I was going to figure out who I was looking for, but when I met the train it was Cathy. We hadn't seen each other for close to two years, although we had written and talked to each other a few times.

She didn't know she was going until the last minute; they'd called and said, "We have an assignment. We want you to be ready to go in a few hours." When she learned where she was going, it hit her that it might be me and she found out that it was. She was supposed to be there for six weeks, boarding with different families. It was some time during these six weeks that I asked her to marry me. Neither one of us is still quite sure how it happened that quickly or what the steps and stages were. The interesting thing was that neither of our families or our friends were the least bit surprised. When we were in Chattanooga and ran into high school friends, they'd say, "You two finally got together." It seemed like everybody had known it for a long time but us. We've now been married 13 years and have known each other for 20.

In whatever community we've lived in, Cathy's been involved in all kinds of things. After we were married, she taught first grade in southwestern Virginia, while I was still in college. She loved the kids and loved teaching, but she hated the system because she was much more a secretary than anything else with all the paperwork and things that had to be done. She's worked in many varied jobs, but it seemed to me the thing she always enjoyed the most was working with preschool kids. So when she was offered a job in Arlington, we decided to move there. We both were a part of beginning a couple of day care centers, because we saw a screaming need for kids whose parents were just a little better off than the poverty level. We joined with a group that tried to pick up where Headstart left off, and started centers that are over ten years old now and still running.

My first job was with the Virginia Manpower Commission, as an interviewer. I had been there only a short time when I was given some special training and promoted to what they called an employment counselor. I dealt with senior citizens, high school dropouts, prison parolees, mental dischargees, the physically handicapped, anybody who had a problem in getting a job. I liked the work and was doing a good job, but I had the same problem Cathy had with the educational system. There was the damned paperwork and all the forms. I resigned shortly before they were going to fire me.

After that, I sold typewriters and calculators for a little over a year. Cathy was working at that time managing a satellite office for a mail order firm. We were talking about giving up and going home because I couldn't find anything I wanted to do. On the other hand, we were happy because we were together and because living near Washington was exciting.

I remember our first summer in Washington we practically starved for a week because we bought tickets to see Bernstein and the New York Philharmonic with guest soloist Eileen Farrell. We had never been anywhere where there were live concerts by well known people. There were all kinds of things in the Washington metropolitan area that we liked, but we didn't think we were ever going to find a niche that we'd fit in and be able to afford. We would have gone back to Tennessee when we found that Cathy was pregnant, but that sounded like running home to both of us. If we'd gone home with no children and no pregnancy, it would have been going home because we wanted to. The other just seemed like we'd failed completely and were going home to admit it.

So we stayed, and I took the first job that offered me any kind of security at all. It was in insurance adjusting, and I did that for seven years with two different firms. I never put in more than 20 or 25 hours a week on the job. An insurance adjuster generally has his schedule pretty well set, and as long as you show up at the right meetings and turn in the right forms, nobody questions you very much. I used the time that was left over to start day care centers and become involved in community kinds of things that were going on. But in the last few years, I was very actively looking for a job that would pay me to do what I was already doing in the community as a volunteer.

By this time I didn't hate the church any longer, and I was part of an organized church group trying to get day care centers built. It seemed to me there were Baptists and Methodists and Catholics who were all trying to do the same thing, but none of them were big enough or had enough power to get it done. So I worked with a handful of people that formed a parish, a council to which churches elected officials and contributed according to their size. Most of the eductional and social action things that were done in that area were handled through this larger body, which represented more than 30 churches.

My activity in church affairs was primarily for two reasons. It was to be involved in social change because, at that time, a lot of it was done through the church. And it was also for a sense of community, to be with people who cared about each other and enjoyed each other. As I look back on it, I guess it was kind of strange for somebody who really didn't believe any more than

I did to be chairman of the Committee on Christian Education. At the time, I felt that a belief in Christ was not important to me but a belief in his teachings was.

We have had a lot of background on interracial things that helped to prepare us for Underhill. I was working part time selling household appliances and met this black fellow at one of the social affairs the company arranged. Wives came along to some of those things and so Cathy met Bob's wife, and we all liked each other a lot and enjoyed the same things. We were roughly the same age and our backgrounds were really quite similar, except that both of them were better educated than we were.

We kept finding ourselves being drawn into a close friendship with them and, at the same time, finding it was difficult for us to handle an interracial social relationship because we'd never before had a chance to. But we finally worked through the problem and became very close friends. During the various civil rights legislative days, I think I was probably able to see some of the points through black eyes as closely as most any white could because of our close association with this couple.

I'll never forget the first time Bob asked Cathy to dance. I still don't know how I sat there because I was furious. A black man was not supposed to touch a white woman and you touch when you dance. Intellectually, I knew that was absolutely asinine, but from the gut level I was having trouble dealing with it. Somewhere in the middle of all this, it dawned on me that etiquette says when a man asks your wife to dance, you are supposed to ask his wife. It didn't take long for June and I to find out that we simply had four left feet. So over the years the pattern was that Bob and Cathy would dance while June and I watched.

One night, we had gotten involved in a very philosophical discussion that went on very late. We all needed to go home but wanted to continue talking, so very impulsively I invited them to our house for dinner the following Friday, and they accepted. It was after we got home that we realized this was a black couple we'd invited to our apartment, and we didn't know what the landlord or our neighbors would say. We were quite concerned about it but decided that we liked them, so we were going to do it.

They came to supper on Friday night, and we enjoyed them very much. It was a very relaxed evening together, and they left in the wee hours the next morning, with a return invitation to us for the next Friday night. Although the management office said nothing, our neighbors immediately stopped speaking to us; they were either cold or rude for the rest of the time we were there. The following week, we got to laughing on the way to visit Bob and June, thinking they were sitting there with the same thoughts, worrying how their neighbors were going to react to this white family. Later in the evening we asked them, and sure enough, they'd had the same hesitations and the same doubts.

This was in the midst of the civil rights march in Washington and some of the major civil rights legislation that came in the Johnson years. I opposed a lot of it because I didn't think you could legislate things like that. I thought people simply had to change and do it because they wanted to, not because it was the law. Bob kept trying to convince me that if we waited until then, it would be another 300 or 400 years, at best.

I remember a fascinating evening when Bob gathered some friends of his, I gathered some neighbors of mine, and we met in our backyard. We had copies of several of those bills and we hashed them out. I think an awful lot of what drew me to favoring the legislation and lobbying for it was seeing it through Bob and June's eyes. One was from Texas and one was from Louisiana and, when they wanted to travel home, they showed us how far out of the way they had to go to find a hotel that would accept them and where they could get a hot meal. This made it very real to us, and we were able to see that legislation from a black viewpoint.

We became very involved in fair housing in Northern Virginia and did a lot of door to door canvassing, educating, discussing, and talking. We were escorts for blacks trying to move into exclusively white suburbs. After escorting them to a home that was for sale, we would be their white front to help them get in. One of these families moved in 6 or 7 blocks from us, and we got to know them quite well.

During the riots in Washington just after King's assassination, something happened that was both very funny and very pathetic. Our son, Allen, had a plaid bathrobe and, to be funny, he tied the sash to the radio aerial of our car. We noticed it but didn't get around to taking the dumb thing off, so it stayed on the car about three days. Our neighbors didn't like us because they knew of our connections in the black community and our civil rights involvements. But on the third day, one of them came to tell us word had spread through the neighborhood that the particular plaid on our radio antenna meant we were safe from the car being attacked by blacks during the riots. Although it meant absolutely nothing, everybody had been frantically looking for something that matched the plaid from our four-year-old's bathrobe.

Then Cathy became pregnant with Jeff and in the middle of delivery, her uterus ruptured, and we came very close to losing both of them. It was pretty clear that we couldn't have any other pregnancies, but we both loved kids and wanted more. That's when we took in four black foster kids, three that were brothers and an older girl that was not related to them. Our own children were then six months and four years old, and the foster children ranged from four to 12.

The need was largely for black kids, so we asked for black kids. We probably would have gotten them anyway, but we asked for them. We figured this was a way of showing what we believed in without our saying a word, and maybe this could accomplish something. It was also related to our frustration at not being able to move fast enough in civil rights.

The children reacted to the experience in different ways. The younger they were, the less impression there was of any kind. The older they were, the harder it was on them. It was particularly hard on Louise, the 12 year old. The boys were four to nine, and they could handle it because so much went over their heads. They were the first black kids ever to go to the elementary school in our area.

Louise did pretty well that first year because she's gregarious, attractive, and intelligent. Even though she was considerably behind academically, she had basic intelligence that was very good, so she did quite well both academically and socially. The following year, she went to a junior high school that was about 50-50 black and white, but the whites were largely middle and upper middle class, while the blacks were largely poor and lower class.

There was an awful lot of racial tension there, and Louise didn't fit anywhere. She was being raised in a middle class white home, and that's what part of her identity was. And certainly a part of her identity was black, so she was torn right in the middle between these two groups that were warring with each other. Probably the closest friend she made was white, and the two of them did an awful lot of crusading, campaigning, and really gutsy stuff for her age, when peers are so important. They would purposely walk to school together, go for a hamburger together after school, knowing they were going to be laughed at, yelled at, and sneered at. But they both were saying, "We're friends and it doesn't matter what color we are."

And then they put together an interpretive dance for a gym class; it was put to a kind of moody rock music with words in the middle portion. They had done the choreography and written the words themselves. Before there were any words, they touched in many ways, fingertips, elbows, toes, hips, shoulders, linked arms, just about every way two people could touch. In the verbal part, they kept repeating, "Okay, gang, here we come, ready or not." The moral was that one was black and one was white, and they were together.

The teacher was so impressed with it that she brought some other teachers in after school to have them see it, and they ended up doing it in an assembly for the whole student body. There were some who were too stunned to react; there were some who catcalled, jeered, and booed; but the majority of the students stood up and applauded. I remember it as being a real high point of when Louis was with us. She felt she had really worked to make a statement; she had made it and it had been heard. But it was tough on her.

As for our own children, the baby never really knew that anything was different. He was six months old when they came and a little less than four years when they left, so the difference in black and white never really hit him at all. Louise was his older sister; she wasn't black or white or anything. The boys were his brothers; they adored him and he was crazy about them. But Allen was just old enough to get kidded and taunted by the neighborhood kids and school kids. He had to battle verbally and sometimes physically for introducing the boys as his brothers, but he always stood up to it very well.

Of course, we saw an awful lot that none of the kids saw. There was a petition not to sell the house to us that went to the realtor from the neighbors. We went around to people to try to tell them what we were doing and why we were doing it. Finally, we kind of reached an agreement with five of our most immediate neighbors, that if we kept the kids in our yard they'd leave us alone and that was good enough.

We had a lot of threatening and obscene phone calls, and a minor cross burning that must have been from the KKK. Our own families and some of our friends sure had a hard time dealing with it, but over the years an awful lot of people began to accept it. Some of the neighbors who had petitioned to keep us out had become very friendly; some had become much more tolerant; some had only moved from totally ignoring us to saying, "Good morning, how are you?" But that was still progress.

By the time she was 15, Louise's behavior was a problem to us and to the school. She was beginning to deal with gutsy black and white issues and with her own identity and confidence, and that's always painful. It was hell to live with, so we went into family therapy, and the team of therapists were very pleased with what was happening to her. We saw it as healthy and good for her, good for us, and good for the family.

But the social services agency in Washington saw it as something they couldn't live with at all, and they decided to move her practically overnight. They didn't ask her if she would like to leave; there was no input from her at all. They didn't ask us either; it was just that she was going to be moved. They told us on Monday that she was to leave on Thursday. And they didn't even tell her; they left it up to us to do that.

I can only conjecture about the reasons for their action, but I think we understand it better now than when it happened. We were very threatening to the whole agency because we disagreed with them frequently and loudly. If they wouldn't let us do something for the kids that we thought needed to be done, and they wouldn't pay for it, we found a way of getting it done. At that time, they were also under a great deal of pressure from several black militant groups who were against interracial placements, and that was an additional factor. Another thing they used was that Cathy had fallen and fractured her pelvis and was in bed and a wheelchair for about four months. They said she was not able to care for the kids, but things were going very smoothly.

We talked to Louise then and said that since she had no family, it might be good for her to go to this teenage halfway house. She would learn to become much more independent and still be able to visit us when she wanted to. We had previously discussed this idea with her as a way of having the best of a couple of worlds. But the place they moved her to was run by nuns who were very strict, and Louise didn't want to go there. So her leaving was extremely traumatic to all of us.

Louise had been hurt so many times that it was actually hard for her to love or be loved. I don't know whether there had been an attempted rape or beatings or what, but she didn't like to be touched by anybody, particularly by men. In the three years we had together, there were very few times that there was any kind of physical touch between the two of us, unless it happened at a time that was extremely spontaneous when we were very excited or happy about something. We would both be surprised that it happened, and there was always a moment of tenseness afterward.

The morning she was to leave, I had purposely arranged to go to work early to avoid being around when she left. Somehow she found out I was going to do this, and she slept on the couch in the living room so I couldn't go out the door without her hearing me. When I started out the door, she got up on the arm of the sofa on her knees and said, "Come here a minute." I walked over close enough for her to reach me, and she put her arms around me and held me very tightly. She kissed me and said, "I appreciate what you've done and I love you, daddy." I knew that was very difficult for her to do, and it made her leaving even harder. But it also made it easier because I realized she had known we cared about her and we had tried.

She called almost daily the first few weeks after she left us, and a couple of times she snuck away and came to visit. She didn't like it where she was and wanted to be back with us. She kept wanting us to do something about it, but we were totally powerless; there was nothing we could do. Finally, we mutually decided it would be much less painful to have no contact for awhile. We had indirect contact through friends who kept in touch with her, and we knew she was doing pretty well.

We saw Louise once more a little over a year ago, when she spent the day with us. She was adjusting beautifully, doing well in school, and working in a day care center. She kept talking about things she was now involved in and relating them to the experiences we'd had together. She was telling us, "I learned these things from you," without actually saying that.

If we had it to do all over again, I don't think we would have taken someone at Louise's age with her emotional problems. From the age of four until she came to us, she had not been in any one spot longer than nine months. She had all the effects of institutionalization and all the self-damning attitudes of somebody who's been kicked around and never loved or wanted. I think, too, that in the state she was in, it was too much to add the kind of cruelty she was put through in the junior high school. She survived it and she may be better off for it, but I'm not sure that I could knowingly put another human being through it again.

The boys went home to their own mother and her boyfriend two months after Louise left us. We knew for months that they were leaving, so we at least had time to deal with it and talk it through in family therapy. We were told it was because their mother was ready to receive them, but we still don't believe it. Their mother's condition was no different than when they were taken from her. They had one home visit that the mother had known about for at least two weeks, and she'd done nothing about food preparation. She gave them some money and sent them several blocks away through all kinds of horrible traffic to get potato chips and Pepsi at the supermarket. There was never any indication that she wanted them back or that she could possibly provide anything for them.

When they left, the boys were very verbal about their feelings. They did not want to leave us, but they did want to go to her. There was this need to be with their real mother and a desire to stay with us. They wanted to do both, which was totally impossible. Jeff couldn't figure out what was going on because these were his own brothers and his sister. He also got very confused about this talk of a real mother, and he wanted to know who his real mother was. If the boys and Louise had a real mother somewhere else, then he must also. But Jeff was young, and so he bounced back pretty quickly.

Allen was seven by then, and it was more painful for him, particularly losing the brother that was his own age. At the same time, he was kind of pleased to have his daddy back. The amount of time I spent with the others meant that he was either sharing that time or didn't get any at all. So when they left, he was suffering the same kind of ambivalence of wanting them to stay and glad they were leaving.

We couldn't stand staying in the house we had bought, and this seemed like the chance to move. So we rented the house for the summer and sublet an apartment in Columbia. Our plan was for me to go back to school and work part time, and for Cathy to work full time. We had been interested in Columbia for years, particularly in the concept of the "people tree" that's the symbol of the town. It's a sculpture in the form of a ball that's made up of people joined to a trunk at their feet. They're all stretching and extending themselves outward with their hands and fingertips touching each other. It's a tree made of people, and to me it said this was a town where all kinds of people could interact and that interaction could create a better world.

We had read about the construction of the Underhill project in Columbia, but when we came out to see it, there was nobody who could really help us. There were several months of trying to get information on how to rent an apartment there and not being able to. After seeing a lot of well-meaning people who didn't know what they were talking about, I finally got very frustrated and angry and hand delivered a fairly detailed letter to the developer. Then I spent almost two hours with his representative, who is kind of a troubleshooter for the entire operation. It didn't really dawn on me that she wasn't just routinely handling my complaint but was getting to know me a lot better. The next day I got a call from somebody who wanted to interview me to manage Underhill. I was working at several part time jobs but really didn't have a career of any kind, so I decided to take it on.

In the beginning, I was almost 100 percent social worker. I have moved gradually away from that to being more and more a manager and having social work handled by other people, agencies, and residents. I am now at the point where no more than 25 percent of my time is spent in the social services area, and some moves are being made to make it even less than that. I think it's only economics that's kept these developments from having at least part time social work staff. For the size of this development, part time would do, maybe 20 hours a week, with a fair amount of that being evening hours.

It's exceptionally confusing to the person in my job to try to play two roles, because they're so different. And I think it's also very confusing for the majority of residents. When they walk into this office, I don't think they're quite sure who they're talking to, Archie the social worker or Archie the manager. They look at them differently, perceive them differently.

From the time the first families started moving in, I was called on to provide social help. By the time a year was over, there wasn't a public or private social service agency in the county that I didn't know, including its director and most of its staff. I began having office hours two nights a week, and people would come in to chat about nothing of any consequence. The pattern was almost always the same, like they'd rehearsed it or learned it from each other. They'd say, "Can I close the door?" and then Archie, I've got a problem." They'd sit and talk and I'd sit and nod, and then they'd get up to leave and say very sincerely, "Archie, I sure do appreciate your help." I didn't do a damn thing. I listened, that was all. But that happened so often that it showed me there was a need for a listening post, for somebody that's just there that you could talk to.

We'd been open less than a year when someone brought a woman in here who needed housing immediately. She had no money and no furniture, and she and her three kids needed a place to live. She had a husband with a big drinking problem, and the night before he had been exceptionally violent and injured her slightly. So she felt for her safety and her kids' safety that she had to get away from him right away.

Within three hours we had her moved into a unit. We had the basic furniture she needed, a long term loan to pay her security deposit and her first month's rent, and food to last her for a week. This was done using two public and two private agencies. But it was unusual that things fell together so well. The various agencies all have their own bureaucracies and usually can't respond that quickly. They can respond in ten days or two weeks, but most of the time they can't handle a crisis thing. So there are an awful lot of emergency situations that I've dealt with myself by default, even without the right kind of background and training.

Then there are people who have needs and are not aware of them. They may desperately need budget or marital counseling, but they're not willing to admit to themselves that they need it when even an outsider can see it. It's difficult to find a way kind enough or subtle enough to convince this person or this family that they need help.

I've talked to a couple of agencies about tying counseling in with the renewal of a lease, and giving the family notice that their children are misbehaving or their own behavior is disturbing the neighbors. I felt we could tell them we weren't going to renew their lease unless they agreed to counseling, but the staff from the agencies told me not to try it. People would cooperate in order to keep their apartment, but they'd come with such a fence around them that it would do no good whatsoever.

Later, the Childrens Aid and Family Services Agency asked if they could bring in a mobile counseling bus. I said they could give it a try, even though I felt the residents would react negatively to it. It was one of their ways of trying to bring the service to where the need was, but it wasn't accepted because people didn't want to be seen going in it. When the van didn't work here, they parked it at the village center. They also set hours to use a room in this office, and I know of four families that are being counseled on a regular basis. This agency has probably been one of the most active and aggressive agencies in Underhill. They've passed out fliers and leaflets and used the bulletin boards for posters and handouts. They also had group meetings to explain their services, and they've offered counseling individually and in groups.

There have been a number of other agencies that have handed out brochures saying they would like to help people talk through their problems, but it's hard to know the extent they're being used. The confidentiality between counselor and client would keep the counselor from telling me that he was here. One of them told me he'd run into two professionals from other agencies, so evidently some of the residents are using these services.

In the early days here, I had a bias against the County Department of Social Services. I guess it was because of my dealings with the agency in Washington, where they were at least 50 years behind the times. I just kind of assumed that all agencies were like that one, and my dealings with this Department began with a chip on my shoulder. It didn't take long for me to change because of the caliber of most of the people and the dedication they have. But they're constantly hamstrung by lack of money, lack of staff, and regulations that don't make sense. Still, they have been very helpful to the lower income people of Underhill, and they've even wanted to meet some of the needs of the more moderate income group. But they're slapped with all kinds of federal restrictions that keep the limits very low. There isn't a great deal of common sense in the manual they have to live with. So there have been times when we've twisted things a little bit to make it better for the client.

This Department is the one that takes applications for public assistance grants, food stamps, medical assistance cards, and other needs. They also provide a lot of information and do referrals to other agencies. What's most impressive is that they do an awful lot as individuals beyond and above the call of duty. Like I had a call here last night after hours from one of their workers. She had talked with her client who's a resident here, and that person was having trouble getting draperies installed. She had the curtains but she wasn't physically able to get the traverse rod up, so she was using a sheet over the window. The agency worker asked if I would arrange for someone to do that work, to charge the client a couple of dollars so she'd think she was paying for it, and send the rest of the bill to her. It's typical of that agency to be genuinely concerned about the individuals they work with. We had asked them to send someone over here on a regular basis, but they told us they simply couldn't afford to do it.

Transportation to Social Services is a problem; that's one of the reasons we wanted to have somebody over here. The Community Action Agency offers a station wagon service, but unless it's a real emergency, you have to call a day before. They come pick you up, take you, wait for you, and bring you home. They ask for a donation of a quarter or 50 cents if you can afford it, but if you can't afford it, that's okay. That same service will take you to the highway shopping centers, but it usually tries to plan that with groups of people. They'll take you all kinds of places, but they won't take you from one spot in Columbia to another spot in Columbia. The service is used almost daily by someone in Underhill. It's intended for people at poverty levels, but to keep from embarrassing anyone, they accept a call from anybody here, even though we have different income levels. When someone calls and gives them an Underhill address, they just accept it without asking any questions. This transportation is available in the daytime, but it still doesn't take care of evenings and weekends.

One of our more effective agencies is a sheltered workshop; it's a place that offers employment for people with physical, emotional, and mental disabilities. They now have 14 clients and five of them are from Underhill, including the bus driver that picks up the clients and takes them to and from work. The idea behind the workshop is to get subcontract work from industry, things that have to be done by hand that take a lot of time and cost industry an awful lot. Hopefully, the workshop can do it at a price cheaper than industry can do it, but still enough to pay the client something. We have a deaf woman from here who got 80 cents an hour plus something extra for how many pieces she got done. The problem was that the Department of Social Services found out about it and had to deduct what she earned from her welfare grant, so she stopped working.

The Christian Women's Thrift Shop has been one of the most helpful agencies throughout the history of Underhill. I think one of the big reasons is that they have no bureaucracy. There are a couple of women who make all the decisions, so you can call them and get an immediate answer. I call them miracle workers because they've never told me no on anything, and they've always come through on whatever they said they'd do. They've loaned money for rental payments and for educational purposes at a very long term and with no interest to at least 20 families in Underhill.

Recently, however, they've put some conditions on that. They'll loan you money if you'll meet with their counselor to make sure that you're budgeting your money properly. They had a number of people who did not pay them back, and they felt part of the problem·was that families needed budget counseling. So they have a professional who's volunteering her time to do this kind of counseling. There's one family here they loaned some money to at one time, and it wasn't paid back. They asked them again for money and were told they had to accept counseling to deal with their budget problems. The wife in that family called me two days ago to say she was absolutely amazed at what she'd learned from this counselor. She was helped to cut corners in many ways by changing some things that were costing her.

They also have been very helpful with furniture and clothing. A big portion of the money comes from a thrift shop they operate, and other money comes from donations from individuals and about 15 churches. If a family moves in with no furniture, they can outfit an apartment with the essentials. It's not going to be a lovely apartment, but they can do it with a day's notice.

Several times, the Salvation Army has come to the rescue of a family who needed food for a week or medical help they couldn't get elsewhere. And the County YMCA has offered employment to some of our teens in their summer day camps. In addition, the Community Action Agency has been aggressive in trying to find ways of meeting day care needs, counseling people, and walking them through the red tape of the bureaucracy of other public and private agencies.

The State Employment Service was located across the street from us, and they were very anxious to help. They came over here to tell me what they offered and what their limits were. Any time someone came here looking for a job, this was one of the first places I sent them, and in many cases they found assistance there. Unfortunately, a cut back in funds finally closed the employment office. It sure is missed by residents, especially since the closest place is in Baltimore and transportation from here is very difficult.

Big Brothers wanted to help us, but said the needs were much greater in the inner city. In fact, they look for Big Brothers from Columbia to come to the city. They won't accept the fact that we need help out here. When they compare it to other needs they say, "We're sorry; we just don't have enough men to help you." In a place like Underhill, where we have 41 female-headed families, this is very definitely a crucial need. Many of these families are black, and I have asked the NAACP to try to create their own Big Brother program. They told me they saw the need and the problem, but they've never responded to it.

We needed to get a path put in behind one of the buildings to make it accessible to wheelchairs. The apartments here have steps that go either up or down at the front entrances of the stairwells, so the only way we could handle people in wheelchairs was in the rear. With the help of the Governor's Committee to Hire the Handicapped and the State Department of Vocational Rehabilitation, we got a path in that leads directly to three units and passes a couple of others that could feed off of it at a future date. We also widened the bathroom doors so the chairs could get in. Now we have three units that are specifically geared for residents who are disabled and use wheelchairs.

HUD requires that we give priority to the physically handicapped, but there's no way to give priority to them if you can't get them in. In my mind, this was a mistake on HUD's part. They had to approve the architectural plans for Underhill, and they were approved with no comments about the physically handicapped. But then you can't come down too hard on HUD because Congress hasn't allocated money to increase HUD's staff to the point where they have the time to check on things like this. In the last ten years or so, their staff has increased only slightly while the housing stock they deal with has tripled.

Kind of by default, there's a building here that houses most of our elderly. We have 18 one bedroom apartments that are located in the same building and none anywhere else. I think right now 13 or more of them are occupied by senior citizens, so that the building is sometimes referred to as the elderly building.

Personally, I like to see ages mixed more, but in the buildings where we have senior citizens mixed with younger families and children, there have been problems with noise. The seniors' sleeping patterns and life styles are quieter and calmer and some of them get upset easily by noise. So there are advantages for senior citizens to having a building with no children. I'm glad at least that they're living in a community where there are people of other ages and not totally isolated by themselves. I think they are too.

When I was interviewing for that building, I questioned all the seniors as to how they would feel about having a totally senior citizen building. All of them said they would like to have at least some younger people in the building, that they didn't want to be totally isolated. But most of them also said they would just as soon not have children. In that building in particular, the seniors look after each other and care for each other. The others who are scattered throughout the rest of the development aren't tied as closely as those who live in that building, even though it offers nothing that was designed for seniors. But then it was never advertised as a senior citizens building either.

The senior citizens here certainly miss a place to congregate; it's almost like the teens wanting a place to hang out and the seniors don't have one. They kind of stand out in front of their building and talk to each other, but there's no place for them to sit. Unfortunately, neither the developer nor the Columbia Association has responded to our repeated requests for a couple of benches.

Our County Commission on the Aging has created what they call a satellite group. They meet here in Underhill once a month for a couple of hours, but it's not limited to Underhill people. There's someone from the Commission here who helps them plan recreational and social things. Most of them cost money and that's sometimes difficult for people here. But at least it's a chance for them to get together and to know each other better.

And then there's the Retired Seniors Volunteer Program, which is a way for seniors all over the county to volunteer their services through the Commission to help somebody else. The Commission also arranges to provide cards that allow seniors to get discounts at certain stores.

Legal Aid has been a problem for a lot of reasons. First of all, we haven't had a lot of it in this county; we've had to get it from Baltimore. Then the income levels that qualify for legal aid are unrealistically low. There are lots of people who need this kind of help, particularly women with husbands who won't give them support.

I've had at least a dozen incidents with somebody coming and asking for legal assistance. What legal help we had was coordinated through Community Action, so I referred them there: I usually tried to follow it up and that generally showed that the person didn't get a lot of help. If they really wanted legal aid, they ended up paying for it.

Despite the large number of public and private agencies offering services, there isn't a single agency that has enough staff or a big enough budget to meet the needs of Underhill. If you combine the difficulty of transporting people from here to the agencies and their inability to come here, there's a real problem. But there are services that sometimes aren't even used by people here, and it's because of the missing links. The county is just beginning an information referral service in a very limited way, and we're all glad to see it because it's the first we've had. Everybody has been doing his own thing, and it's much better to have a centralized way of doing it.

As far as Underhill is concerned, there's got to be a catalyst, a facilitator, somebody to help bridge the gaps in the linkages that affect the delivery of social services. In large part that's been me, but the more I've become manager and the less I've become social worker, the less I could do and the less I was trusted to do. And that brings us right back to the need for social work staff.

If I had a reasonable budget, there would be one person here who would be the manager, the authority figure and the rent collector, the one who enforced rules and regulations. He'd write the nasty letters about the kids that urinated in the parking lot and so forth. There would be another person, part time in a development this size, whose job would consist entirely of providing social help, including the delivery of social services, counseling, working with groups, and dealing with racial tensions. That person could work for management as long as there was an understanding of management's role and the person's role, with the responsibilities well defined and kept very separate.

From the viewpoint of the residents, I think they might prefer that the social work staff person come from outside the community through an agency and have no ties to management, not look to management to get paid, and not have to kowtow or answer to them. But the manager would have to be the boss, because the firm that manages the property has the ultimate responsibility. If the development fails financially, all the social work goes down the drain anyway. This could work if the personalities involved had good communication and an understanding of each other's roles.

I don't think public agencies can ever fully handle this country's needs; private individuals and private industry have got to become involved if it's ever going to work. But this won't happen here under the present circumstances, because all fiscal things are decided by owners who are removed somewhere. Social things are left to happen if they can. Like a year and a half ago, I made a recommendation for a social management team, a group of people who would work not only with Underhill but with other 236 projects that were scheduled to be developed in Columbia. I felt they could take a look at us on a regular basis and help management decide where it should be going. Residents were to be represented in that group, so management would have had somebody else to talk to and get advice from. There are so many decisions made by the manager that should be looked at from more perspectives than one person can possibly have. Tenant selection is one of those, and every time I get notice that somebody is moving out, a part of me tenses because I know I've got to decide who is going to go in that spot. It's kind of like playing God.

What HUD has done thus far has not been that helpful. They have a Community Services Department that has visited here at least three times, but it seems they've been trying to learn from me more than helping me. Maybe if they had the right kind of professional staff and enough of them, it would be useful. But I think I would rather see that kind of backup coming right here from a social management program on the local level.

HUD has never developed a manual for the 236 developments, but there are guidelines that leave the manager a lot of discretion. If you followed their guidelines, you'd be on the right track—if you could afford it. But that's what's so unrealistic: the management fee provided the firm that manages the project will not pay for what the HUD guidelines call for. The guidelines assume that the manager is going to be firm, maintain the property, stay within a budget, and be a social worker. That's just not possible.

I had the opportunity one time of spending about 45 minutes with the Deputy Director for Community Services for HUD, and I talked to him about this problem. He said, "You mean you're a combination of an angel and an S.O.B." I said, "Yeah, that pretty well sums it up." He asked if I thought it was possible to be both things, and I said that I felt it didn't work very well. And he said, "Neither do we, but we don't know what to do about it." So I know personally that from a national level there are people at HUD in responsible positions who know that what they're suggesting doesn't work, but they don't have the resources to do anything about it.

HUD has recognized that the process of moving in is one of the toughest periods of adjustment because there are so many things happening all at the same time and each one has to be handled right then. They now have something called "supplemental management funds" of $100 per unit, available one time only, to be used before you're 95 percent occupied. The money can be spent by management in a variety of ways, but HUD approval is required. There are basically three things that it can be spent for: counseling before, during, and after the move; improving the delivery of social services by helping to provide linkages between the need and the agency; and helping residents organize so that they can help themselves. They haven't provided enough money to do these jobs, but I sure wish I'd had even these limited funds.

Underhill got caught kind of in the middle there because supplemental management funds came along after we were begun. This would have been a way of hiring social work staff at least in the beginning. While I can readily accept the fact that the initial period is one of the roughest, I think this kind of help needs to continue at least six months to a year after the project is fully occupied. Hopefully, in that length of time, residents could be organized and settled in enough to fend for themselves a bit more.

The need for help starts even before the family moves in. In only three instances could I find the time to visit a family in the home where they were living. I think it was good in these cases, because it helped me understand where they were coming from and gave them a chance to get to know me a little better in their own setting. It would have been helpful with a number of people who moved here if someone could have spent a fair amount of time with them before they moved, preparing them for the change. There was almost no way for me to do that, to help them plan the move, to answer all kinds of questions about the schools their kids would be going to go to, where they would shop, how they would get around, how to use a flush toilet and a garbage disposal, how to take care of beautiful floors, and how to pay for carpeting the floors that the lease says they've got to cover. The tenants should be told this is a break and a step forward for them, that it requires a positive investment of effort and energy to make it work for them, for their neighbors, and for the whole community that they're going to be living in. If there had been this kind of orientation beforehand, I feel many of our problems would not have happened. And for those that did happen, there would have been someone they knew already that they could call on and say, "I've got a problem; can you help me?"

I made another proposal to the company when I discovered that HUD had belatedly given them more than $10,000 in supplemental management funds to be used for social services. There was a lot of confusion about the money, but I was able to determine that it was sitting in the bank waiting for somebody to tell our accountants how to spend it. After consulting with a large number of the social agencies that have offered to help Underhill, I put together a proposal that allowed some of this money to go toward previous management losses, but left enough to hire a half time social worker for 70 weeks. That proposal was sent to my immediate superiors and it was thrown away; it was ignored.

Someone wrote an entirely different proposal with no input from me and no discussion at all. I was told, "This is the budget we're going to send to HUD and what we need from you are facts to back it up." Their budget applied the entire $10,000 to back management losses. The arguments used were valid, because all of the things that the guidelines said this money was spent for, I had done in one way or another. So while it was totally within the guidelines, it was one more time that my bosses were saying, "Dollars and cents are so much more important than flesh and blood." They were saying that what I was asking for could be done by nonprofessional volunteers who would be paid pocket expenses but no salary. I'm all for volunteers and I think an important part of our national heritage is based on volunteerism. But volunteers were not going to do the job that I saw needed to be done, certainly not without professional guidance. So I have finally gotten the message loud and clear. I am being told over and over again, "Get done whatever has to be done over there, but don't bother us and don't ask for any money."

It was very obvious early in the game how little I knew; so I asked the area HUD office where I could get training and was invited to two or three sessions with them in the local HUD office. They were helpful to some extent in explaining HUD process and procedure, but nothing further than that. Then they suggested that I seek training from the National Association of Housing and Redevelopment Officials and from the Foundation for Co-operative Housing. I registered for a number of courses but they kept being cancelled for lack of participants. It wasn't that there weren't people who wanted and needed the training, but most people couldn't afford it.

Then the Administration created something called the National Center for Housing Management, and I was invited to take part in their first course. We had classes for a period of 12 weeks, alternating a live in situation and commuting. Part of the curriculum was built from our own experience. There were a number of shortcomings for me personally and, I know, for a number of the other participants. We needed a graduate course in human behavior, and they were giving us a kindergarten course. Our evaluation sheets kept telling them this, and the program did begin to change toward the end.

One of the things I had hoped to learn was how you organize residents. It's one of five things that we spent the most time on, but the only answer we came up with was that you do anything you can possibly think of, but don't be too surprised if it doesn't work. I've met no one who has a really well functioning organized residents group except those where it's truly a house organ, where it was organized by management and run by management. Then it simply becomes residents saying, "Yes, we're beginning to agree with you."

Probably the most beneficial thing of my training program was the interaction between those of us who were participants. All of us had at least some experience in management and some had a great deal, so we could share joys and sorrows, things we tried, funny stories, and all kinds of things. There was a great camaraderie that grew out of all this and a real desire to do something about improving the whole situation of housing management.

The teaching staff and the participants agreed unanimously that we all needed social workers. Certain people talked about what they had been able to do in their particular community or what they had tried to do that hadn't worked or had worked partially. We learned a little bit from each other, but we just didn't know where to find the money for staff.

We did a lot of brainstorming of what would you do if you were in Congress or if you were President, and we agreed that one of the first things we'd tackle was the Office of Budget and Management, which insisted on keeping one agency from talking to another. For example, when Underhill was built, HEW should have been informed well in advance by HUD and planned a multipurpose center with a day care unit in the midst of it. I think it could have been done, but OMB didn't allow HUD to talk to HEW.

There should have been some advance planning of day care for children, particularly for working mothers and families where there is no daddy.

Some are getting help by having neighbors keep their children, and some are getting it through the several day care centers that exist within Columbia and the county. A few are getting it with financial assistance from the Department of Social Services, but the day care need is still not met.

It simply would have made things much easier for an awful lot of people, plus providing employment for some others from Underhill, if we'd had a center here. It could also have helped in building a feeling of community because it would have been a place for a lot of people to come together and get to know each other in a natural way. I have been told by Community Services people at the national level at HUD that they think it could happen if the various agencies could ever communicate with each other, but the federal bureaucracy just doesn't show it.

Some people in the Community College had an idea for a day care program that would be more concerned with growth and development than babysitting. They proposed training a number of women in Underhill to take care of kids in their own surroundings in a couple of experimental programs. We were excited for a while because the regional HEW office said, "We think this is a great idea; it ought to be tried." They told us they could only provide $50,000 of the $80,000 needed, and that instead of cutting the figure, we ought to go to HUD nationally and present it to them. They responded quickly in a letter that was extremely encouraging and sounded like, "You're funded, but there are some technicalities." They asked half a dozen questions that they wanted more clarification on. So we scurried around and answered them all in like 48 hours and delivered it back to Washington. Then we sat and sat and sat, and we didn't get an answer. We had to go digging and finally found out we weren't funded but not why.

Another thing many of us talked about was the need to get rid of all income limits, because they made no sense whatsoever. Under federally legislated income guidelines, I can have a family walk in here that's a few hundred dollars over the annual income limit for moderate income rental, and I have to say to them that I can only rent to them at market value. It might end up costing them more to live here than elsewhere, and I can't really believe Congress meant for that to happen. We all agreed that if a family was no more than $100 or so over the limit, you weren't much of a manager if you couldn't find a way of hiding it. Although it was illegal, we still felt we were following the intent of the law.

The 236 program is probably the closest we've come to having a reasonable way for a family to stay in the same spot with rent going up or down according to income. I've had families who came in at base rent whose job situation improved, and their rent has gone up $30 or $40. Then there was a layoff or something happened to decrease their income, and they've gone back to base rent, all the while living in the same unit. In public housing and other programs, there are ceilings that force people to move when their incomes go up.

But there are problems in the 236 program, too, particularly when re-certification comes up and rents have to be changed as incomes have changed. I can lower rent at any time during the year if a family is above base rent and their income decreases. The only time that I'm required to check their rent to see if it needs to be raised is once a year. It's very possible and totally legal for a family to move in with the daddy working, and the week after they move in, for the mother to go to work and their income to be doubled. This gives them a year to have a higher income with a lower rent, and it's a way of allowing a family to move upward. It fits in with my perception of the program that a family be allowed to better themselves.

Now if they are both working at recertification time, the rent would go up. So it's possible for them to work for a portion of the year and not be working at the time of recertification. There's nothing that requires me to check on people's income except once a year. I think there are a lot of managers who kind of see it as their role to make sure that nobody gets away with anything. But I see people trying to make a living for themselves and to have what we all want, a certain amount of economic security.

From the beginning, I saw the separation that had happened with some other subsidized developments in Columbia and the fact that they were not seen as an integral part of the community. There was also a tendency on the part of some people to look down at Underhill, but I didn't think the attitude was as strong as in some other communities. I firmly believe there is more acceptance in Columbia of people of different economic and racial backgrounds than there is in most any urban area. Still, we had merchants who complained to us about vandalism and theft, and sometimes it was our kids and sometimes it was somebody else's kids. It was hard to convince them that some of the ones they were complaining about did not live in Underhill and weren't poor.

We also had aggressive efforts by others to pull Underhill into the mainstream of the community and to help me find ways to keep us from being isolated and cut off. The Columbia Association frequently called to discuss ways of getting our kids interested in neighborhood centers and making facilities accessible to them at rates they could afford. It bothered me that we were looked at differently at all, but I still thought it was hopeful that the difference was less here than it was somewhere else.

One of the things I saw as my role here was to integrate Underhill into the neighborhood we lived in and the larger surrounding communities. So almost from the very outset, I was active in village meetings, committees, all the schools the kids are in, groups dealing with housing throughout the county, and agencies dealing with social services, so there was a link between this community and the rest of the world. All along, my hope was to move residents into those roles, but it was very hard to have that happen early in the game. In the last few months we've made some progress, and there are now residents serving at various levels in nonelective positions throughout the county. Part of their role is to try to dispel myths and stereotypes about us.

One example of the kind of problem we face is the very high rental property adjoining us that's been open roughly the same amount of time we have. It's on a hill with a beautiful view of downtown Columbia; that's one of the things that makes it rent for so much. Management there was very concerned that we were next door to them. They were afraid we'd hurt their image and that our kids would give them trouble. I had several meetings with them and said if they did have any problem, I wanted to hear about it immediately and I'd do my best to handle it.

I've never had a call, letter, complaint, or anything from management there, but the reverse has happened. We've had at least four kids from there, all from affluent families living in expensive apartments, who've created all kinds of problems for us. They've vandalized playground equipment; they've harassed kids and cursed parents; one has threatened kids at the bus stop with a switchblade; they've done all the things that are supposed to happen from poor black folks. They are middle class kids, both black and white.

Of course, we've also had some incidents including Underhill children. There were two brothers in this family from the Virgin Islands that were a problem in the school, in the village center, in the community center, in Underhill, and in their own home. I tried to work with that family and got very little cooperation. I had at least four different agencies trying to work with them, and they never could get any cooperation. Last December, I had to give them notice that I would not renew their lease because they had not in any way tried to modify the behavior of these kids. I made it very clear in my letter and my talks with them, that if there were any effort to work with the kids, I would reconsider. But the misbehavior continued, and they were doing absolutely nothing about it.

I'm still not exactly sure how they reached HUD, but somehow or other, the letter I had sent them got to the area office. HUD was very up tight about my doing it and insisted that we give them another chance. The family did finally agree to some guidelines, but they continued to ignore them. I was at the point of defying HUD when I learned they were going to move anyway. When they left, the whole community kind of breathed a sigh of relief.

A serious problem arose later on, when several residents wrote to the developer asking for my resignation. They listed a number of reasons to explain their request, but one was very important and that was where the problem was. I was accused of keeping extremely personal, opinionated, biased, and discriminatory information in my files that I was supposed to be using against residents to keep them from getting jobs and for all kinds of other reason that were all dirty lies.

Fortunately, my boss was very supportive of me throughout, and tried to find some positive aspects to the situation. He came over here with another company executive to meet with a group of residents and to talk through all the things they wanted to discuss. It was strange that the entire community was never really aware of it, but word did begin to spread a little bit. This was not something that was openly talked about, but was whispered behind closed doors.

I had written an answer to the Residents Council, but had refused to see them because I said I had nothing to defend. It's my understanding there were 25 or so people here for the meeting. There were a handful of people who were determined to get me out, and there were a handful who were determined to see that I stayed. Then there were a number of observers that were waiting to see what happened. As the night went on, more and more of the observers realized they didn't like the process and didn't like the way things had been handled. They felt that even if I were guilty of what I'd been accused of, no one had come to me, and it had all been done too secretively with most residents having no input into it. The mood of the whole evening changed to being pro-Archie by process of elimination, if nothing else.

Then there was a HUD investigation, and the guy from HUD spent about four hours here going through practically every file I had. He never gave us a written report, but that's not unusual. However, he did say to me and to my boss that he did not find anything derogatory or discriminatory. In looking through my files, he found every evidence that this development had a caring manager, and the people should be glad that I was here. So both from HUD, from the developer, and from the residents themselves, what was done to be detrimental to me turned out to be a positive thing that increased my value.

I kept pretty careful files because I felt it was important to maintain records, and also to protect myself, if a family or social worker were to accuse me of something if a particular situation didn't work out to their satisfaction. If I had a complaint of one neighbor about another, or if someone asked for help, I wrote it down. I haven't kept anywhere near the amount of written material in the file that I'd like to; I just haven't had time.

What I have done has helped me to see the way things are happening and to understand the patterns. An example is that over a period of months there might be several people complaining about one person or one family, so it becomes pretty obvious there is a problem. On the other hand, if I see that one person is complaining about a lot of different people on a regular basis, then it's that person that has the problem, not the other people. It's easier to see that when it's in written form and you can go back and look at it and document it rather than keeping it in your mind.

Another reason for record keeping was to help me understand how I reacted to particular kinds of situations, to know what worked and didn't work. It was a tool for me to figure out the best way to handle certain kinds of problems. I've had the hope that some day others could learn from our experiences and avoid the difficulties we have had.

HUD did suggest that some personal and confidential stuff ought to be kept separate from the regular residents files. We've moved some of them to a different spot and have taken a lot more security precautions. The files are locked; the doors to the rooms where the files are have locks on them; windows that can be jimmied have bars on them. None of these security measures were taken before.

Over the last year, I learned largely by accident that most of the people involved were from outside of Underhill. The gal who had been elected chairman of the Residents Council just a few weeks before was weak and immature. She came to me within a month after that all happened and told me she knew she had been used. It turned out to be a racial thing with outside black influences wanting a black manager here. These people were concerned with me because I wouldn't be a puppet for them; I was too independent. While it was blacks who were instigating it and who helped get stuff from my files, it was whites who made the accusations. Race didn't appear to be a factor, while they were actually trying a build a black power base.

HUD management guidelines say that you are to be receptive to some sort of tenant organization and, if it doesn't happen naturally, that you will encourage it. What HUD doesn't do is tell you how. I'm beginning to find out they never tell you how because nobody knows how.

I started from the very beginning saying that I wanted residents to have input into management, to understand the budget process, and to help make decisions. If a rent increase came around, I wanted them to know beforehand, to understand why it was needed, and to help decide on how it would happen. I said this until I sounded like a broken record. Very few of the tenants believed me because of the age old distrust of the landlord. The distrust of my white face by some of the blacks moved them to say, "We've never been treated fairly by a white man, and we can't really believe that you believe the things you're saying."

Other things also made it hard for a community like this to get organized. Some of the people here are living better than they ever dreamed they would, so why should they organize to improve their quality of life. What have they got to strive for when they've already arrived? And as in any community anywhere in the world, others wanted somebody else to do the work so they could reap the benefits. So it was a constant uphill battle to try to get the residents organized.

We finally did get a Residents Council off the ground through a core of about six or seven people who put together a system to elect a representative from each of our stairwells. This was done in two identical meetings held on different nights of the same week, to make sure that everybody could attend and be part of the planning. On the day of the election, the polls were open from 9 A.M. to 9 P.M. That night, those who had been in charge learned that the voter turnout was just over 50 percent, and they really wanted it to be more than that. Of course, our national elections don't get any more than that. So the next day they divided up the names and phone numbers of the people who had not come, and everyone was contacted and urged to vote. The polls were left open till 5:00 the next day, and we ended up with something like a 73 percent turnout.

The first time the stairwell representatives met together, I gave them a list of things I thought they should consider. I told them they could call on management for any kind of clerical assistance, to get information, or to get help from people with expertise. They spent an awful long time putting together a very complex system of bylaws that were then voted down because they were too complicated. They never did get rewritten, so there were no bylaws that were in effect. They did elect a chairman, a co-chairman, secretary, and treasurer, and they have a bank account. They've sponsored several functions like a Halloween party, a rummage sale, and a picnic, and have done some cleanup in the project. While they did cause several things to happen, in recent months it's kind of fallen apart. There's a core of people who are still functioning, but they aren't the ones who were elected; they aren't the officers.

At one point, the residents here asked for help in organizing, and a couple of people from the Community Action Agency came over to a meeting. The feedback I got was that the residents who wanted the meeting said, "They wouldn't help us." The staff people from Community Action said, "The residents wanted us to do everything for them. They weren't willing to see that we would be glad to help them organize, but we were not going to do their work for them." I've often wondered if Community Action had pushed a little harder whether our residents' organization might be in better shape now.

I still think involvement of the tenants is necessary and that the whole development would profit from it. But it requires a change of attitude from people who are at the very bottom of the totem pole economically, educationally, and experientially. There is the feeling that they can't be heard, that there's no sense to try to be heard because they can't be. There are all kinds of people in Columbia who'd like to communicate with Underhill, but we still aren't organized enough to do it.

The problem is complicated by the fact that decision makers don't always listen. For example, the community as a whole is pretty much in agreement that we really need a paved area other than the parking lot for kids to roller skate and to ride all kinds of wheeled things on. They looked to me to get this done, but I've tried to explain to them that I can't do it alone. I've tried repeatedly to talk to the Columbia Association, the developer, and agencies that might fund it, with no success. It's one person trying to speak for a community of 107 families, and I haven't had any influence. I've urged them to organize in written form and choose people who could verbalize the need. This could carry a lot more weight because it would be coming from them directly. They nod like they hear me, but either they don't believe it, they're afraid to try it, or they're not willing to devote the time to trying.

The problem of keeping pets is a real touchy one, not just in Underhill, but everywhere. It's a big issue in apartments all over this geographic area. As more and more people live in multifamily units, there's a push for them to accept pets because they're part of the family. The owners and managers view pets as a real difficulty because they create noise, they cause damage, and there's always a problem with waste. Some places have solved it by having pet walking paths, but in this development the HUD model lease suggests no pets.

There are things in the HUD lease that we must do and other things that are merely suggested. When we were writing this lease, my boss and I were sitting in his family room. There was a cat in his lap and one of his dogs had his head on my leg and I was patting him when we decided "no pets."

We were two animal lovers saying "no pets," but we did it both from a manager's viewpoint that pets were problems, and from an animal lover's viewpoint that apartment living was not for animals.

In the first few months after we opened, I realized we had a dog and cat in Underhill. I turned my head and pretended not to see them, but that was a mistake because in a matter of weeks we were flooded with pets of every size and description. Some of them were leashed, some were kept inside, most were properly cared for, but they still became a big nuisance very quickly. The residents who didn't have pets and who didn't want to live with them really raised a clamor.

We have three women here who are absolutly petrified of cats; being near a cat just sends them into hysteria. So it's certainly not fair to them to have to live next to a cat. You have to balance that with a 12 year old girl who's had a cat for four or five years and I say, "You can't bring the cat when you move in." That's not fair to her either. I think any time you talk about multifamily living, there's got to be an awful lot of giving up and a lot of tolerance. But with pets, I just think there are many more disadvantages than advantages.

We had a problem with two families, one that had an old French poodle and another that had two cats. The family with the poodle was subsidized, and they gave their poodle away. The family with the cats paid market rent, and they were being pretty stubborn about the whole thing and going over my head to fight it. I was at least giving that family the chance to fight it, knowing full well that I was going to be backed up. But it took longer than I expected, so to the family that had already gotten rid of their dog, the two cats still being here looked like favoritism. The charge was made that if you paid full rent, you could do what you wanted to. But that wasn't true at all.

I guess it took about five months for me to get rid of all the pets. At first, we explained to the whole community by mail why we had the "no pet" policy and that all pets had to leave. Only a few left, so we then sent individual letters saying, "Your pet has to leave." After that we sent threatening letters, but it took a long hard fight to get rid of them. Some apartment developments have a pet building or other ways of handling it. But I still think, by and large, apartments are not for pets.

I think most of the residents want rules and regulations, but they just don't want them to apply to them individually. If we didn't have rules and regulations, life here would be much more confused and hectic and much less pleasant. But when it comes down to enforcing one of those rules with a particular family, that family always has a reason why the rules shouldn't apply to them.

Still, I've tried to be flexible to the extent possible. For example, the lease lists the names of the people who are occupying a unit and if anyone is added or subtracted, this office is supposed to be notified. There are many reasons why we are required to give approval for any new person moving in.

There are county and state laws dealing with the number of people in a unit. Also, if the new person coming in has an income, that has to be considered part of the family income on which the rent is based. I've had some situations where I've said, "No, this person can't stay." Sometimes it's been overcrowding of the stairwell; sometimes it's been overcrowding of the unit; sometimes it's been the habits of the new person that are not welcome to the majority of the development. But then, there have been cases where I've said, "Yes, that's fine," like a grandmother moving in or somebody's niece moving in for six months because of illness in her family.

There's one particular case where a mother with several children had a boyfriend that she wanted to move in. They both came and talked to me about it, and I agreed to let him in. A large part of my reason for saying yes was that I felt the woman needed his companionship. She needed something besides just the kids because she'd had a pretty tough life. I thought if this is what would make her happy, that was all right with me. At the time, he had no income so I knew it didn't change the rent pattern at all. Also, two of her children were away most of the time, so there would not be too many people in the unit. That particular situation has been thrown up to me several times by others as playing favorites, but I still feel like my reasoning was sound. I just refused to discuss it; I told them that was a decision I made based on facts they didn't know about and I was sticking with it.

While Underhill people are slowly beginning to develop contact with the civic and religious groups that abound in Columbia, a number of them still have very close ties with where they came from. There's a woman who has lived here for over a year but has never been involved in our community life. She's friendly, knows all of her neighbors, and her kids play with the other kids in that stairwell. She's not antisocial about it; she just hasn't been a part of anything formally organized or planned in Underhill or anywhere else in Columbia.

This same woman is very involved in her church in another section of the county. She's part of a choir that sings in her church and goes on tour to sing for groups in other cities and counties. She does a lot of work with youth over there, so practically all of her spare time is spent involved with her church. But there are some encouraging developments here. For the last two summers, Underhill has had a female baseball team, but there weren't enough girls from just here. So they went elsewhere in Columbia and found some others, and this has helped to create ties with neighborhoods close to us.

Politically, we've had a couple of people who were involved in the presidential campaign passing out leaflets, getting people to meetings, and helping to coordinate transportation to voter registration. Almost three times as many people voted from Underhill in this last election than in the one preceding it. They began with absolutely no participation, and it's gradually increasing to the point where I think we are now as involved as most any apartment community, although apartment dwellers generally are not involved people.

A major source of community power is the Columbia Association. It's a mechanism created by the developer to fill the gaps and to create things that federal, state and county agencies have never been able to do. Through the Association, we have a number of neighborhood swimming pools, an ice rink, an indoor swim center, tennis courts, and bike paths. The open space is deeded to the Association, and eventually all of these things will be totally community owned and community run.

Community control is being phased in. At first, there was a 15 member Executive Board, all hand picked by the developer. With each few thousand dwellings units, the residents got to elect someone to that Board. We now have several votes, and if the development process stays on schedule, we'll get the eighth person on that Board and gain control in a few years. In the 1980s, we'll have all 15 elected residents, and the developers will be totally phased out.

The problem lies in the machinery that governs Columbia, because there are things that nonproperty owners can't vote on. It has to do with the covenants that all property owners agree to before they come here, and the only ones who can vote on certain issues are those who own property. This excludes Underhill residents and other apartment dwellers from participating, and I don't like that at all.

A few of our people are part of the religious life of Columbia, but even here, there are obstacles to full participation. Religion is largely ecumenical, with facilities shared and services often held together. Because it's a totally new approach, there are many traditional people in Underhill who are turned off completely by modern services, by buildings that don't look like churches, and ministers that don't dress and talk like ministers. So the religious life of people takes place mostly outside of Columbia. Another problem is that the Interfaith Center and most of the religious organizational life is physically separated from us by the highway that divides the town.

One immediate recreational shortcoming was that we had practically nothing in the way of play equipment for the large number of preschool children here. We did have a very innovative, creative, and exciting playground in the woods behind us, but that's been vandalized to the extent that it practically doesn't exist any more. I'm convinced, some by proof and some by assumption, that at least 90 percent of the vandalism has come from outside this community.

There is certainly plenty of recreation in Columbia, including neighborhood centers with all kinds of things going on. They have classes that are either free or very inexpensive and, in the summertime, the lake front has something every night—from movies to jazz, to rock, to everything imaginable. But it's always amazed me the number of free things that residents here don't take advantage of. Some of it may have to do with transportation, but an awful lot of it is within very easy walking distance, and they still don't take advantage of it.

Maybe C.A. is planning things that don't fit the needs of people here, but I think a big part of it is the stigma of living in subsidized housing. This has been blown out of proportion in the minds of people who live here, so they don't leave. They go to school, go to work, or whatever, and they come back here and stay. I see it changing, especially this summer when the lake front has been much more organized. Last year, I don't remember ever seeing anyone from Underhill on the lake front, but this year, I've seen two or more families there on several occasions.

One of the neighborhood centers had a talent show last week, and I know of at least nine kids from here that were involved. So they are beginning to take advantage of more of the free things. When it comes to the things for pay, like the pools, the ice rink, and the health club, they are used much less, and part of it is certainly money. The activities are quite inexpensive when you compare them to other communities. Membership in the pools for the summer is $45 per family, and you can use any of 12 pools. But in many cases that's still $45 more than a family here can afford. Two years ago, I was part of a group that developed something called Earn-A-Membership; this was a way for families at low income levels to work for C.A. at the rate of $2 an hour and pay off their memberships. Unfortunately, not enough families are taking advantage of the opportunity.

They're considering a new kind of arrangement for the pools on an experimental basis to see how people react to it. It's a sliding scale with the amount paid adjusted according to family income. The low income family can pay the greatly reduced fee or still use the Earn-A-Membership program. I'm convinced that the Columbia Association and the population in general want everybody here to be able to take part in all things that happen. They don't want the poor kid with his nose to the window pane looking in, but it's a matter of how you do it without its looking like charity.

We joined the Columbia Medical Plan within days after we moved here, and we've had nothing but just great experiences with it. When I first came to Columbia, I was paying the premium myself. Then, at the time the premium went up, I became an employee of the company and it was a benefit. We've always found it very efficient and friendly and have liked it very much. There was an emergency one night when we had been a plan member like three weeks or so. We just simply called the clinic answering service, explained that our son had split a kneecap, and the surgeon was back on the line to us immediately. He met us at the clinic in three minutes, gave Allen the stitches, and the entire process took 25 minutes and cost us $2. I don't think there's a city in the world that can boast that.

As I began opening Underhill, I saw all kinds of medical needs and realized that 90 percent of the people here could never begin to afford that plan. I had gotten to know the director, and I knew him to be a very caring individual who had a crusader's feeling about reducing the high cost of medicine. He very much wanted the plan to be available to more people, and was able to work out with the state that medical assistance cards would be accepted. This took care of our people on public assistance and those who qualified for medical assistance. From the inception of the plan, elderly people over 62 who had Medicare coverage could join for like an additional $12 a month. But at least 50 percent of the Underhill community still has no way of affording the plan.

The clinic has moved to a new hospital within the last few weeks, and there is an emergency room that is open to anyone, plan member or not. There's a fee of $20 for such visits, but that's pretty reasonable. Several times, I can remember distinctly asking them to evaluate an emergency situation for an Underhill family that couldn't afford to pay. The director never refused those families, and I know that one of them has had continuing care for a baby that had some serious problems. They didn't have medical assistance and couldn't afford to pay for it, so they were never billed.

Psychiatric or psychological care is limited under the plan, with your first 15 visits at the usual $2 fee, and after that going to a higher fee. There are also a small number of psychologists and mental health counselors that work individually and with couples and groups. Then there's a woman who does psychological testing of children and a child psychiatrist who deals with children and does family therapy.

Other than that, the county has a Department of Mental Health that handles all phases of psychological difficulty, including drug and alcohol addiction. But because of a lack of money and staff, Underhill people practically have to have a crisis situation to get service. If it's somebody who just simply said, "My wife and I are having trouble communicating and we'd like some help," they'd probably wait for a year before they could ever be seen.

There are some other groups that have counselors available. The Family Life Center trains people in counseling, has classes in effective parenting and better communication in marriage, and arranges family groups where children and parents learn to communicate better. The Community Action agency also has counselors, but all of them have such long waiting lists. There still aren't enough public or private agencies or enough counselors to meet the need.

As I look back at the Underhill experience, I think, generally speaking, I was on the right track from a manager's viewpoint. But I was entirely too soft and kindhearted. I've allowed people to think I was being kind to them, while I've really been unkind, although with the best of motives. An example of that is allowing somebody to get behind in their rent. The truth is they have to one day pay that rent or be evicted. So I have changed my way of handling rent collection, and it is much better for the development and for the individuals who live here.

One woman had been behind in her rent, and I agreed on a payment schedule that brought in a proportionate amount of dollars each week, to keep her rent current and pay a little toward her back rent. She was even behind in that schedule and told me all the reasons why she couldn't pay and a million and one problems she was going through. I listened to all of it and then very calmly but firmly said, "When I first called you, I said that I had to have $75 before 9 o'clock tomorrow. If I don't have it, I'll take your file to the attorneys and you'll be evicted. I'm sorry about all the other problems, but there's nothing I can do about them." She paid her rent the next morning.

We've had a number of complaints about tenants whose homes were so dirty they brought roaches into the buildings. Some of that is exaggerated but, even where it's true, it's not easy to deal with. Regular inspections of units would have caught some of this before it became as large a problem as it is. I have not done this because it seemed like an invasion of privacy, but I see it now as very necessary in a community like this. The guidelines are pretty vague about how to handle this kind of situation. They mention the possibility of a yearly inspection but that would not be enough. If you're going to do it, it needs to be done three or four times a year, because an awful lot can happen to a unit in a year.

If you want people to conform to certain ways of living, you first have to try to educate them. This might be done through home visits by staff persons from the Department of Social Services, Community Action, or the social work student who may be placed here. I think you'd first have to teach people why they need to be cleaner, recognizing it's a slow process. If that's working, even if it's a gradual thing, I think that's all you can do. But if they're resisting all help, and their behavior and degree of cleanliness is not changing at all, I think you have to take steps to remove them from the community. The consequences are that they have to go to worse housing elsewhere.

We're talking about people who can't make it here. When we don't renew their leases, there's really no place for them to go where they can live with as many conveniences and as nice a place for this amount of money. So they probably go from here to substandard housing that hasn't been condemned by the county. It's tragic from that family's viewpoint, but you have to look at it from what's good for this community. Somewhere along the way, we have to accept the fact that there's a person or a family that's not salvageable, at least not now, in this community, with the resources that are available.

We do have some success stories, however, like the family that moved here from an absolute hovel. They'd always lived in a hovel and their house had been condemned because it was so very bad. The first few months they were here we had just tons of complaints on the behavior of everybody in that family, from the mother on down to the smallest child. Neighbors objected to the noise, the arguing, the screaming, the foul language, the dirtiness, and everything imaginable.

I did a lot of counseling with that family and so did Community Action and Social Services. They wanted to learn and they've changed. They'll never be at home with the Vanderbilts, but they aren't the pigsty kind of people they were a year and a half ago. I think they're happier, and I know the community is happier with them.

On the other hand, there's the family from the Virgin Islands that there was no way of helping. We had practically every resource that existed in and out of that unit and counseling with them. They just didn't learn anything and didn't want to learn anything. That kind of family you finally have to give up on and get rid of because there's no hope for them here.

It's hard to get rid of a family unless they don't pay their rent. Regardless of life styles and cleanliness, if they pay their rent, it's very difficult to do, particularly if the family challenges you. If you simply do not renew a lease and they accept that and move, there's no problem. But if they challenge you, if they get legal help and it goes to court, it's a very long, involved legal process.

The question of invasion of privacy is exceptionally difficult. Maybe it's like teaching our kids about the relationship between freedom and responsibility. The more responsible you are, the freer you are and the more privacy you can have. Tenants have to ask themselves, "Will this harm or disturb anyone else?" It's necessary for the well being of the community as a whole, to make it a better place to live for all of us. But it's a very difficult problem, and each case has to be weighed on its own merits.

This raises the question of how far management should go in relating to the behavior of tenants. I can't help but think that some of this is management's responsibility, even in conventional housing. Management has to be related to people; it's got to be people oriented. Our world is so dehumanized and so depersonalized that there's got to be an authority figure that's reachable.

I think I had trouble communicating what I saw as needed, and management had trouble hearing me. This was largely because they just didn't want to be bothered with it; they didn't want to hear it. I think they believed there were processes within existing public and private agencies that would handle these things. There's merit to this argument, but the point that's missing is that there has to be a facilitator and a catalyst to get the needs and the resources together. It doesn't happen automatically. In big cities all over the world, they're trying to figure out how to deliver social services, and I don't know anybody who's really hit on it. Since the urbanization of the Columbia area, there has been a higher degree of need than this rural county has ever known before. Their agencies aren't equipped to meet it. The county is filled with dedicated, hard working employees in public and private agencies, but they simply do not have enough dollars and people to adequately meet the needs.

It's my contention that it's the developer's responsibility to see that the gap is filled. But I don't think there's anybody within the developer's whole team who will buy that concept. They have some valid points, like the example of teaching a child independence. The longer you do something for a child, the harder it is for him to learn to do it for himself. They argue that the residents have got to learn to stand up and fight for their rights.

That comparison is true to a point. But using the parent-child analogy, before you allow a child to be independent, you've got to make sure you've given him all he needs to make appropriate decisions. There are people in this development who aren't capable of handling things for themselves and need help. In my mind, the responsibility for this assistance in any community is both public and private. At the same time, I can't help but feel in a community that so loudly publicized it was a place for all people, a big part of the responsibility for seeing people's needs are met belongs to the developer.

When they were first planning Columbia, they spent an awful lot of time on social planning. I think a lot of that got lost in the physical planning and marketing, although I don't believe it was intentional. It was a matter of priorities and people having difficult jobs who just couldn't do everything.

The Columbia Association was created with a very broad charter that goes beyond swimming pools, ice rinks, and tennis courts. It essentially says that it's to fill in the gaps between what is routinely offered by our county, state and federal governments and what people need. It is not in any way limited to recreation. C.A. has to act as a facilitator to put pressure on government and to say, "Here's a need not being met. Where are the resources to meet it?" We should try to make existing agencies live up to what they should be doing instead of our doing it for them. But if acting as a facilitator doesn't work, human needs and social concerns still can't be ignored.

They also didn't do enough planning in Columbia to take care of the needs of the kinds of people they were required to bring in under HUD guidelines. Someone like myself, but with more training than I had, should have been involved at the blueprint stage of the physical development. An expert on social problems has got to be a part of the team, along with people experienced in physical design and fiscal management.

As an example, the laundry rooms here were planned for one washer and one dryer for 18 families. That was somebody looking strictly at dollars and cents and not at common sense. There's no way 18 families can cope with one washer and one dryer. That same laundry room also housed the hot water heater, the main plumbing valves, the telephone equipment, and all the electrical equipment for the building. After the fact, I was able to get three washers and two dryers into that space. By threatening legal action against the project builder, not the town developer, I was also able to get cages built around the equipment, both to protect it from vandalism and to protect children from being hurt. All of these things would have been so much easier if they had been done at the blueprint stage.

Among the priorities we're charged with from HUD is to give priority to the physically handicapped and the elderly. Yet no thought was given to the physically handicapped or the elderly in the construction of these buildings. There are no grab bars in the bathtubs to keep them from falling, and they have the most inconvenient laundry room of any of us. They have to walk seven steps outside into the weather and then go down 24 steps to the basement. That's bad laundry facilities for anybody.

With no place for those seniors to sit and chat, and no play area for preschoolers, I've wanted to see this island in the middle of the parking lot become an area where mothers could bring toddlers and where there was a sitting place for seniors. That would have created conversation and involvement across three generations.

If we had planned properly, the project office would have been open at least four months in advance instead of less than one month. It could have been an orderly process of interviewing people, getting HUD forms filled out, and verifying income, with a great deal of orientation of residents before they ever moved in.

We actually did a lot of one to one orientation as people moved in, but in the beginning, it was not very organized at all. When anybody had a question about anything, he called me and that's when he got oriented. When I got the same question five times, it dawned on me I needed to answer this before they asked it, so we put together a fact sheet to hand out as people moved in. Then, when the first building was occupied, we held a meeting and the agenda was pretty well centered around the questions I'd been asked the first few weeks. We also handed out welcome packets and told them who to contact for what.

It was primarily nuts and bolts kinds of things, how to get your kid enrolled in school, how do you get around without a car, and what you do if your toilet backs up in the middle of the night. Later on, we began to deal with where to shop and where to find things at reduced rates.

If I were opening this development again, I would have a series of orientation classes that would help people understand why they need to work together to better their lives and the whole community. I'd offer these classes during the daytime, in the evening, and on weekends, so that everybody could come to them, and I'd make them mandatory.

What I'm saying may be unfair, because the company has been a hundred times more human in its approach than most private corporations. But they should not have made the very dramatic, beautiful kinds of statements of what the town was hoped to be, if they weren't ready to follow through with everything necessary to make that happen.

I think the marketing of Columbia has had a fallacy; I've tried to talk about this, but the marketing people are pretty defensive about it. They have a slide show that makes you think this is Shangri-La or the greatest place that ever existed in the history of mankind. All you have to do is move here and lie on your patio and enjoy it all. The marketing implies that no effort is needed; it's already a great world. I'm not convinced that you're going to lose sales by challenging people to be part of something different, that calls on them to contribute to make a better community.

I've accepted the fact that my job here has changed over the years, and that I had to become much more involved with fiscal and physical responsibilities and much less so with social responsibilities. While I could live with this, it was extremely frustrating to see the process that had begun in Underhill dropped. So I sent a memo to the top people in the development corporation and the Columbia Association on our responsibility for meeting social service needs. I gave some examples of what had been done and what needed to be done as my position changed. I emphasized the importance of having a staff person who would be concerned with the delivery of social services in Underhill and in other subsidized developments in Columbia. I reminded the developers of their promise to create a city that nurtured individual human growth, a garden city where people grow.

They responded by calling together a meeting essentially for all the deliverers of social services in the county, as well as management from the other assisted housing developments in the area. Their attitude seemed to be, "You don't know about all the services that exist; all you need is to find out where they are." So I ended up going to a meeting with people I'd known for years and worked with practically on a daily basis. The purpose was for me to meet them because I was not supposed to know them, and for them to tell me all the services they offered. There wasn't a single soul in the meeting that I didn't know well and hadn't worked with.

It was almost as if the developers couldn't ignore me but didn't want to answer me either. I was asking them to take a more positive role in the area of social services, and they were saying, "We're not going to because we don't need to; it's all here for you." I was not asking that they compete or overlap with existing services. I was suggesting that they assist and encourage existing agencies to plan for improved delivery and coordination of these services. Since there was no one in the public sector doing this, I felt they had a responsibility to follow through.

The job is big enough that it's never going to be done properly; I don't see us ever having totally adequate delivery of social services. To get anywhere near where we should be, we will have to assume a collective responsibility. It's going to take the volunteer housewife, the professional social worker, private industry, public and private agencies, religious institutions, and civic groups. It's going to take all of us, and we won't get anywhere by arguing over whose job it is. Everybody has a responsibility, but I feel this developer has a particular responsibility because of the goals that were made for the city when it first began.

Even with the problems that exist, I still strongly believe people in Underhill, particularly the children, have a much better opportunity for individual human growth here than in inner city ghettos or some poor rural area. There are things available to them here that wouldn't be available elsewhere. Despite the frustrations that are part of living here, the advantages outweigh the frustrations. Some families had no access to nature, and here they've got tons of it. There was no access to recreational facilities, and here they do have access, although it could be better. Their schools were inadequate, and although I don't think our schools have arrived, they are better than the schools these kids were going to. Many of our families have been frustrated because of unmet needs, but I'm sure they have benefited from advantages that are at their doorsteps. So I still think we should continue to fight to make it a city for all people.

Some people in Underhill are very satisfied with the quality of their lives, especially where there's enough money to keep a roof over their heads and food on the table. They feel they have pleasant, relaxed surroundings and the convenience of a place to shop, things to do, and people around that they're comfortable with. There is also some access to fairly good schools, medical facilities, mental health care, and all the things that fall under the social services umbrella, although the linkages and the delivery are weak. Then there are people who aren't satisfied and don't use these facilities at all.

We also have people at the lowest levels of income and need, who are looking for things that most of us take for granted. A 68-year-old woman is not too excited over the amenities in the town. She's looking for transportation and for adequate medical care that she can afford. People here are worried about how they're going to feed their families next week, so they can't be too interested in something philosophical like building a sense of community.

They've got to move a step at a time, and I think I've seen some of them grow from survival concerns to levels of interest in the well-being of others. I do think that most of the people here are looking for a sense of belonging. There are residents who show a real pride in living in Underhill. They feel, "It's a great place; it's home; it's my community." Then there are those who just sleep here, and others who brought a lot of problems with them— marital problems, teenager problems, and racial problems.

There's been a lot of confusion and frustration on the racial issue, because the generally accepted idea of Underhill, which came largely from me, was that we all wanted integration. There are people in Underhill who agree that integration is what we've got to have. But there are whites who aren't for it and blacks who aren't for it. I think I may have had to convince them that they ought to give it a try, or maybe they've tried to convince themselves to give it a try so they could have a place to live. Their need for housing was great enough that they could put up with living with somebody of a different color.

One instance that comes to mind is a black woman who had been here five or six months. She's a prime example of somebody who essentially lied to me, saying, "I accept your concept," and then after she got here decided my concept had some value. She came in to pay her rent one day and said, "For the first time ever, I've had several months of living next door to a white family. I would never have dreamed that we could have had the relationship that we have. We keep each other's kids and we go shopping together occasionally. If she bakes a cake, we get half of it and if I bake a pie, she gets half of it. We're real neighbors; we like each other."

There are black and white kids who play together here in Underhill and all over the city who really aren't that conscious of color and are buddies. They may fight as kids do, but it's not racial. And there are black and white kids who are very aware of color, and it's a problem to them probably because it's a problem to their families. Then you've got out-and-out racial antagonism and all those gang fights in Columbia. They range from elementary kids on up through the whole age gamut.

There's a black majority in Underhill because there are more black children, even though family-wise we have a white majority. When you look at the statistics, you see that whites here are younger and on their way up. The blacks tend to be older and moving up much more slowly. What this says to me very loudly is that blacks stay poor longer. You've got a white majority among preschool children, but in elementary you've got a black majority of around 60 percent. At the junior high level, about 80 percent are black.

A lot of the black children came from the county and were either related or already knew each other. The white children came from diverse geographical areas and didn't know each other. So what you ended up with in the parking lot was a large majority of black kids who were already close, and they immediately said, "This is our turf." Time and time again, the black kids would tell the white kids, "This is our playground; this is our parking lot and you can't use it." It would be six blacks to two whites and the whites couldn't fight back.

Sometimes they came to me, sometimes I heard about it from other people, and sometimes, I'm sure, I wasn't told. When I did hear what was happening, I went into the middle of it and tried to deal with it as best I could. It's something that's hard to handle, particularly with a gang of kids, so I dealt with the parents. I felt that the majority of parents wanted the kids to play together and certainly didn't want the fighting and haggling that was going on. It was hard for them to deal with this, but there were many who tried valiantly. Some black and white parents who got involved because of the kids are now pretty good friends, and they shop together or share babysitting or something else.

Things seem to have improved recently, and I haven't seen or heard of a single incident between kids that was racial. Kids have fought and gotten into scraps, but even if it was a black and a white kid, there wasn't the racial name calling. It was two kids who knew each other and were fighting over something.

But there are racial problems all around us, and some forms of separation are emerging. I personally can't accept a facility that's exclusive to any group. If a bunch of black teens congregate in one spot, and that's a pattern that happens, that's one thing. But if some white teens pass by and want to join that group, for them to be excluded is just as bad as the reverse situation, which we've lived with for generations. It's happening and it bothers me that it's happening.

I picked up a white teen a few days ago when I was coming back from downtown Columbia, and I asked him if he'd been in the teen center that had recently been renovated. He said he hadn't been there because it was all black and he wasn't welcome there. He said, "I don't like it and I wouldn't want an all white center either. I'd like anybody to be able to go and feel welcome, but it's not that way. I've tried to go and some white friends of mine have tried to go, but it's been made very clear that we're not wanted. I think that's sad; it's leading to more and more problems."

I can accept there being an area where people who wish to live with others of their own culture, background, or ethnic identity can do so. But I can't accept someone from another ethnic background being terrified to walk through that spot. Separation continues the idea of our looking at each other as completely different, and I can't buy that. I'm not asking anyone to give up his identify, but it goes against the grain for me to back anything that's separatism or exclusiveness. The world gets so much smaller every day, and I think we have to learn to appreciate each other's uniqueness.

My learning about people hasn't stopped with coming to Underhill. I've learned an awful lot through the training I finally got in housing management. Although I know I accept people as people and am not that conscious of color, religion, and differences, I am finally beginning to accept the fact that most people can't believe that. They don't feel my views are real. I think probably the thing that brought it close to home was the experience I had with the group I was in training with. It was painful but it was good for me. The majority of the group was black and I enjoyed being with them. We went out to supper together and we partied together.

One morning about 2 A.M., several people had been drinking a good deal, enough to be honest but not enough to be incoherent. I was the only white in the room and there were four black men and two black women. They got to discussing race relations, and I was kind of fascinated with their differing ideas. Then the whole group turned to me and discussed me and my being there and my relationship with them. The essence of it was, "Archie, we think you're a great guy. We like you and enjoy being around you. You're a lot of fun, and you've added a lot to our learning experience here, both from a technical and a human relations viewpoint. But you're white and we're never really going to trust you. So you might as well stop trying to push yourself on us."

I hadn't consciously pushed myself on anybody; they just happened to be people that I enjoyed being with. It was a very upsetting and painful experience, but I think it also helped me. I began to understand that they might like me and think I was okay up to a point, but they did not and probably never would trust me.

I think that's sad, but when you look at it from their viewpoint, why should they? How many whites have given them reason to trust? That's still a big hurdle that we've got to cross some day, but some have done it. There's a black woman who was part of the group that night who realized what it meant to me. She talked to me about it several times and told me she didn't feel that way. She saw me as a person and not as a white, and I saw her as a person and not as a black.

I have been very idealistic about this and allowed myself to become vulnerable. I feel like I'll continue to take the risks involved in reaching out, but I'll be more cautious. When you keep sticking your hand in the fire and keep getting burned, somewhere along the way you learn to put something protective over your hand before you stick it in the fire. I'm not saying that I'm at all ready to stop. I'm just going to be more careful.

Things have happened here in Underhill that couldn't happen somewhere else because of the new idea and concept that was part of our basic
philosophy. I felt that what we wanted could happen, and I think it is happening. It just isn't happening nearly as fast as I thought it would. There
are also things that aren't being dealt with; there are racial undertones that
you can feel. It's hard to verbalize them; it's hard to pinpoint them, but
they're there. Occasionally they are verbalized, or they explode in one way
or another. Essentially, I'm the only one to handle them, and there's no way
that one person can deal effectively with 400 people.

I think I've given Underhill as much as I can give. I've done as much as
can be expected of one person, and my family has done as much as can be
expected. The most important thing we've learned is that the community
can only be as good as each person makes it. There are a lot of people here
who thought the community could only be as good as Archie Conover made
it. That's an awful lot of responsibility to carry around.

COMMENT

Archie's background demonstrates the depth of personal commitment
that is required if anything like satisfactory levels of effectiveness are to
be achieved in his joint roles of housing manager and social worker. Despite
his strong commitment, however, Archie leaves the job after four years for
one where he can separate his work and community roles and enjoy the
satisfactions of private housing. He gives up the sacrifices of his former
situation and moves into middle class America. The conflict in his roles is
the most obvious obstacle and perhaps the primary reason that we simply
cannot expect long tenure in such a position. Yet governmental programs
characteristically combine such roles because of their widespread suspicion
of welfare recipients and constant emphasis on surveillance and control.

Adding to these frustrations is the extraordinary fragmentation of public
and private welfare efforts. The specialization and narrowly defined character of most programs leaves people like Archie with the enormous, frustrating task of constantly petitioning and trying to coordinate a poorly
assembled bureaucracy. The number of contacts he must maintain, both
formally and informally, is mind boggling and time consuming, even when
only minor loans, services, or exceptions are at issue. The welfare state in
the U.S. seems to have grown only additively, with each program creating a
new set of offices, a new bureaucracy, and a new set of personnel. Coordinating these programs is either left to the poor or near-poor themselves
or falls onto the shoulders of an occasional person like Archie, who attempts, by hook or by crook, to see that the programs are brought to the
clients.

The magnitude of his task is also increased by the nature of his clientele.
The near-poor, the working poor in particular, frequently cross the multiple

lines of eligibility that welfare agencies have established. The frequency of recertification, of minicrises, and of changes in income status is probably much greater in this marginal population than among the persistently destitute. Such people sorely tax the inflexibility of governmental bureaucracies, so that workers like Archie function in a twilight zone of legitimacy. Thus the welfare system casts doubt on its own moral worth, both in the eyes of the wider public and in those of such dedicated people as Archie. The problem does not seem to lie in a lack of good intentions, on the part either of governmental legislation or of those who attempt to implement the programs. Rather, the core issue is our fundamental conception of the poor as people who must be both helped and watched. Conflicting roles, conflicting agencies, and inflexible bureaucracies all reflect this ambivalent conception.

Chapter 3

WALLY AND MAY BONNOLI
In and Out of Poverty

WALLY BONNOLI

I'm 26, but I feel like a man 50 or 60 years old. I think May and I have experienced enough heartaches and problems at the age we're at now than most people go through in a lifetime. I mean I had my good times, my ups and downs, but livin in a place like Underhill, I don't know.

I had a chance to travel around to see how other people act and their styles and ways. I met people who didn't like this or that, people who were b.s. artists and little guys with a lot of authority. If you want somethin done, you give me somethin; give me a trip to Florida or a case of booze or a piece of tail. Everything's materialistic, finaglin. Phooey, the hell with it. It's just not right.

Columbia, they say, is the well planned community, of which the developer and the rest of the company sat down with an idea and came up with somethin. It's just hard to believe what they came up with. But I think that people in Columbia don't know the total concept; I don't think I even know or can really explain it. They just can't get it together. They don't relate with one another or know how to be friends. The guy next door is prejudiced, the man down the street can't stand Jews or Catholics, and I bought an $80,000 house and they're puttin poor people in over here. They don't understand the concept of a planned community where they have whites and blacks and greens and purples and people of all religions. They have the rich, the mediocre, the poor, the professional people, and the trades. It's gonna take time and they might not ever do it, gettin it together.

Look at it this way, there's a rich white neighborhood somewhere and a rich black family moves in. I mean, who's got the right to stop em? It's the law. But those people can make it tough on em; they can make it downright dirty. Take down here where you've got mixed races, mixed everything, like fruit salad or vegetable salad. It's what the people make of it. If they want to live here, fine. They know what the consequences could be. They know it might be hard. But if they want to put up with it, sweat it out, fine.

In Underhill, everybody knows it's a project. Everybody's in there for one reason or the other. They got sick kids, or they just can't cut the mustard, or the jobs they handle are not producin them money, or they're in debt and they can't finance a problem.

I think about 90 percent of people that live in here have seen other facets of hard life like the ghetto area, very, very low income, or not even havin a pot to pay for. And the other 10 percent have led a sheltered life. We lived in a project on the other side of Columbia. I would read in books about the Bronx in New York, or the ghettos in California, or in Mississippi, or out in the Midwest, and I'd look at that place and say, "Whew, I don't know what those people went through, but it's probably twice as bad as what I'm experiencing."

I tell you this right now, that people who have seen the rough spots of life, who know that this is a little better than what they had, can get along with people much better than the other 10 percent, who have gone from somethin to nothin and lost it. It's not easy if you haven't seen what life is all about, or haven't known what it's like to live next to a family with screamin kids, or a family with no calm in it, a family with no mother, a family where everybody works, and a family that's poor. I don't think the people are ignorant; I just think they're sheltered.

Right next to where we lived, they came in and built some town houses, $40,000 town houses. Beautiful. So right now you got kids walkin through the lawns, doin this, doin that. So I say to myself, "I wouldn't live in a town house." But if a person wants to buy a home there, all right. Let him make the best of it. They know what they're movin into is low income and they're gonna have problems, just like they were middle income and they moved into a rich neighborhood, keepin up with the Joneses.

Well here's the thing. There was whites; there was blacks; there was Mexicans; there was Puerto Ricans; there was everything. It was a combination of mixtures. But the thing of it is that people didn't control their children. They didn't care about the children. The children would go out and play late; the teenagers would hang around; they would cause trouble; they would steal. To me it was a breakdown in communication between the town and the children. And when you tried to correct another child and say somethin, the child went back and told his parents and the parents would go into orbit. They would come over to your house, and they would raise so much hell with you you'd think you went through the first degree. And I said, "Phooey, forget it."

My philosophy is "Life is just too damn short to fight and cut up and carry on and razz one another." If I can't get along with the next guy—I don't care what his nationality or his color is, what he does—if I can't get along with him, forget it. I don't wanna live this way. I wanna be able to come home, and to have my family, and to love my children in the flesh, and I wanna be able to say hello to my neighbor and show respect to him and have him show respect to me.

Here in Underhill, you have problems to a certain extent, but everybody tries to put forth an honest effort in correctin em, in tryin to get along with one another. I tell you some of our neighbors are the greatest people in the world. It's like a small town; everybody knows everybody else to a certain extent, not real intimately, but everybody else realizes that you got problems and you depend on one another. If we run short of cash during the week, we call a neighbor next door and ask, "You got a dime to lend us? Fine." Friday comes and you pay him then. Downstairs across the hall, do you have a stick of butter, or do you have this, or do you have that, or can you run me to the store, or can you pick me up afterwards. We try to get along and we do.

When we moved in, everybody had disagreeances and had problems. So we all sat down like adults and we put our heads together and we said, "It just can't be this way; we're gonna have to work a solution and work out all of our problems." The only way is to confront a person, to face one another, to sit down. We don't holler; we don't pick up clubs and arms; and we don't say, "I'm not gonna talk to you for a week or two." You got a problem; we sit down; we talk about it; we take in both sides. "You're right here, but then on the other hand, you got to consider this. We wanna be fair between both parties, and this is the way we're gonna solve it. Is it agreeable? Do you think it's a good plan? Do you think it'll work? Well, let's try it. If you have somethin else that comes up you think is better, call me and we'll go another way."

We had a noise problem and everybody got their heads together and said, "We're gonna do this and that." We didn't know if it was gonna work or not. We hoped it would and let it go at that. It worked for a couple of weeks, but everybody started stretchin out of their bounds and out of their territories, and so there was a lot of ill will and animosity to come about, and one thing led to another. There was a lot of stink about it, and a lot of people who were good people got hurt and stepped on. When it came to the final point of takin some people to court about it, everything was more or less dropped and we went back to tryin on the original basis.

Like the people downstairs, on a weekend they might play their stereo. They play it loud. And if I've worked eight or ten hours on Friday and worked all day Saturday, then that's the last thing I wanna put up with till one, two, or three o'clock in the mornin is a stereo. I say, if you ever had a chance to know me, I'm crazy. I got on the phone last week and I told him, "I'm not gonna put up with this shit tonight." I said, "Turn it down." It would have been nothin for him to say somethin to me, and I was goin down there. He would've probably licked me, and I would've licked him. But I would've got the best of him. I'm just crazy or stupid enough to do it. I mean, I'm a nice guy and I try and get along with people, but I got a boilin point. And when I blow, man, I'm like a maniac. Sunday I saw him out here and apologized. I said, "I'm sorry, man; I was all drunked up and didn't know what I was sayin." We shook hands and we talked.

I feel that if you've got a problem, you've got to confront the source or the other party involved and work it out between the two. It doesn't do a damn bit of good to have troubles in this building, or this stairwell, or in Underhill, and have a mediator come in from another building to be nonpartisan. If you can't work it out between the most of you, forget it.

You know, things come up and we get on one another's nerves. But it doesn't last. We got to live together; we're here; there's no other place cheaper, no other place to go. So if you can't get it together and work your problems out, you shouldn't even be in here. I try to use a type of professionalism as to certain tactics. I don't approach people to say, "You're a slob; you keep a dirty house; you got roaches." Everybody's got roaches that live in apartments; I don't care who they are. And we've got em worse, really; for a number of reasons. So I use tactics. I like to call at the house and say, "We got a helluva roach problem; do y'all have em?" You know, talkin to the guy, talkin his language, his trash, his thoughts, on his level. He says, "Yeah, we got em," and I say, "Somethin's gotta be done. For me to go home and find a roach in my child's crib, I'm not gonna put up with it, I don't care who it is; I'm not gonna do it." I say, "What would you do?" And he says, "I wouldn't put up with it either." I say, "Well, listen, I think some of the other people are fed up with it; I think we're gonna get the places exterminated. How about it? He says, "Sure. You just tell my wife the time of the day that the whole deal is set up." No problem.

Every now and then it might not work, but eventually the people come around. Give it some time with some age and some jelly, it's gonna be there. They're not the type of people that you can say, "Well, you're a dark ball; you look dirty and the kids are dirty; you never brush your teeth and you never take any baths." You got to use some type of tactic or be sly about it, puttin yourself in with everybody else, so he's got to play ball with you. You got to be like a junior con artist. The people here have different levels of education, and some can't even read or write. In order to converse with em, you gotta talk their talk, their kind of trash, their hillbilly accent, their southern accent, in order to get em to understand you, for you to understand them.

Like the people next door, the Turnfinders. I feel sorry for em at the bottom of my heart, I really do. Because the guy can't read or write; he's goin on 50 and she's only 20 or 21 years old and they have two kids. She's sly in certain ways and stupid in others, but it's just downright bein lazy where she won't fix the children anything to eat or a bottle. She won't clean. She'll buy them clothes and buy herself clothes, and when they get to the point that they can't stand the damn stink, they'll put em in a bag and shove em away. And then after they can't stand the stink somewhere, they'll throw em out. The other gal that lives over there, who's their aunt, is clean as a whistle. She told us they went away and she was away herself for a couple of days, and they had left food out that had spoiled and stunk, cookies smashed on the floor. They went away on a Friday and, as of Monday, there was raw chicken sittin out, that was to be thawed. That gives off a real nice odor. And the roaches. I feel sorry for the people, I really do.

I went to high school in the Baltimore metropolitan area, and from there I went to college. It took me approximately five and a half years to get through, and I graduated with a degree in management. Then I went into business when I was very young. There was times where I'd work six and seven days a week, 12 to 16 hours a day, buildin it up. This idea of duty was brought on by workin with my father.

I worked for a man who put me in charge of the business, to run it completely on my own. Then he sold me corporate shares of stock which May and I were to purchase at so many shares per month. Eventually we would own the business completely, because he was gonna retire within the next number of years. But certain problems came up, the business went bankrupt, and we were out on our ear.

We had enough money for about five weeks for me to look for a job. I traveled all up and down the eastern seaboard; I was only offered one job and that was with the proposed Alaskan pipelines. But May was pregnant and I couldn't relocate because she was due within about six weeks. That was the only job that I had offered to me, and right now I wish I had taken it. There are jobs around, but as soon as somethin comes up, it's filled within a matter of hours. In order to get in, you have to know somebody where you're gonna work, somebody's uncle, somebody's brother, or the girl you went to school with.

You know, we have a family joke. Our last name is Bonnoli and the second "o" you don't pronounce. Now in Italian, it's Bonnoli, so the family joke is Bonnli is a high class guinea and Bonnoli is a low class guinea. So this is why when I was in business, and I met various people, they'd look at my name and look at me and say, "It doesn't sound like the way you pronounce it." And I'd tell em that joke and they would remember me right off the bat. I'd associate their names with other things, too, because when I was in business, I used to meet like 35 or 40 people a day and it was hard for me to remember certain things. I would use name association and appearances, somethin like that. But this was brought up through the family, and I got people to remember me by this name.

My father had lots of brothers and a couple of sisters. It's a huge family; you wouldn't believe the number of grandchildren. We were all matzoh balls, all wops, you know. Matzoh ball is a personal joke between May and I, in Italian. When I was in the Fire Department, they used to call me matzoh ball, so this is why she picked it up.

I grew up near Baltimore in a township called Morgan Hills. There was five of us boys, and I was the oldest. I was expected to be an example for my brothers, to work hard, to go to school, to get good grades, to be the man of the family when my father wasn't around, to tend to problems and help my mother out. Like when I grew up, my mother taught me how to sew, how to cook, how to bake bread, to clean house, to do all this. I was the oldest, and it was expected of me to learn this, to help around, even though it was a job for a woman.

Everything that was taught me I use nowadays. When May doesn't feel good, I'll chip in, and three or four times a week fix dinner, wash dishes, help her clean the house. If she's had a rough night with the kids, or they aren't feelin well, or she wants to catch a couple hours sleep, I'll take over. There's no real problems to it; she knows what I can do and I expect so much of her. If it doesn't get done, then I want an explanation of why. When I was growin up, my mother tended house and it was spic and span; it was spotless. I tell you with five boys it was darn hard to do. And I expect this of May. I know it's a lot with us havin four children, but if she tells me somethin the night before like, "I'm gonna iron," and when I come home it's not done, I'm gonna know why. And what the reason was, whether she's been sittin around and talkin to somebody or whether she's been havin a good time.

I do plumbing work on buildin new homes. They're not prefabricated; everything is stood built from the ground up. I mean I go out to work eight or ten hours, like today we put in a 12 hour day and I really feel beat. But I don't mind, because I know that we're not foolin around, that we're work-in. We don't play when we work; we get out and we do it. And the money's decent. But May, to a certain extent, likes somebody who's gonna work eight hours and come on home and that's it. Me, I was taught to work and work hard if the work was there to do. So for me to go out and work six or seven days a week, I couldn't care less. If it's there, I'll do it. But she has different feelings.

Me and my real mother, we don't hit it off at all. I mean she doesn't call me and I don't call her. To me, the only family that I've got is the family that lives over in Morgan Hills, my real father and my stepmother. From about six until I was 14, I was with my real mother after my parents were divorced. But the first year and a half, I lived on a farm in Virginia with a man and his wife who raised me and my real brother. Now there's five boys in the family but the other three are half brothers. I consider em as bein brothers because we're so close to that family and to my father and my stepmother.

My mother was livin in Washington, and she couldn't afford to keep us even though she had us, so she put us on this farm. The old man and old woman, they didn't give a damn about us. We were there and we brought em $20 a week or whatever she paid, and that was it. There was no recre-ation, no play, no nothin. We were allowed to have our toys only on the weekends. When the old man and woman wanted to go visitin, my brother and I would stay out in the car while they would go in and visit. I remember that just as clearly as if it was yesterday.

Then my mother remarried, and we traveled around with my stepfather who worked for a big company. We got a chance to go to Alaska for four years and to Germany for three, and all over the United States and Canada. We saw how other people lived, traveled the countryside, met people, took slides, and collected souvenirs. The travelin and visitin the various areas was an education in itself.

When I was 12 to 14, I started callin and writin my real father, but my real mother and my stepfather never knew about it. They weren't gettin along, and I wasn't gonna put up with no guff even though I was young. I mean the difference between he and I is like night and day. He's a German, very, very cold.

So I just said the hell with everything. We were in Alaska when the end of the tour of duty was up, and we traveled back. I had saved up enough money, and I left them in San Francisco. I stayed with an uncle for awhile, and from there I came right back to my father's house.

My real father was a taxi driver, and he was proud of it. He used to tell all the guys, "Some day, I'm gonna own this company." He drove a taxi for five years, and when my grandfather died, he willed my father and his brothers his money. My father and my uncle bought this company. It lasted for 15 years, until the point where it grew so much and so rapid, with so many headaches, they sold it even though the money was there. The company is still there to this day, and it's a boomin business.

Now my father is in the construction business; he has a syndicate which is made up of primarily Italian people which they develop industrial land. He makes a lot of money, but he works for it.

My father was born in Sicily. I give him a helluva lot of respect, which is part of me bein the oldest son. I mean I have to stand up and do certain things and try to shine over my brothers because I'm the oldest. When I go over there to the house, I'm very respectful of him. We sit down and we chat, and we talk business first. Then we talk pleasure, maybe, or somethin along that line. But it's a relationship where we're close. If he needs somethin done, a favor or somethin like that, and he says, "I need some help," then I call him right away, no matter what the problem is, because he doesn't ask that much. We try not to call on each other, but when he asks, I'm there. In an Italian family, we're close.

My mother's family is from Italy, but she was born in Virginia right close to Washington. My stepmother is also Italian. She's another woman who's a very hard worker, raisin up five boys. She put up with a lot from us, but she kept clothes on our back, she ironed and sewed. It's actually my stepmother who I consider my mother.

All of my family and relatives lived in about a mile radius and once a week, everybody'd get together at my grandfather's place. He had like a small farm, and he had vineyards and he had goats and made cheese, and he raised figs. Generally it was on a Sunday, all the kids, the husbands, the wives, the cousins, everybody would get together at Mama's for a big dinner. We'd have a great big salad, spaghetti, lasagna, and the grandparents would spoil the kids. We were like brats when we were growin up; we'd get away with murder.

We stuck together like a pack of rats, and if someone in the family had problems and they needed help or money, they could rely on one another for it. It was like a small knit clique of people, so to speak. And each and every person either had a trade or a profession, and one would help out the other. I have an uncle who's a lawyer; I have another uncle who runs a restaurant; I have an uncle who's in the fruit business; I have another uncle who owns a truck and drives for a big outfit. There's carpenters in the family, barbers, plumbers, and so on.

To this day, the land and the property that my grandfather had over where I was raised, they still have it. We own eight blocks. Every year around Christmastime, every one of the grandchildren in the family gets $1,000. That's a helluva lot of money. This is what we get and we been gettin this now for the past four or five years. What they do is they put everything in a fund and pay off all the bills, the mortgages, and the taxes. At the end of the year, they split up the profits to each one of the kids.

The town is all Italian. They have Italian food stores, Italian restaurants; they have a grocer who's strictly Italian, who makes up all kinds of Italian dishes. The Fire Department, all the guys in there are matzoh balls. They fix pizza every Friday and Saturday night to raise money. And then there are guys who think they're big wheels; they're with the big boys. They play the horses, and one's a bookie. It's all there, everything that you read about, the Godfather and everything else. It's no bullshit.

We know other people of different backgrounds and nationalities, and they're friends to us, but I don't feel the same way with them as I would with my own people, Italian people. Because to me, they understand what I understand. They've been taught and raised the same way, and we can get along with one another. Like if you know people who live across the street and they're Polish, or Turkish, or Irish, or somethin like that. We hit it off as far as bein friends, but we don't understand each other's feelings, or each other's backgrounds, or how we were raised, or how we show respect or homage. I still feel lost bein away from my town. I call the family once a week and say, "How are you? How's everybody? What's new? What are you doin? How's everything with dad?"

We go back to visit and bring the mob, too. By the time we leave there, my mother looks like she walked through a wind tunnel, like she did when she was raisin us. We have a good time. My mother told me that I was the worst out of the litter. And my oldest girl, Cathy, is the same way. I mean, she looks like me and she talks like me; she's got the same teeth, the same nose, the ears, everything. She's the spittin image of daddy. And when I take the family over there, she tears the place apart. My mother she kind of snickers and puts up with it; she's good about it. When we leave, she says, "Now you know the trouble and the problems I went through when you were little."

My real mother expected me to marry an Italian girl. The thing that blew the knob off the head was when I mentioned May to her. She didn't want me to marry her; she didn't care for her. She never even met her. There was opposition there, but to me it was like the breeze blowin through the walls.

But my father, no. He says, "Never marry an Italian woman. You know what I got when I married your mother; we never see eye to eye." Of course he was jokin, because he loves my mother very dearly. But he says, "Never marry an Italian woman; it's like marryin a mule. You're gonna bump heads; you're gonna fight with her. And if you knock her around, she's gonna knock you. You're not gonna get anywhere. For Christ sake, don't marry an Italian woman. Marry a Polish girl, or a German girl, or somethin like that."

May's family isn't real, real Polish as far as bein tightly knit. Well, on her mother's side, yeah, on her father's side, no. Our parents have only been together a few times. They were together at the wedding and about a half a dozen times in five or six years. Once in a blue moon, her mother and my mother call one another, and they'll exchange cards. But there was a strong, cold feelin. My family had their ways, and her family had their ways.

Like in my family, the man of the house, the husband, he's the provider of the family. He's the worker. As far as the liberated woman bit, my feelin is you can take it and shove it. In my book, there's no such thing as a liberated woman. A woman, she has children; she fixes the man's meals; she does the ironing; she takes care of the children. But May, to a certain extent, isn't this way. I'll help out; I'll clean house; I'll bake bread; I'll give a hand doin this and doin that. But I don't look at myself and herself as bein liberated.

Right after we were married, her mother come over to my house and sat down and intended on tellin me how she was goin to run my life. No way. I told her, I said, "Bull shit." I said, "There's the door; hit it. If you think you're gonna come over and sit down and tell me how to run my life, you pack your daughter up with her bags and get her out of here." I said, "I come from an Italian family, and when I say 'drop it,' she either drops it or she's gonna get clobbered for it." That's just the way Italians are; they're hardheads.

I think if her mother knew me a little bit longer before we got married, she would have said no. Because her mother only saw the good side of me, naturally. She never saw me in action, or what I did, or what I believed or what I wanted. I think she had her own views, whether they be ethnic or personal from her background, and I had mine. If you're a man and you stand up and you believe what you believe in, there's no problem. If you're somebody who's a mama's boy and you've been led around by the apron strings, and you come from this background and marry into that background, you're gone. Because the person who's domineering in that family's gonna rule your life. You're gonna gradually do everything what they say and do this and do that. And to me, I'm the domineering part of the family. I believe it's done this way, and it's gonna be done this way. It's been done this way in my family for years and years, and nobody's gonna change it. That's it.

I don't think the mixin of ethnic backgrounds has to be a problem. Sure, they'd have a different opinion, but to me, as far as it goes now, no problem. As far as I'm concerned, my children have May's parents for grandparents, and they have my real father and my stepmother for grandparents. That's all they'll ever know. To me, it doesn't make any difference who they marry, as long as they're happy and get somebody who's gonna treat em right and be a good provider. I don't care what color they are, what religion, what background, really. As long as it's somebody who's good.

I'm serious. When I was in college, for a period of time I roomed with a guy who was Puerto Rican and another guy who was blacker. The black guy, I knew his family and used to go out there for dinner. I worked for a man who was black; I worked for a man who was Puerto Rican. He's a man, you know; he's got eyes, everything else, just like me. His beliefs, certain things are a little different, but I could care less.

I enjoy Polish jokes; I get a big bang out of em. They do the same thing with Italians and other ethnic groups. I mean I don't have any prejudice or anything like that against other groups or backgrounds. I haven't seen that much, other than what I know from May's family, but I can tell you those Poles, they're tough people, they're crazy. When her family gets together for an outing, these guys 60 and 70 years old sit around and drink a boilermaker, which is a shot of booze and a can of beer. They pass a quart, not a fifth, around to all the men. The old men and the young boys who are 20 or 21 and over are allowed to drink in her family. They drink a shot and they kill the can of beer right then and there. They don't sip it.

I remember when we were up at her cousins, and they had a big family bash up there. Food, oh my God. They had about a 30 or 35 foot basement, and one whole side was just covered with Polish dishes, everything under the sun. There was breads, pastries, salads, meat dishes, macaroni dishes, everything. You can believe it that Polish people eat and like to have parties. Man, they would dance, and the women would dance and they'd have a gala time. They didn't have a care in the world. When they got together with people of their own background and people in their family, they would live it up. It reminded me a lot of my family.

I think the Poles and the Italians, they try to bring up their families and their children in more or less the same way as far as havin respect, bein a hard worker, a good provider, and the work and the play part. But I look at it this way, each to his own. I feel more stable if I'm with my own people, with the Italians. I don't know how I would feel if I went over to Little Italy in the city. To me it would take some adjustment, because with the Italians, you have large families and you have names. Like in the city you might have two or three big Italian names, and then you have a family tree all down the line. It's the same way with my people. But to me I would feel better, like I'm with the people who know what I'm like, and what I like to do, the food I like to eat, and the wine I like to drink. I like to work hard and play hard and be with my family, my mother, my father, my uncles, and my cousins.

I don't see anything wrong with a planned community. They got to cover all minorities to keep from discriminatin. I don't care if it's a band of 50 people who are Indians or Mexicans, who are Jews or Catholics or Protestants, or what the hell they are, they got to put it in here to cover them. But the only way a planned community is gonna work is if the people can get it together, if they can stand livin with one another. You can plan this and that as far as the materialistic point of the community, like buses, schools, housing, shopping centers. That's all fine and well, but you can't plan human beings. I mean you could put those people there and these people here, but every person is made up different. They've got different reactions, and it's up to those individuals to either make it or break it. Everybody knows the ground rules. It's up to the people to get along.

These people who plan these communities are not stupid, they're geniuses. They say, "Here it is; this is the Garden of Eden." It's like in the Bible, the bringin in of the sheep. They say, "This is a better place than what you've been livin at in a ghetto. Here's a convenient shopping center where your kids don't have to walk through a bad neighborhood. Here's sidewalks and here's tunneled areas to keep em away from the street. Here's a fine place to live, but you've got to make the best of it."

We're in a planned community, and for the time bein we've got to live this way; we've got to live on a low income. We can't afford luxuries that other people have. I had a good education which I've still got, but I can't put much of it to use. We've seen some good times; we made good money; we're tryin to bring up our children right. What happened, happened, whether it's fate or destiny or God's will, who knows? Every night in the paper, I'll look at the jobs, new jobs, somethin that might come out, somethin that might interest me or I might be capable of doin to better myself.

I sit down about once a week and draw up a house plan; that's my dream home. And I think about what I can build it for. I eat my heart out. If I only had the money, or if somebody only gave me the opportunity. I don't look at anything pessimistic, it's always optimistic. I always look at everything on the bright side, that it's got to get better and it's gonna get better. It's wonderful to be free, to be married to a wonderful woman like May, and to have four children. I'm here to do whatever it may be, whether it's to be plumbing for the rest of my life, or to own a business, or to be somebody famous, or to have a lot of money, or to be civic minded.

I tell May I grew up from the school of hard knocks. Like when I was goin to college, my father gave me $500 for one semester and that was it. He taught me to be a hard worker. He used to say, "You want this? Fine, save your money, and you'll get it some day." So I went to school and paid my way, and then we were married when I was in school. I wouldn't appreciate it on a silver platter; make em work for it. If it's given to them, nine out of ten times, they're gonna abuse it. But if you work for somethin, you're gonna appreciate it more.

I'd like to have a small piece of land and build my own home, not buy one, unless I could find a real steal. I'd build a house and put in it what I'd like to have in it and be proud of it. I'd like to have a house which I can say that I built myself. And just be where I don't have to put up with congestion, where you don't have to contend with city traffic and you don't have pollution. If I came up tomorrow mornin with $50,000, I'd buy a piece of land and build a house out in the country for the peace and quiet.

I don't care what the next guy does; whatever turns him on, fine. But when it boils down to where it might interfere with what I'm doin or bother me or upset me, then I might show a point of view, or dislike. I work all day with a group of nice guys; we carry on and have a good time. But everything is do this and do that, and when I come home, I like to sit down and have a cigarette and a cup of coffee and read the paper and listen to some soft music. I don't wanna listen to horns blowin and beepin, and fire engines, or loud music of boom, boom, boom playin, and kids runnin through the buildin. I wanna sit down and I wanna relax. I got hobbies, plenty of em that I love, but I got a champagne taste and a beer pocket and I can't afford it. So the only thing that I look forward to every day is to come home and just say the hell with everything.

Life is life and you got to put up with it and do the best you can. I mean, you sit down and you knock yourself, and you feel that you're not doin it right. You know you got to give yourself just a little bit of credit every now and then or else you fall apart. I got the hustle and bustle all day, and when I come home, I like to forget about it. Who wants to come home after workin eight or ten hours a day doin that kind of work and have the same thing home? You need a chance to relax, to get away from it all.

Still, of all the stairwells and all the problems in Underhill, I think ours is the only one that's really worked out. The rest of the people here couldn't give a damn.

MAY BONNOLI

I don't know why my next door neighbors are in Underhill. They're low income and I know that maybe this is their last ditch try. I think they dislike any kind of organization, any kind of community spirit, and they fight everything Archie does. He can do no right; management can do no right.

I think that I am a very unprejudiced person, but these people rile me no end because every other word out of their mouth is "nigger." I feel like putting my fist through them because I didn't move here to be prejudiced. I knew that I would be living with all kinds of people; I grew up with all kinds of people. I don't look at somebody and say, "You're black and I'm white." You're a person and I'm a person—that's the way I feel.

Any complaint they have, a broken car mirror or something else, is because of the "colored" children around here. Well, my God, some white kids could come along and knock it off just as easily. And they're one family that feel anything coming from a Residents Council or from management is trying to bug in on people's personal lives. Well I don't feel this; I feel that management, Residents Council, it's all for your own good. It's working for you; it's trying to give you some better things in life, activities, a place to go, somebody to talk to.

I'm not saying that everybody should join in; that's your privilege and that's your perogative. If you want to, fine. But I don't think you've got any right to fight it or knock it when other people are trying to do for themselves. I get kind of irate at times when I look and see the way some people just knock every little effort you try to do. There are some families here that are against being organized and against any community spirit.

Just as an example, we had a great problem with roaches. It's something I've never had till I moved here. And we have one family in particular that's causing the problem, the Turnfinders next door. I've reported it because I don't want them around my children; I think roaches are positively the dirtiest thing on earth. So we all agreed that we would have our building exterminated at the same time. We went ahead and had the extermination, but they wouldn't be exterminated. So as a result I had roaches; even after the extermination, my walls were covered with them.

So I went and I said to Archie, "What now?" And he said, "Have a bug bomb." I had to move my children out for 12 hours; six of it was necessary, the other six I felt essential because I've got little children. But I was over in this apartment the other day, and it's so dirty you stick to the floor. I just don't understand why people want to live like this when you're given a new apartment, a chance to better yourself and come up.

Every kind of thing that we try to do in this building, there's always this one family that causes the dissension, that says, "We're not gonna participate." We've also gone to Archie and told him that if he can't do anything, we'd like the Health Department to move in. Their neighbor downstairs, Ada Harris, she is an elderly lady; she's got a husband that's bed ridden constantly. And I mean she's petrified with these roaches because she's scared to death it'll bring other bugs, bedbugs, stuff like this. I just don't think it's fair to have one family drag five other families down with them and create this kind of problem.

Still, I find the people out here, with the exception of a very few, if you've got a problem, they're ready to bend over backwards and help you, right here in Underhill more than any place I've ever lived. Right here in our building, it's nothing to have a neighbor say, "Hey, I need a ride to such and such a place; would you mind?" And if I can do it, I'll do it because I know what it's like sometimes.

My husband, Wally, is a plumber. We've been married for seven years and we're both 27. If he can get a ride with somebody else, I use the car. I have a child that goes to the doctor three days a week for allergy treatments, so I kind of depend on it for that. But otherwise, I use their public transportation, the call-a-ride. Though you have to reserve a week in advance, they come right to your door, and I can take her this way. So I never really feel completely at a loss for transportation out here.

And babysitting, too; it's great. I've got a deaf neighbor downstairs, and she babysits for my three youngest kids. She's just as good a babysitter as somebody who has both ears. Archie suggested her, and I said, "Well, gee, I don't know." He said, "Give her a try." And I said, "Well, okay." I was amazed at the results. She'd never want money for it, just maybe a ride to the store or here or there. It's kind of a cooperative thing; you do something for me and I'll do for you.

We've lived in other low income housing on the other side of Columbia. We didn't care for it because the people were not together. You were there fighting for yourself, and there was no common cause. You didn't stop to realize that your neighbors might have problems. Of course they have a problem; they've got one management for five or six different projects. Now they're trying to get their own management going within each individual group, and maybe work up to something like Underhill's got.

We have our own man here, and there's not any kind of problem, whether it's social, financial, or what have you, that you can't go to Archie and talk to him about it. He'll either give some kind of suggestion right off the bat or say, "Let me call you back and I'll have a suggestion for you or an answer to your problem." He's not a landlord; Archie is a friend. He's there to help you if you need it. I'd hate like the devil to see it ever change. You feel like you're dealing with a human being and not some God that is gonna stand there and pass judgment.

You just don't get this consideration in very many places at all. I know because we started out on top; my husband had his own business. He had a silent partner that robbed him blind, and we went bankrupt. So we went from living in our own home to a project in Columbia and then to Underhill. But I don't feel that Underhill's a step down; I think for us it's a step back up.

When I first moved here, I allowed myself to get overinvolved. I tried to help build a better community because basically I like people, and I like to get out and do things to better my life. I was spending 90 percent of my time away from my family till one day I said, "Whoa, this has got to stop." Around here you've got maybe 25 percent of us that are really interested in doing things that'll bring the community up, give people a place to go, things to do. And you've got another 75 percent that are willing to participate if somebody else does the leading. But then a problem comes up at home, and you get involved in your own personal thing. The community projects fail because everybody just sits and waits.

We've tried to talk about how you get people to fight for themselves, but we really have no positive answer. It's kind of a shame because right now we've got the Community College over here ready and willing to bring courses to us in Underhill, if we can just get the people together to say this is what we want. We've tried approaching them; we've tried having mass meetings. I get kind of aggravated, to put it very mildly, and every now and then I just drop out because I get tired of fighting a no-good system.

I can point to some positive things I think we've done. Archie had a fire last year, and even the people that didn't do anything were on the phone asking what they could do. It's kind of sad in a way that you have to have some kind of personal tragedy hit a family in order to get everybody moving. It lasted for as long as Archie and Cathy needed help. We got together just in this building along these three stairwells, and we had a painting party. Everybody chipped in and got their whole place painted and cleaned up. The wives got together while all the men were up there painting. We cooked dishes and had a potluck supper. And we thought maybe somebody would get the idea of doing something for somebody else, but it didn't catch.

And then last spring, we had our cleanup in the parking lot island over here to create a play area for the younger children. I would say about ten percent of our male population and some of our women showed up to clean it. But now you turn around once again and everybody's wiling to use it once it's in, but not to do the work to help clean it. This just doesn't seem fair. I'm not gonna grouch because I went out and worked and say, "Well, your kids shouldn't use it because I went out and did the work." I just feel that if people want these things, we could do even more if everybody would group together and work together.

Right now, I think in our Residents Council there's a lot of deadwood and a lot of dead promises. People say, "Well, I'll do such and such," but it never materializes. I think it would be wise to disband them. Maybe then we should try to have a community get together, even if it's a picnic, where you could get to meet everybody, decide who you like and kind of form opinions. Then we could have a general election again, try to set up a new board and see if we couldn't get something working with new faces, new people that have just come in who have ideas they'd like to see implemented.

I think it would be very helpful if you could get one person to go around to the families and try to decide who wants what, even if it turned out that the person had to be salaried from an agency. I know one gal down at Community Action that has come out and tried to start a number of projects, but of course she has limited time because Underhill is not her only project. We need someone who could get out day after day and work with the people. Nobody here has the time to go round from family to family.

Archie has limited time, but I have to give him a pat on the back. There're times when he doesn't get around when he should because he's really pressed. He's one man working with all these people. But you have to give him credit for the size of the development and being only one man with a hundred and some families.

Living in a neighborhood like this, we're a unit within ourselves. We've all got common problems or we wouldn't be here. If we had one person that could coordinate us, it would be easier for everybody to work together. Archie's got a problem because he's got 50 percent of the people that are behind him and another 50 percent who say, "Well, gee, he's trying to run us, and we don't want a manager running us." They look at him as the old landlord figure, which is something I think he's fought to get away from. If I had a problem, I would think nothing of asking him for help. I think there's not a family in Underhill that could claim he would not do it.

We had a rummage sale that was one of our more unsuccessful projects. People were very free with giving out old clothing; this part of it was a success. But we only had four people that actually worked on it. We couldn't get one person to transport the stuff from here to up the street to the Village Center. There was difficulty getting people just to take posters. We worked two consecutive Saturdays right down here at the office, and I think we only made about $30. The purpose of having the rummage sale was that we wanted to give our children a special Christmas party. This irritated me because I thought, "Wow, this is for the kids; this oughta really spark it." Instead, we wound up with our children transported to the County Christmas party.

There was one other project, when the government decided they were gonna recertify us every year rather than every two years. This meant that they looked at your income to see if it changed so they could raise the rent.

We felt that a two year limit was very fair; it gave people time in which to put some money away before they raised rent. There're numerous families living here now that after a year their rent's gone up. It's cheaper living here than if you were someplace else, but that doesn't matter if you're low income and still trying to make it.

Well, everybody was up in arms so they called a community meeting. We had about a 90 percent turnout, which was a real shock to everybody. I think there was as much positive thinking and work as could possibly be done when you're bucking the federal government. Letters were written to HUD, but we got the runaround—we never got any place, even with promises of help from different tenant coordinators. I don't understand why HUD did it; I don't feel they were completely fair.

Some wives work until recertification and then quit their jobs. We just got our letter for recertification, and in a way it'll benefit us. My husband's making less money than he was last year at this time because he had to take a cut in salary. Our rent won't go up, and starting next weekend I have a job, so that we'll both be working. And he also gets a raise next week. We have to get our recertification in before that, which maybe sounds underhanded, but somehow you've got to get ahead. A lot of people moved out after this recertification thing came up because they found that their rents were going to be more. They just felt that if they were going to have to be paying more, they'd rather be someplace a little bit better and paying more there.

With most people, you know you're going to be here a year, two or three years at the most, until you can build up in your finances, so that you can either get a better apartment or a home of your own. Most of the people I knew who have moved away from here have gone to either a better apartment or a home of their own.

Our goal is to put enough away in a year's time to buy a house, whether it's old, new, falling down, or what. I think this is what most people's idea is when they move to Underhill. Most of the people I've talked to around here are not satisfied with just living in an apartment for a lifetime; they want a home. I think when you get married this is one of the things that you work towards. Of course, we had kids a little too quick; but that's how it goes.

We've got library facilities down at the project office; people have brought books in by the carloads, but we can't get enough people to sit down and organize a catalogue. We have one gal who works all day, and she'd go down there a couple of hours every night and try to catalogue. But it's a pretty large job. And with working and children, it was a little hard on her. Plus she's divorced and didn't have a husband to come home to and say, "Will you take over while I go do this?"

At Christmastime, the development company donated approximately 30 children's books; it was a terrific donation. But the last time I looked, they were sitting in a bag waiting for somebody to put them on a shelf and catalogue them. The bookmobile comes around once every two weeks, but their supply is limited. We've got more books down in that office library than the County Library has on their bookmobile.

Underhill has to learn to deal with the black and the white situation. I think most of us can take a pretty positive attitude towards it and not feel anything one way or the other. But then there're some who definitely have racial feelings. Out here, it's nothing to see an interracial marriage. This is what the whole concept of Columbia is, where everybody could live together regardless of who or what they are.

I felt good when I first came here, because when I went to parochial school, some of my best friends were black. My husband worked with black people, with Indians, you name it. And I don't feel that we've ever distinguished and discriminated one from the other. But I know this isn't so with everybody around here.

In our stairwell, we've got blacks, we've got whites. It's a melting pot right here in our own stairwell. I think that Verna downstairs had to learn how to deal with white people. She came from a small town that's 90 percent black. She always felt that she couldn't come to us if our kids were making dirt in the hall because we were white and she wasn't equal. She would go to Clara, her black neighbor upstairs.

So Clara would come down and say, "Verna's afraid to come to you because you're white. She's afraid that you are gonna look down upon her because she's complaining." So finally one day, I went down and talked to Verna and I said, "What's with you?" I said, "I'm no better than you are, and you're no better than I am. This is ridiculous." Well, it took Verna about four months to really work out of her uptight feelings there. I think that we effectively dealt with it because I took the initiative to go down and talk to her. But I think she still has her reservations. It's the same thing with Archie. She won't go to him and make suggestions or complain about anything because he's white and she feels that he's above her.

Clara's done a lot of good around here as far as racial problems go, because neither she or her kids ever look at anybody as being a different color. Everybody's the same. I know Clara's worked with different families around here trying to get them to see this. Now next door to me, there is definitely a racial problem with the Turnfinders. I think that part of this is caused by ignorance, by lack of education, by background. When you come from the hills in West Virginia and you don't have much education, you're taught that black people are garbage. I disagree. I think it's fine if you've got a racial prejudice to keep it within your walls and talk about it among yourselves. But the man over here has the habit of going right up to kids if they're on the steps and saying, "Move, niggers." I don't think this is fair because I think children are easily hurt. We've tried to have stairwell meetings to try and talk to them. Well, several times they've refused to show up. The rest of the time they just sit down and not talk to you. They've got one positive thing going for them. They've got Aunt Matty, and she's got a lot more on the ball, a lot more education. She still has no control over what Elmer says to the kids or anything like that. But I think she's trying to help

Nancy out to the point that she will at least look at a colored person and speak to them without Elmer's nasty snide remarks.

The Corbins upstairs were prejudiced against black people, or just prejudiced against the whole basic idea that we were here because we had financial problems. They were here because they were flooded out of a home. Once their flood problems were over, they rebuilt the home, sold it, and made a pretty good deal on that. So basically they were uninvolved with the community.

When you hung around them, you got a feeling that they felt they were better than you were. We knew we had been discussed at one time, and we both felt that they were a little bit above us and they couldn't really relate. Mrs. Corbin was against two of the black people in our building; I heard her voice it to me.

I always felt that she was removed from us. But she would ask how the kids were, something like that, if she knew they were sick. She never really went out of her way to become involved in any of our stairwell activities or even community affairs. She had her life outside of here.

And this Mrs. Harris downstairs. I've never met a woman more fantastic in my life. She's in her seventies and has an invalid husband. I know that woman must go from 6 o'clock in the morning till 10 o'clock at night caring for him. You never see her that she doesn't have a smile on her face, no matter how hard things go. And I've never heard her say, even when the Turnfinders were making noise. "Oh, they're white, and that's why I'm having trouble." It's just, "They're people and I'm having trouble with them, and they've got to understand my situation." I think she's just a wonderful person.

It's kind of hard to screen people in public housing. This project was created for low income people, and they have a right to it. You can't deny em that privilege, regardless of what their views are. As a result, you get people like the Turnfinders in here. They were moved in under emergency circumstances because their place was either being condemned, they didn't have running water, or stuff like this. I believe somebody like that would feel, "I've been given something better than what I had. I should be appreciative; I should make something of it." I've never really had contact with a family that has been this dense to get through to. I just don't feel that Elmer gets along with anybody, period. He told me one day that he was sick and tired of the whole world. Everybody was against him. So what do you do if you get somebody like that where he's convinced that everybody hates him?

We had one family that's no longer living here; they were West Indian and there was a communication barrier. They had several unruly children, and she really didn't know how to discipline them. They didn't know how to come and fit into a new lifestyle from what they had originally. There was a great deal of racial tension there because they were black, and the kids would go out and cause fights with the white kids all the time. They finally were evicted for nonpayment of rent.

We have a Turkish family living up here that have difficulty dealing with blacks. They're getting a little bit better; they're a little bit more tolerant, but we've had trouble with them. I'm not saying that I'm against foreign people in any way, but the American people raise their kids basically along the same pattern. These two people work and they've got two sons who are left to run from early morning until late at night. There's no discipline whatsoever. I mean there's not a mother on this block that doesn't pull her hair periodically because they're the gang leaders of any trouble.

Some of the kids here without parents may fight a lot harder to get what they want. I don't mean illegal things; I mean just simple everyday things. I don't feel that they're nasty, but they have a tougher road. I have never had any of them really be out and out disrespectful to me. If I have a grouch, I come right to the kid and say, "I wish you wouldn't do that." I've never been backtalked, so I just really don't have a beef about the kids. Sometimes I feel it's the way in which you handle a situation and the way in which you look at it.

Well, I will say this; I've heard plenty of foul language. I've heard, "hell," "damn," "shit." You show me any kid from five years on who doesn't experiment. I've even had the occasion where they've tried it on me as an adult, like a three-year-old saying "hell" to me a couple of times. But I don't think it's ever been used maliciously, at least to me. I think that what fighting there has been between black and white kids is parent oriented. They hear it coming from within the family, and if this is how mommy and daddy feel, then this is how I'm supposed to feel. Basically, I feel that the kids get along very well, that what fights there are, they're just childhood fights.

Now when I was in the other project, there were perpetual fights between whites and blacks. It was definitely racial, and I mean it was dirty racial. It just wasn't little, picky things; I mean kids would get beat up. I rode in the ambulance one night with a white boy that got beat up, and it appalled me that human beings had to act like this. The child broke his nose, and it was all over something stupid. He was delivering papers and some kid said something about, "I don't want any of your whitey papers." He said, "Oh, shut up, nigger." This created a major battle and this kid, I mean, he was blood from head to toe. I just thought, "God." But this is common there; I talked to the people that were my old neighbors and this still goes on. I think that we deal with our problems much better over here.

We left that project mainly because of inadequate housing; it was just too small. Plus the fact that the racial bit got me. My son couldn't go outside without getting beat up just because he was a white child. I had toys stolen, things like this; I'd never faced this before. I heard them all the time call him "honky kid," and of course he'd come in and ask, "What's that?" I'd have to try and sit down and explain to a four-year-old why this was going on.

I don't know if it's a more militant type of black person, a more militant type of white person, or what. As far as income goes between there and here, I think we're the same level and we should be of the same intelligence. But here we've got Archie pulling us together; maybe over there you just don't have anybody pulling for you. If we have a hassle, like it's too major, we go to Archie, and he either acts as your mediator or gets somebody from the outside. I've seen him do it in different stairwells.

I think you could say that Archie does screen his families to an extent. He sat down and asked us point blank what our feelings were towards blacks, whites, and what have you. I can't believe anybody moved into Underhill without knowing there would be all different kinds of people, it being a 236 project. He also told us, "I want you here because I think you and Wally would be good for the community, because of your attitudes, and because you're a family situation." He said, "I'm not against divorced or separated women, but I've got more than enough here right now. I need more men that'll go to work with the kids and do things around here." I think he had a good idea. I've noticed since then he has tried to get in more family situations, and in a way it's been helpful. But the men still haven't pulled together with the kids like I think he hoped.

I have only one beef with this apartment, the construction in general. They don't just construct them so that they're noiseproof. No place is gonna be noiseproof, but in here I think it's a little bit cheaper construction than a lot of places. You get up and go to the bathroom at night, the person in the room below can hear you. They've dealt with the problem of outside noise pretty well. It was explained in the memo they sent us that rules would have to be followed or sterner measures would have to be taken by management. Archie could take measures even to evict somebody if it really grew to major proportions. When spring first came, I thought, "My God, will my kids ever get to sleep?" because there was so much noise, kids playing outside, adults with radios, stuff like that. The kids are a lot more curbed now, it seems to me. You don't have any of this noise and carrying on after 10 o'clock in the evening.

We had a meeting one time because the noise hassle in the stairwell got to be so much. Clara would play her hi fi so loud that my floor would jump; it drove me up the wall. She's got a teenage boy with a guitar and amplifier upstairs, and you'd feel like, "I'm gonna go crazy." I got accused of not liking music, and I said, "Oh, boy, are you off base." I said, "I like classical. You can have some of your hard rock, but I'll be honest, I don't like it."

Clara complained because my kids were too loud. They're little and they yell like the devil around the house. We went to Archie and he said, "I can't be impartial because I know all of you." Then he had a mediator, but that didn't work because everybody clammed up and felt self-conscious. So one night, we said "Come on down in our living room." All of us got together and we sat down here. We didn't holler; we didn't act like kids. We acted like adults and we discussed what the problems were. We did some pretty positive thinking. Everybody showed up except for the Turnfinders next door. We talked the problems out, and we just decided some of it you've got to live with because it's the construction.

Well, I think as a result, they turned the hi fi down. Clara put a marker on her thing so she knows how high she can turn it without it aggravating.

I know that I can't let the kids yell around the house to the point they were. I get on them and we curbed that. We talked to Gary, and fortunately Clara's teenage kids are out of this world; they're just as nice as can be. He understood the problem that my kids have to nap at some point, so my kids nap between 1:00 and 3:00, and from 5:00 to 6:00 he plays his guitar. We don't have that hassle any more. We got together because we had such a good relationship that we didn't want to see it go to pot.

It's worked out beautifully. Clara will come in from work and say, "Hi, any trouble with the kids today? Were they too loud? How'd the day go with you?" There's free contact. Like if I have to go to the store and I know Mrs. Harris is down there by herself, I'll call and say do you need anything. Or she'll take a walk while somebody watches her husband. I know there are times when you can run out of things, so I check in with her. I even check in with the Turnfinders, like their baby had been really sick over the weekend and I took aspirin over. I said, "Please take him to the doctor," because the kid was burning up. Well, I never did get through, so I guess by the grace of God he's getting better. But I stopped over with freezer pops and said, "You've got to get some liquids into him." Even though we don't get along to a certain degree, we keep the avenues of communication open.

Those Turnfinder children don't go out from one end of the day to the next. I'm surprised that they know what the outside is like because she won't take them for a walk. She doesn't like the people around here, so therefore she won't go out. This isn't fair; they've got to get out and to have air. As a result, they're constantly sick.

I think Archie's up a tree with them; he's tried every way on God's earth to move these people. He even had a public health nurse offer to come in and help work with this gal. She'd never cleaned, never done anything like this. She came in here one day and said, "What do you scrub walls with?" I said, "409." She said, "What's that? Will you buy me some?" I went out and I bought her some and showed her how to scrub walls. Of course you can help people so far, but people have to help themselves.

Maintenance is a problem around here. This building burned at one point, before anybody moved in it. I think they rewired it backwards; they never did anything right with it. So when we moved in last year, our air conditioning wasn't working. This year it went out for four weeks while I hassled maintenance every day. I finally got mad and said, "You either fix it or I'm calling in a private contractor. I'll deduct it from my rent or you will have to pay the bill yourself." The next day, bam, I got reactions. It's nothing around here for a toilet to stop up and the next day to still have it stopped up. This is something I think Archie would like to be able to control more, but maintenance is a separate unit. It's like fighting God to get them to move and do things; it's really ridiculous.

Underhill is one of the prettiest spots in Columbia, especially the woods. I like the area; I really think it's just lovely. And the apartment, God, it's just enormous. You know I feel like sometimes I'm gonna lose myself in it because it's got a huge bedroom here and a walk-in closet. I wanted a nursery for the baby when we moved in, so I just moved all the clothes out of the walk-in closet and set up a nursery. Archie said, "You're illegal. You don't have a window in the bedroom." And I said, "Are you gonna do anything?" And he said, "No."

What bugs me is that there are residents that have pets. The Turnfinders right next door have a cat, and this cat invariably plants itself either outside my front door or comes in here. The cat comes in and pees all over the floor, you name it. People just don't stop to think of the neighbors enough. I hated to be the fink to call Archie and say, "There's a black and white cat here; would you please do something about it?" But I have done it. Of course, he's been assured that the cat's gone, but the cat's still here.

Archie and I only have one hassle. My little boy and his friends have a tree down here where they dig, and they've dug down to the roots. I don't agree that they should be allowed to do this. But I have begged and begged, "Couldn't we please have a sandbox?" Well, Archie is all for it, but there are so many people around here that are worried about pinworms and all kinds of worms in the sand. My son has been playing in sandboxes since he was old enough to toddle, and I've yet to see any adverse reaction. I always go out and buy this special sand in the bag. I said, "I will be willing to donate two bags of sand and my husband will build a sandbox." Still no good. So, of course, Archie and I got into a hassle, and he said, "They've got to stop digging." Later he said, "All right, let em dig in the woods." I don't like him back in the woods that much because he's too little and I can't supervise. But he's back there because little boys are gonna dig.

I wish they had maybe one more washer or dryer in the laundry room, because it gets to be a hassle when everybody's trying to get in there to do their wash. I've tried every day of the week, and I've yet to find a good day. Also, we're not allowed to have dishwashers; I have a dishwasher that I can't hook up. That bothers me when I have company, like at Christmas and Thanksgiving. I can see the merit behind it; it's gonna cost more for the additional water use. You can also have a vibration from it that's gonna drive somebody nuts. The one rule I don't understand and can't abide by, they won't let you have a freezer. And boy, for a family my size or a family like Verna's size with all those kids downstairs, this would be a real saving. It would be worth the initial outlay to have a freezer and be able to stock up stuff when they've got sales. I can't see that a freezer would pull any more electricity than, say, a guitar amplifier upstairs or your air conditioning.

The day we moved in, Gary, the young kid upstairs, asked, "Can I help you move furniture?" You know, it was Wally and myself moving couches, beds, the works; we had no extra help. People came down the whole day and said, "If there's anything I can do to help you let me know." Even neighbors from down the street said, "Nice to have you here; if you feel like coming down for a visit, please come by." This is how I got to meet people. In the afternoon, after I was finished in the house, I'd be out walking with the kids and we'd sit and rap for awhile. I felt pretty good about it right from the beginning.

There was really no orientation; we were pretty much Columbia residents already and we knew where to go for the things we needed. Archie never sat down and said, "read verbatim" every paragraph of the lease. This is something that I myself did. Archie would sit down with people that were not from here and go over things a little bit more thoroughly with them. But with the Turnfinders next door, I think he could've been a lot more thorough. There was quite a hassle with their lease; they didn't understand this and that. They finally brought it over to me one night and I went down paragraph by paragraph. It all depends upon Archie, how much time he's got.

Entrance to Underhill is based on financial convenience for most people. We've got some girls here that are on welfare, and they know this is what's going to be for them for quite awhile. I know several gals here that are divorced, not getting much money, and Underhill's a chance for them to sock away what little they make out of a paycheck. They're also going to school in order to better themselves. There's no place else in this area where you could build yourself up like this.

Most of the people who come in here, even the ones who move out shortly thereafter, have done a good deal to try and get something working. If they know they have to make the best of it, and they want to work for life as it is right then and there, they'll put an effort into the community. Of course, you get some that are going to be here a short time that say, "The hell with it; I'll put a little in or maybe I won't put anything in." For some families, Underhill is rock bottom.

If you don't join in, and you're not part of the activities or the community voice, you kind of get snowed under. People will look down on you in a way if they think you're a dead beat and can't be bothered with community affairs. Outside of Underhill, everybody has a right to live by the lifestyle that they like. But you can't survive in a community like this, as close as everybody has to be here, if you want to be by yourself. It's not for the individual seeking a solitary life. Whether it's to buck management on some kind of proposal they've got or whether it's to buck the government, you've got to provide a united force. Underhill is like its own Columbia, and each stairwell's a small cul de sac. You learn to give and take and weigh one thing against another.

I'm very glad that we have the relationship we've got right within this stairwell. If Wally's working late at night and I have a problem, I know that I've got four or five families I can call on and have an immediate response. And it's the same with them. We've been called out at night when Clara's child, Julia, was having trouble breathing; she has asthma. Julia split her head open one Sunday, and Wally was there within a couple of minutes. One night my child had trouble; she had pneumonia and we had to take here to the clinic at 12 o'clock at night. I called Clara, and in two minutes we were on our way to the clinic. It's a good feeling in times of trouble when you've got a neighbor to help.

Even when things are good I'll say, "Hey, Clara, come on down and have a beer," or, "Let's sit down and talk," or, "Verna, come up for awhile." You can sit there and have a smoke and exchange of ideas, just sit down and relax for awhile to have some company. No one in this stairwell has ever seen any reason to feel lonely. Mrs. Harris downstairs, she knows that; all she's got to do is dial our number, and Wally can be down there in a minute before the police could even get here. You know you've got friends.

But when it hurts other people, then it's time to bring in somebody from the outside, be it Archie or a mediator. I think somebody's got to deal with the problem next door, because they're hurting five other families with the dirt and the noise. I confronted Archie the other day. I said, "What in the name of God are you going to do about the dirt and the bugs? I've had it." Archie himself says, "I don't know what to do; I don't want to evict them. I know they need Underhill." I'm sympathetic to this, but still, how do you combat people that don't want to participate in any way in helping to improve conditions?

I said to Archie, "If I was in your shoes, I'd evict them." But then, Archie's Archie, and he said, "Well, if I evict them, where do people like these go?" He remarked to me one day, "You know, I play God." And I said, "You know, I think you're right." And he laughed. At one point, we had two senior citizens drop dead just about within a week's time. One woman who was also a senior citizen came to him and said, "Archie, what in the name of God are you going to do about all these senior citizens dying?" And that is just about what his role is supposed to be, that of the Lord Almighty.

I spent most of my life not far from here, in a suburban town where I was born. We lived in our own home in a middle class neighborhood and had relatives that lived right on the street. It was an atmosphere something like I find in Columbia, where as neighbors you help each other. As a kid growing up, I made some fine friendships that we've kept through the years. It's the kind of neighborhood I would look forward to raising my children in, where you had pleasantness and kind of a relationship with all your neighbors, where you could visit back and forth. When I was growing up, my parents used to get together with different couples in the neighborhood, go to dances, play cards; there was always something going on.

My father is a pretty great guy; he's what I think would come under the old cliche of a self-made man. He came from parents that were low to middle class in the same area. He put himself through college, but he never completely finished. He's one of the few men I've ever met that if there's something broken, be it electrical, carpentry, you name it, if he doesn't know how to fix it, by God he'll go find out how. And I think for somebody that has not really gone through a complete college education, he's really done terrifically well in the business world. I have never met anybody, and I have met quite a few of his business associates, who didn't have high praise for him and think he was a really nice guy. He's got a personality that works, and he's got the gift of gab to kind of get around and do the saleswork.

My mother, she and I aren't always close. I don't know why. Ever since I was growing up, I went to my father; he was more the listener and more the wise man of the family. My mother tends to explode a lot; she doesn't take anything calmly. I think basically she's great; she's a good grandmother.

We're different though, because I'm not satisfied to just say that I'm a housewife. I like to think that I'm a housewife, a mother, a wife, but that I can also broaden my interests. She's the kind of woman that's just perfectly satisfied with her life. She finished high school, went to work, got married, had kids, and this has been her whole life.

She expressed the opinion to me one day that she didn't care if she never worked, that she never had any desire to further her education and was perfectly happy. She didn't want to be part of the women's lib movement—which she feels that I am. I said, "I don't really think I'm part of women's lib; I just feel that a woman doesn't have to stay in the house and just cook and clean and take care of kids." You're a human being and you have a brain just as well as the male has. You should have every chance to go out and broaden your horizon and become a better person for it. To me, she leads a pretty dull life because she's just a stay at home type. Whereas with me, I still feel that I'm young, and while I'm happy with my family and my life as it is, when my children get older, I'd like to be able to go back to school and either go into social work, nursing, or something like that.

When I was in grade school, after all my exposure to nuns and all the talk about vocations, I decided in fifth grade I was going to be a nun. I went through all kinds of vocational counseling towards this goal. I think it was suddenly around the eighth grade it dawned on me that there were boys in the world, and I figured out that I couldn't be a nun and have boys, too. So that kind of changed things.

I took a general course in high school because I wasn't really sure of what I wanted to do. I was really good in English; I could pull straight A's without even studying. I loved to write and I did some short stories. I thought I'd like to go into some branch of writing or something to do with English. There was one really great teacher who kind of convinced me that teaching was a pretty good vocation.

When I got out, I want to the University for one year, but my father did have some kind of fallback in funds, so I went to work as a secretary for a big manufacturer. I found this completely fascinating. So I've gone from nun, to English teacher, to secretary, and I've found that each time I've changed, it's been pretty interesting.

On my father's side, I think my ancestors came over from England. I don't know too much more, except that it was a pretty large family. And on my grandmother's side, it's definitely Polish. My mother was born here, but I think her mother and father came from Poland. My grandfather is dead and my grandmother has lived with my mother and father now for 15 years.

I don't know how you go about doing it, but to me it would be very interesting somehow to trace the family tree. I don't know where to go to obtain the information because basically once I get past my grandparents on either side, it's very sketchy as to where my family really came from.

My mother's maiden name was Ganiecki. They must have at least a hundred of them living right in this one area in Baltimore. That's definitely a Polish section because as each family has grown up, they've kind of built right around there and gotten the old homes. At least once a year we all get together, and you've never seen such a gang in your life. They're very fun loving people, and you never go that you don't have a good time. I think they're really fine people, and they would bend over backwards if they knew a member of the family needed it. They have given us help when we've needed it, even if it's just to pass on secondhand clothing to the kids.

But it's not the same way with my father's side; they're a little bit colder kind of people. This is kind of surprising to me because my father's a very warm, open person, whereas with his own father, he's not very demonstrative in his feelings. He just assumes that you know he cares. And they're not as close knit as the Polish side. They're scattered more, too; they're not in one neighborhood. Maybe every couple of years we happen to have them together and you have a good time, but it's not the feeling of warmth that you get when you're with the Ganiecki family.

I knew that we were of Polish background, Polish descent, but I didn't really feel that they brought it up that they were definitely Poles or anything like that. But it is interesting to note, with the exception of a few of us, they kind of carried on the Polish tradition of marrying a Pole. I married an Italian, so we always have a big laugh because when we have our family get together, they have their Polish dishes and I bring my Italian dish. They, of course, have the traditional dishes, but I myself don't know how to cook them.

I've got a cousin named Claudette who's been very interested in Columbia and in the development. She and her husband have five children, and they're outgrowing their present home. In the Polish area there really are not too many houses for sale right now, and they may have to branch out. She's been out here several times and I've taken her around. They might miss the old neighborhood because of the way they've been brought up, but I think they also realize that they're gonna have to move. They would like to make it a wise move, someplace where they would have neighbors and friends, along with the old neighborhood to go back to, which wouldn't really be that far away.

I don't really feel that my mother has any strong Polish feelings. I feel it was more in my grandmother and my grandfather, more in the older people my mother was brought up around. There is a close feeling between my mother and her cousins and friends, but I don't really believe she goes out of her way to show that she's Polish. I guess you could say it just exists.

I always got the feeling that my grandmother was very proud of her Polish background. I know I've seen her feelings hurt very much on occasions when my brother's friends would come in and start spieling off Polish jokes. She made the remark one day, "How are we any dumber than Americans? They had to have come from some background in Europe, too." I think it definitely stepped on her toes. It's not fair to take a particular crack at any nationality; you know there're Italian jokes, too. I just feel that sooner or later you're going to find somebody that feels strong enough about their background that you're gonna really hurt feelings. There are plenty of jokes in this world that leave out the backgrounds of different people.

We were brought up in an area away from it. We went to St. Jude's, which was a Catholic Church for all people. Even when we went back to Baltimore to visit, we never went to the Polish church, cause most of the time it was early afternoon or evening and church was over with. They had several Polish priests there, and most of them were real characters. On occasion, my mother would take my grandmother and go with her. I know my grandmother still likes to go back. They definitely do it for Christmas Mass, and they also do it around Eastertime for the different services they have. My grandmother wouldn't miss that.

My family still lives around here, and we're all fairly close. I think that since we've gotten married we're closer to my parents; I visit my mother a couple of times a week. Wally comes from a split family. His mother lives in one place and his father in another. There's a lot of friction, so there's really no chance for us to get together too much. The father and mother I speak of is Wally's father and stepmother in Morgan Hills, the Italians. His real mother lives out here in this area; she's Italian too. She's presently divorced from his stepfather, so it gets to be very involved. We visit with his real mother maybe a couple of times a week, more than Wally's stepfather or even his other parents. We're invited to official functions with Wally's parents. They're the kind of people that I think basically have a healthy attitude. They would prefer that they remain uninvolved, that we should lead our lives and they lead theirs. We get together for birthdays, holidays, and things like that, but it seems to be the trend that we're invited to my parents for most of the holidays, and this is where we spend them.

My family didn't feel anything at all about my marrying an Italian. I think they were mostly concerned that I made a good marriage and that it would be a marriage that lasted. But Wally's family weren't too thrilled; they really weren't. They would have preferred his having an Italian wife. However, I think I've proved that I can cook just as well as the rest of them. When I first met them, they were kind of standoffish and, being a direct person, I said to Wally shortly before we were married, "What gives?" And he said, "You're not Italian. They really wanted me to marry an Italian girl." I said, "You have got to be kidding; have they somebody picked out for you? I can't see where it makes any difference."

I think that they're learned to accept me. They include us in some things, and they burn me up in other ways. I've had all four of the children christened, and I've had just a simple church service. Well, according to Wally, I blew it with the first child, because they always have a real bangup church service, formal, the works, and a big Italian party afterwards. Of course, I didn't know about this custom, and he didn't tell me. They were very hurt and would not show up for it. I just had a christening party with very close members of the family, godparents. I asked one of Wally's brothers if he would be a godfather, and he was the only one that did show up. He was one of the younger members and I think he felt sorry for me, the poor Polish gal that married into the Italian family. There has definitely been a little friction there because I'm not Italian. I always get a little dig whenever I'm there.

I've had a lot of exposure to their ways and they're really something. They're not as open with their customs, I don't think, as the Polish or the English people. Like with a recipe or something like that, his mother will not part with it. If it's an old family recipe, you can get down on bended knees and beg for it and there's no way. It's something that her mother gave her, or somebody's mother gave her, and you won't get it. But I think that Wally's pretty satisfied. I don't think that when he was younger, he was indoctrinated as far as the Italian way of life went. He went on to college and got to meet all kinds of people, so I don't think it mattered a hill of beans to him whether the gal was Italian, Polish, or what have you. We never really have any discussion about it, but he always kids me about the lasagna i make. He tells me it manages to taste Polish. But he did tell his mother that he married me mainly because I could cook good spaghetti.

Since the time we've been married, Wally and my father they're like carbon copies; they get along beautifully. So it's a real chance for him to have kind of a father figure, somebody to discuss problems with. They're really wonderful grandparents; the kids are all treated fairly and equally. And babysitting, all I gotta do is call Mom up and say, "Hey, wanna babysit?" My parents are frequent comers and goers; they're in here all the time, because down in Fenton City, where they live now, you don't have facilities and recreational things like we have out here. My brother and sister spend more time up here in Columbia than they do down towards Fenton City.

I would say for both of us that we came from middle class backgrounds. My family was more permissive, more giving, whereas with Wally's family, the idea was you had to work for it. He wanted to go to college and his father flatly refused any financial help, so he worked all night long practically and put himself through school. He got a degree in management, and I admire him for it. It took him seven years where it would have taken most people less.

When we were first married, we were living in private apartment housing and paying a pretty good price for a two bedroom apartment in Fenton City. I found that on the whole, life there was 100 percent different from Columbia. The people came and they went, and you never really knew your neighbor other than to say, "Hi." There was no socializing. Basically, I never felt as I did when I moved here, that if I needed something I could knock on my neighbor's door and say, "Hey, can I have a helping hand?"

We are very easy going and people know if you want to come visit us, we're here. If you suddenly get the urge to come walking up, you come on in; that's the way I like it, the more people the merrier, usually. We have no trouble keeping in touch with people. Saturday nights are usually our kind of visiting night. People pop in; it's just kind of a free and easy thing.

When I was a child, I had several good friends I would bring home, and there was never any question about bringing them home. And then we moved out here, and I eventually went to County High School, where we had a pretty good black population of students. I had one guy that was a very good friend of mine, who's a minister now. He'd drop over Friday, Saturday evenings, and we'd sit around and rap for awhile. It didn't make my parents uptight; they were used to it. They were used to him bringing his girlfriend over and we'd doubledate. We had several groups like this where we had blacks that we were friends with. I will say that it made our neighborhood very uptight. Most of the people that were living out in Fenton City were not ready to see a white girl having black friends.

I think my mother was a little bit uptight about it, but my father had very fair and open feelings. My mother to this day doesn't have the open feelings that I have about black people; neither does my brother. Maybe it's exposure to my father, who's always been under the impression that everybody was created equal. He didn't look at them as anything other than a person. I think this is where we got our feelings from. My father has never been anything but cordial and natural with any black person that I every brought in the house. My mother was always cordial, but you could feel the edge to it. It's not really explainable, but if you're there you can feel that she's uncomfortable. Just like when she'll come up if Clara's here, she always feels very uncomfortable.

When I was growing up, my mother had two black maids. I noticed the color difference as I think any child would do, but I can always remember them as being very fine people and very nice. I don't think I ever was afraid of them or felt the difference particularly, except that maybe I did grow up with the idea that black people were there to serve white people. As a matter of fact, when we had our own home, I had a particularly rough pregnancy and I had to be in bed for four months. We hired a black gal to come in and help take care of the baby and the house. I never looked at her like I looked at my mother's maids; she came in and we were the best of friends. She was the kind of person that was attuned to white people; she liked them just as well as she liked black people. And to this day we keep in touch.

My relatives don't agree with Wally or I in our feelings; maybe this is their background. They grew up in Baltimore where there're a good deal of blacks, and I'm sure their children had to go to school with them. They won't come right out in front of me and say "nigger." I've heard it whispered, and I've heard the kids down black people. But I would rather not get into a free for all. I have my beliefs and they will always have theirs; I don't know really if you could change them or not. It seems to me it's a very narrow-minded point of view and a very narrow-minded way to live. I mean, it would be just the same to me as if I had been raised around Chinese people. Why should I feel any different towards them than I do toward whites, blacks or what have you?

In Baltimore, the Polish people are very much opposed to the blacks moving in. You've got your Polish section, your German section, your Italian section very much in evidence. There is some resentment in the old neighborhoods of having the blacks move in places where their grandparents and parents lived before them. You have all your ethnic groups and your old family groups, and I don't think that the people really know how to deal with it. They resent the different cultures coming in because they don't stop to realize that maybe black people have a culture of their own. This was something that I didn't realize very much until Clara and I talked one day, and she said, "All you white people think of is Martin Luther King." She sat down with a book of black American history, and there were numerous people that I hadn't even thought of that really entered in. They have a history and a culture all to themselves, just like the Polish, the Italians and whatnot.

It's very good to have different kinds of people living together; I hope that it's just not the Columbia area. Maybe someday in this United States, where we're supposed to be very open-minded people, everybody can learn to a degree to accept it. This is what America should be, and I would like to be part of it. This is where Wally and I differ in our views.

Archie tries to keep management out of resident oriented projects. His main objective seems to be that he wants the people to work for themselves; he doesn't want to feel that he has to do it. I don't feel that he has intervened in any way in any of our projects or told us how to do things. Archie will make suggestions, but they are just that.

He has never come to me, even though he's heard whisperings that I had a problem; he's always waited for me to come to him. I never heard Archie say, "Hey, you've got a problem; come talk to me." It was always up to the individual resident. There's a gal here, she's got one boy right now that's in jail because he's had all kinds of problems; everybody in the community knew about it. Archie went to bat for her and tried to help out only after she came to him. It's a secure feeling to know that if things got really heavy and I didn't know what else to do, I could call him and he would help me.

Archie has a wealth of information about help that's available, but sometimes I feel the Residents Council should have all this information. I've often thought there should be some way that we could put this in a booklet for people, so you wouldn't have to sit there and sweat things out all on your own. These facilities are available to you, most of them for nothing; a booklet would be a big help for people around here. I've passed the word on as I've used something, telling people if they've got a problem to contact this agency or talk to these people. Through personal experience, I had a chance maybe more than most residents to find out just what kind of facilities we had available.

Archie's tried to get the office set up as a social service center. I think one of the first projects was the tutoring bit out of Community Action. They have people available for tutoring in different subjects, like if you're a slow learner or have poor English. I knew several families that used it, and I think they thought it was a success. But I felt that not sufficient announcement went around, and very few people made use of it. The counseling service got off to a blooming start in the back office. There were enough people and there was enough need, and I think gradually people got the counseling they needed. But some people may have been too shy to use it; maybe it was the fact that it was in the office and they had to go past Archie. Some of them said, "Well, gee, we don't want Archie to know we've got a problem." So then they set up counseling in a trailer, which was basically a community thing, not just Underhill, but the last I heard there was a lack of participation.

At one point, Archie was trying to work with our County Department of Social Services to see if he couldn't get them to set up some kind of branch for welfare, food stamps, medical assistance, this kind of thing. I think it would be a terrific thing because we've got numerous families that are in need. Now you've got to go all the way down to Fenton City, and if you don't have transportation that's a real bummer. It would have been a real boon to a lot of people around here, but with the Department of Social Services, you're bucking the county government and it's a funding problem. I guess they felt they would have to supply extra funds in order to set up an office.

We've had help from the Christian Women's Thrift Shop; it's supported by a group of I think seven churches. They also run marriage counseling, budget counseling, and family counseling. If you're a family in a pinch and you get really far behind in your rent, they will evaluate your situation to see if you're using your money wisely. They will chip in and help you with your rent; they've done this for me. When we got in a bind, they contributed $100 to the rent, which was like God sending down a present from heaven. They are a terrific organization.

The budget counseling we had was very interesting. She said, "Well, you've really got a problem with a lot of bills that were back. You have to take care of your priorities first." She made hints as far as cooking things, like how you could cut down on money. I personally found that it was very excellent to use, plus the fact that it was free.

If you get a family where paychecks are tight, they're short on food, short on rent money, Salvation Army has a branch out here in the county where they will go to bat for you. And the Catholic Church over here, if you have a counseling or financial problem, they'll help you out and make you a loan to get you on your feet, even if it's $25. We had a rough time at one point and they really got us out of a financial hole. I asked them, "Are you doing this because I'm a Catholic?" And they said, "No, we've had Protestant and Jewish. If people are in a bind, we're here to serve the community, not just our own." This made me feel good because I thought, "I hate to feel that something is just for one particular group of people."

There's one other group, the County Health Department; they have terrific facilities, which I didn't know about until Archie told me. They've got a clinic program where you can take your children for all their immunizations and not pay a penny. There are mental health facilities down there, too, that if you're wealthy, you pay; if you're not, you either pay on a sliding scale or nothing.

We also had food stamps at one point; I think they're terrific. We were on food stamps on month-to-month eligibility. So as soon as Wally started making $5 or $10 over the level, they cut us off. This I didn't think was fair. I think they should have tried to continue us for a month, maybe two months, until we could build up enough surplus that we really could be on our own. It's the same with Medical Assistance; as soon as you're making it, they don't give you a month or two to get caught up and really be on your own. They completely cut out all assistance immediately. I know, cause it happened to us and to other families; it's a common gripe. They need the funds and the facilities for other people, but still, I know several families that because they've cut them off so quick, a month later they've had to reapply and be certified for it again. To me, it's just making additional paperwork for them and additional trouble.

I had mental health care at one time. Wally lost the business and let's face it, it was really rough. Wally had the attitude, "We do what we can." Well, me, I'd sit there at night pulling my hair out. And it finally got to the point when I was spending more time sitting there worrying about bills and crying and being upset, then I was taking care of the children or worrying about my husband. I called down there and they initially refer you to a psychiatric social worker. She and I had several talk sessions where I did the talking and she did the listening. And she'd make suggestions, just kind of be a shoulder to cry on, whatever you want to call it. After about three sessions, I felt like a new human being. I really felt like I could deal with my problems.

It never cost me a penny, even though it was a time that we could have afforded to pay for it. But they felt that considering the situation, they just wouldn't charge us. The lady in Community Action said, "I think you've used just about every facility we've got." Well, to be honest, I said, "I feel it's there to be used and if it can help, fine."

We belonged to the Columbia Medical Plan when we had Medical Assistance, but we don't right now because for a family our size it would cost about $68 a month. I know I'm running up this much per month seeing private doctors, but I can't chunk up $68 right in one flip. Still, I think it's a terrific facility. When my kids were there, I felt really confident that they were getting the best care available. For an example, my baby that's a year now, I had trouble with her until she was four months old. She wouldn't sleep. Archie said, "Take her over to the clinic and talk to this doctor." They hit on her problem right away. Now she sleeps, eats, and performs like a normal baby, and she isn't crying and screaming. With the other child, they pinpointed her allergy, and they got her on the right track. Their health care program is fantastic, and their emergency facilities I think are just great.

My husband makes too much money now, by about $10, for us to get Medical Assistance, but they are reconsidering. I spoke with a man the other day about re-enrolling us. I told him my daughter's bills would be in the thousands by the time we finished with these scratch tests and everything. It could really become hairy for us without being on Medical Assistance.

I can see why in a way they've kept it an exclusive thing. I wouldn't want them to open up the clinic services to everybody because I don't feel that you could have the individual service per person that you do now. But I think when you get a low income family that really can't afford medical treatment, they could do it on a sliding scale. Right now it operates, let's face it, as a middle income, high income facility. It's not really concerned that much with low income families. And these are the people that I think really need it. If you're borderline like we are, you have a problem.

We have four women here that are really what I consider competent babysitters. They have a day care center set up in their apartments and they're chock full. I mean they've got more kids right now than I think some of them can handle, but they're trying because they know the mothers have to go to work. If Underhill could get a day care center going with these four gals together and maybe two more gals, you could have a real good thing here and not have to charge a whole heck of a lot. You could help out a lot more mothers. My own babysitting problems aren't that many because I've got my mother down the road, but others do need it.

We have a playground out here, and we're working on our "tot lot," a kind of juvenile swing set thing. I think there ought to be some kind of play program during the summer for the younger kids, four or five, because they're still too young to participate in the school age activities. I don't think their interest span is long enough. I heard that we had one young man from C.A. who was going to work up some kind of recreation for us, but that's the last I've heard of it. I've asked questions and nobody seems to know where he is or what he's doing.

As far as the swimming and stuff like that, it's entirely too expensive for most of the families. It's $45 or $55 for the summer, and if you're working on a tight budget and you've got things that you need first, you can't do this. For some families, the C.A.'s Earn-A-Membership program helps, if you can work it around the husband's work schedule and the wife's work schedule. Most of the time, they want you to work in one of the facilities, cleaning up or something like this. We had talked about it at one time, but Wally works from 6 o'clock in the morning until 5 o'clock in the afternoon, plus Saturdays and sometimes Sundays. So I just feel that when he's home I don't have any right to say to him, "Here, have four kids; I'm going out and work towards a swim membership." Of course, now they're talking about putting in a sliding scale for low income families. I think this would be great if it comes through. There're a number of people fighting it, and most of them are your higher income people. This aggravates me because they've had a chance to get ahead; so why not let the little guy get ahead, too?

Some of the tennis courts are open to the public, but most of them are not. Up here at the ice rink, you have to have a membership in C.A. to belong to that. It kind of gripes me because I think there ought to be some way that your common facilities are open to everybody. I know plenty of people around here would like to take advantage of tennis, swimming, health clubs, volleyball, the works. But if you're low income and can't afford it, and you don't have the time to work for a membership, you're out of luck.

Most of our recreation is family oriented; it's just a ride someplace or we'll take the kids over to the park for a walk. We really haven't got the funds to get out, but if they have some kind of family activity over at the lake, we take the kids. In the summer, they have a band concert at least once a week, and we are able to get out to that because it's free.

Subsidies would really help our kids out a lot, especially in the C.A.'s preschool program. We enrolled our son in it for $30 a month. It doesn't sound like much, but when you're young and you've got a lot of kids and you're trying to get ahead, it can be a hassle when things get tight. Well, he stayed in from September to January, and I had to take him out because we just could not afford it any more. I went to the people, and I told them what the financial situation was. They had no grants, no loan system, nothing whereby we could pay so much less and they would help you the rest of the way.

As far as organizations over here, I guess we really haven't had too much chance. Being apartment dwellers, we sometimes tend to feel that we don't have as much say in the Neighborhood Association as the homeowner. Archie says this is wrong, that we should still get out there and fight for what we think is right. That's pretty much the extent of our involvement because we're pretty busy around here with four kids.

We do go to church on Sundays, and occasionally Father calls me and wants me to work with him on a dance or something. They have a children's group that they're getting ready to work up starting in the fall, almost like a Sunday School. He wanted to know if my son would be interested, and I said, "Yes, definitely." Then he asked if I would be interested in helping to run it, and I said, "Well, I will try, but I won't make any promises." You know, I have to watch my time, too.

All the churches have gotten together and built this Interfaith Center rather than each have individual churches. The Jewish faith out here lack the membership and the funds to build a synagogue; this way they have the facilities for their people. I think the Lutheran Church was another one; they could never have built a church because they just didn't have the funds. At first, I felt pretty strange about the idea. I was from the old Catholic Church where you had the Latin Mass, and the changeover from Latin to English felt pretty uncomfortable. Then, when we moved out here to Columbia, it was a whole new concept where there was a lot of participation, where you'd join in the sermon and everything else. It took awhile to get used to. But I think it's a good thing because now you're more involved in religion this way, rather than just sitting back and letting the priest do it all for you.

Columbia residents, to a degree, look on Underhill people as low income. They feel you cause trouble because you're low income. I don't agree with their attitude and I don't like it; I've fought with several people about it. I had friends that lived in their homes out here, and they said, "God, it must be like living in a ghetto." And boy, I jumped. I said, "Wait a minute; it's not like living in a ghetto. It's probably a lot better than living in your own neighborhood situation where you're trying to get ahead of the Joneses." I think they tend to compare Underhill to the other projects. I will say that's ghetto life almost, the way they carry on with fights and everything else. This gives people the wrong idea about Underhill. All you have to do is come spend one day here, and you'll see how the people get along.

Merchants don't look down on you though; they are more than fair. I think some of them recognize that you're a special group of people in a way, with special problems. I know one milkman in particular comes around and offers a fantastic discount on milk that he delivers to the door. It's pretty cheap compared to what you'd get in other home delivery. I think there're several grocery stores that if you can show evidence you live in Underhill, you get a small discount.

I really don't feel that I have to go outside of Columbia for food shopping, but I do for other things like clothing. If you go about five miles down the road, you can get a little bit cheaper clothing and it holds up just as well. I think the price of clothing out here in Columbia is a little bit overrated; it's not necessarily for the low or the middle income family. But as far as the essentials go, diapers and stuff for the children, I do not have to go outside of here.

Last night, I was out visiting friends by myself until eleven-thirty. Wally had locked everything up, and I got in without any difficulty. I didn't notice anything wrong. This morning when he went out to work, he couldn't get the top lock open right. The front door had apparently been jimmied, and somebody made a real good try to get it open. I pride myself on not being a heavy sleeper, so I don't know when in the world it happened. We've had the police to check it out, but there's nothing much they can do. It's the usual story; they really couldn't fingerprint because my fingers have been all over trying to figure out what the devil happened. But they are gonna try to post an extra patrol here in the evening.

I wasn't even sure I wanted to call the police about it, but Archie encouraged me to because he's had so much difficulty in this building. It seems as if somebody's trying to make a wholehearted effort to get into someone's apartment. Late last week, Aunt Matty next door was there by herself. I guess it was around 11 o'clock at night, she came over here screaming. She thought I was at the front door knocking, and she found that it wasn't me. She said she got brave and opened the back curtain, and up here on the second floor balcony stood a real tall guy trying to get in the two back doors. We called the police, and they did what they could, which wasn't much.

The County Police Department got their hands full with Columbia; I think crime has gone up quite a good deal. If you've got a real emergency, like the other night when we had the attempted break-in next door, they respond within seconds. If you have a disturbing the peace call, they can take half a night to get here; they're not really worried about it. They have limited capacity as far as investigative forces go. They always just send a patrolman; they don't send detectives. They don't dust for fingerprints or anything like that, which kind of surprises me. There's always one chance in a million that you can find something to match up with somebody else that tried to do other break-ins. I don't think they're completely effective, but this is probably the county government's fault because of lack of funding.

Columbia itself needs its own police force, or they need a branch of the county force. I know for a fact that they only have three officers at any one time to cover the entire area of Columbia, which is pretty small when you consider the numerous problems, traffic accidents, and break-ins. Then, of course, we have the drug situation that is a whole lot worse. I don't know if you attribute this to the fact that we're a metropolitan area close to the big city. Also, the kids and adults pushing drugs think that they've got an easy move because the county isn't equipped to do the investigations that they need to.

I can cite one example right in our building; I knew of one young man that was pushing it. One day I had occasion to be walking up the street, and I saw a kid going in downstairs and ditch a spoon and a hypo. I came in, picked it up with a Kleenex and brought it in the house. I immediately called the County Narcotics Division, but it took them two days to finally come out; they just didn't have the manpower. I was really irked about it because, I mean, here's a hypo. This to me means real hard drugs that somebody's using or pushing. So I called the state police; they have an excellent narcotics unit and they're authorized to deal in any county in the state. I know for a fact that at least three days out of every week, even to this day, there is a surveillance going on of this stairwell.

I've seen other evidence of it; you can smell marijuana being smoked at times. It's nothing to go to a show at the Pavilion, be it rock, classical or what, and find people popping pills, using marijuana, you name it. It's a very open thing. They have got one agent in the county who deals solely with drug problems. This guy has got more cases than he can handle in a lifetime. In Underhill, from my kind of underhanded way of probing and whatnot, I think there's a drug problem. I don't just think that it's in young adults or teenagers; I know of several families in the 25 to 30 age bracket that are users—of speed, the works. One gal down here, her mind is really messed up because of it; she can barely take care of her kids. It makes me sick to think she's trying to raise a child. How in the world is the child gonna turn out? And there's nobody really watching this except for a few of us around here. Archie, of course, watches it and spreads the word that if he ever finds open use, he'll be the first to call. But will he get any further than I did when I called and said, "Gee, I've got a spoon and a hypo here?"

You know, this to me is a little sad. I hope that the young adults who are using it aren't pushing it; I wouldn't want to see it getting to the kids. I kind of take precautions with my son because young kids have a tendency to pick up a butt. I've explained to him, "Please don't do this; please don't smoke it." I've also told him that unless it's somebody that he plays with constantly, please not to accept candy or anything that looks like candy.

We were around here when Columbia first came into existence. Prior to that, we had heard about certain users and pushers in the county. It seemed to me that once Columbia hit, for some reason it became more widespread; you had a certain group here that was pushing hot and heavy. I've watched almost five years development, and there are more and more cases coming in from Columbia. You don't find it as much in the farm county like you do in a metropolitan section.

From what I've seen, it can hit anyone. In our building, this is a low income family; the boy is around 16 or 17 and the mother's a welfare mother. I've also seen it hit a lot of high income families, especially over on the other side of Columbia in really expensive neighborhoods. Most of the young people that have been drug users or pushers, there's something lacking at home, either not enough discipline or too much discipline. They just feel like they need to have another kick for life other than what they've got.

Before the drug thing, we had the riots, and I was disgusted with white people and black people alike. I felt there were ways of sitting down and trying to work things out without being militant, without burning cities, without acting like that. I think there's a breakdown in communication between the government as such and the people. Sometimes the government is run more for the government and the higher echelon than it is for the people that have to live in it.

Just an an example, the president cut off HUD funds. There are a lot of other programs that I think could have been cut rather than something like this, because you're cutting housing that people desperately need. There's such a shortage; there are so many people in this world that could benefit by something like this. I guess that at times you could say my attitude is disgust. I just wish that somebody would do something positive for the mass of people that really need help, that are trying to help themselves but need a push. I don't think that the government is trying to provide that. I think that a few of us that have managed to get into a place like Underhill, we do have that helping hand. But now it's been cut off to others until somebody else can come up with a different program.

COMMENT

Our images of the poor and of our programs designed to help them are largely based upon the assumption that there is a stable dividing line between the poor and the nonpoor. But there is much movement across this boundary, and large numbers of people hover about on either side. The lives of those receiving help cannot be described simply as "upward" or "downward" mobility, because both courses may occur briefly following one another. For those experiencing these cycles of improvement and crises, there is a deep ambivalence toward both the welfare state itself and the people among whom they live.

For the Bonnolis, this ambivalence is tragic: Wally loses control of himself, beats up May, and undergoes observation in a mental hospital. When Wally is released, the family moves to another state to live with relatives. Both the Bonnolis—like most of the other families described in this volume—can remember "better times," so their lives are based on the assumption that their setback is temporary, to be endured but not accepted as a permanent life style. Despite their professed tolerance of their neighbors, both Wally and May see themselves as a cut above others in the same stairwell. Apartment living is a tolerable alternative only because of the hope that they can eventually build their "dream house." While they accept the aid proffered by public sources because their predicament is "just a setback," they cannot consistently extend the same perspective to others receiving welfare.

This ambivalence also extends to the "better world" which they remember and to which they seek to return. They are frankly concerned about their reacceptance into this world, meanwhile romanticizing its warmth, appeal, and solidarity. On the one hand, there is an effort to cling to what they see as a more civil, more restrained style of life, but on the other hand, there are periodic erruptions of violence and strain. For those at the edges of the boundary, like the Bonnolis, the welfare state is itself a threat to their claims to respectability. Aid is not a neutral element, but something to which families and individuals must adjust: it threatens their tenuous links to other groups of which they still consider themselves members. It is too simple, then, to say that our welfare system is "stigmatizing." What receiving aid challenges depends upon the membership references people have developed in the past. For Wally and May, the respectable, hardworking ethnic community embodies their fundamental conceptions of moral worth. To lose their claims to membership in it is both disorienting and tragic.

Chapter 4

THE TURNFINDERS AND AUNT MATTY
Uprooted from a Regional Culture

A DIALOGUE

Matty: I like Columbia. I've been here since December, and I think it's wonderful. Of course, Elmer and Nancy have their complaints, but I don't see anything wrong with the place. It's just the little things that do happen, but I think that's the manager's fault and those things could be straightened out. I come home and the people are cluttered in the door, the colored people, and they won't move. I won't say anything because I just want to go in. Now those kind of things do happen. And I know Elmer can't find a parkin place half the time. I think with a good manager those things could be straightened out, but you can't just knock the whole city of Columbia.

Elmer: We got a problem here in this place, people raisin hell all night long, and they stop people from walkin on the floor. You're told to be quiet and you get complaints. But I don't pay a bit more mind than the man in the moon. I mind my own business. I speak to em and that's it. If they don't speak to me, I don't speak to them. That's my believin. I don't take nothin offa nobody.

That manager thinks more of colored people than he does of white. His attitudes show it; he's more friendly with the colored than he is with the white. When a colored woman walks up to him, man he lights up like a Christmas tree. Why hell, just watch him sometime when he's not talkin to a white person, just some colored in the project.

Nancy: I've been here 10 months, and it's alright here to me. It's just the damn niggers.

Matty: Well, I think she's right. She's sayin a lot there because they are very ignorant and you know that yourself. They ain't gonna walk up and tell you they aren't.

Elmer: It was alright the first couple of months, but when Aunt Matty moved in there was some complaint about it. I went down to the office and straightened it out because we had enough bedrooms here.

Nancy: The manager jumps on us because we brought a shoppin cart down here from the store. Now the neighbor right upstairs, she brought one and he didn't say nothin to her. I'm pregnant and I push one down, and Aunt Matty, she's awful tired in the evenins. And as soon as we brought a cart here, he wrote our names in the tenants' paper and gave us all kinda hell. But the durn niggers, they can push carts down and he won't say a damn word about it.

Matty: Now Nancy's sayin a lot there. I know that's true because I bring the groceries home. Our colored neighbor could do it but we couldn't.

Elmer: When the kids around here play ball, they bang on my car and everybody's car.

Nancy: But he don't say nothin to the niggers; they still push their carts down. But let one of us, and he walks up and gives us hell.

Matty: I'm glad you brought that up, Nancy, because I was really hurt that evenin. So when I stopped and bought eggs, there was a shoppin cart there and I paid $5 for it.

Elmer: There's somethin else; I've seen it here. The last house down on the corner I've seen five damn hoodlums jumpin in and out of that window.

Nancy: When he was washin clothes.

Elmer: I said why look at them crazy coons jumpin out that window.

Nancy: Like monkeys.

Elmer: All children supposed to be in by ten o'clock, but this colored woman up here she said, "My kids don't have to be in at no 10 o'clock." Now what do you call that? Tonight and tomorrow night, they'll be out here in the hallway runnin till one, two o'clock in the mornin. This cop car come through last night, and they picked up nine colored people.

Nancy: This is a beautiful place. The only thing wrong with it is the damn niggers.

Matty: She's right; Nancy's tellin a lot.

Elmer: This man over here he got three cars, and there's a family of colored people moved in and they got two or three cars. They're all parked right in front, and the manager, he wrote in the paper there's one car to a family. Well, the manager has a car and his wife has a car and they're both parked out here. If he's raisin hell about everybody else havin one car, what's he doin with two of em?

Matty: One night, I was sittin here alone writin a letter to my daughter and readin a paper, and I heard this scratchin. I figured it was the girl next door and I said, "May, May, why don't you answer me? You know I'm alone." And then I thought, "That's not in front of me; it's in back of me." I came over here and there was a big nigger there lookin in the glass door tryin to get the screen off. I called May quick and they called the cops. I asked the policeman, "How in the world did he get up there?" And he said, "Well, that's very easy; he could put a man on his shoulder and bolster him up here."

Elmer: He could jump up here and get ahold of that wall; I don't think it's safe here.

Matty: I said probably the reason I wasn't scared and didn't get hysterical is that Elmer keeps a rod in this door. Now if that rod had of been out, he could of walked right in on me.

Elmer: The man who tried to fix the door pulled the goddam curtain rod and busted the door, broke the door lock. I have been down there a hundred times complainin to the manager, and he ain't done nothin. I'm not afraid myself cause I got a gun. Anybody who walks in my house, he's gonna lay.

And other thing, the light switch on the wall there, they won't fix it. I put more than 15 bulbs in it since I been here, but the switch is wobbly. One time my wife was here by herself, and she kept hearin somethin afryin in one of the switch boxes up there. She went next door to the manager, and he come over and checked it. He called the maintenance right away, and it took two hours for them to get here. He said in another 15 minutes the whole house woulda been on fire.

Nancy: I talk to my neighbors next door here once in awhile, the Bonnolis; they're pretty nice, but they had a lot of trouble with that colored girl up overhead. Clara, the colored girl, come down here once and called us white trash.

Matty: She said we were white trash.

Elmer: She ain't never said that to me yet; she knows damn well not to. I'd tell her what I got to say, and I don't make no bones about it. She kept runnin her goddam mouth. I told that black son of a bitch shut her mouth. She don't own that apartment; I'm payin rent for it. She said, "Well, I'm gonna make you all move." I said, "Well, there be somebody else movin right along with me with my fist in her damn mouth." That's the answer I give her.

Matty: They're still havin plenty of trouble with her.

Elmer: I don't speak to any of the other people in the buildin and that's that.

Matty: Ada, this colored woman underneath, complains. I think she kicked up most of the trouble because her husband's a cripple. He's in a wheelchair and I think he's diabetic. Well, the place for him is in a hospital. They said the little baby up here made too much noise, so then I took a hand in it. I come home here in the evenin and I didn't see the baby makin any noise. But I thought maybe he does it in the daytime, and what are you gonna do with a baby? She carried on about he didn't go to bed, and he was up all night. I didn't do a thing but take him in the bathtub, and I had to hold him down. I broke him in a little over a week, and now he goes and says, "bed, bed" at nine o'clock, and he goes to bed. Ada went down to the office and complained that the baby kept her awake all night. So Nancy went down and told them that her Aunt Matty had broke him to go to bed at nine o'clock and that it was a lie. I don't know what she's complainin about.

Nancy: She's just somebody that bitches all the time.

Elmer: When you make noise up here, the noise goes all down the walls, so you really can't help the noise.

Matty: They kept fussin and fussin, and it went on till I think they got tired about our makin noise. Well, I go to work and I come home here and off goes everything. When I come in, I take my bath, put on my housecoat, and walk barefoot. I usually shop at the grocery store first and come on home about 6 o'clock. I'll fix Nancy and I somethin to eat, and we sit out here and talk. Sometimes I like to watch the news, and she goes to bed about ten. But they kept on complainin and complainin, and I said, "Well, you tell em to come up and see me. Sittin over there on the couch, with the baby in bed and me watchin news isn't makin noise."

Elmer: Well, the manager told me to take my shoes off when I come in the door at night. I told him if I have to take my goddam shoes off, I'll take him and the damn niggers both. If you payin rent, you wanna take your shoes off and walk through the house?

Matty: Well, I think the niggers went down and talked to him.

Nancy: That's what I say; he upholds the niggers.

Elmer: And another thing I don't approve of is the damn niggers marryin whites and the whites marryin niggers. We got some of em up here, and some of em down there.

Nancy: Yeah, there's this nice little white girl; she's got real long hair, married to a black one.

Elmer: And one black child and one white. I don't believe in bein born half blond—half nigger. I got the best damn nigger friends that ever walked where I used to live; we're as close as that. I've talked to em and they say they don't believe in the way of marryin whites and mixin, and they should keep their own color. But these here is the worst trash you ever seen. I still believe God Almighty didn't put em on earth for marryin whites and blacks.

Matty: I don't think any colored people should be over white people, but there isn't anything much you can do about it now. I'll tell you, I was terribly prejudiced when they were first comin out with black teachers over white kids.

Elmer: I sure say you should belong to your own people. Cause God Almighty didn't put em on this earth for mixin. I don't believe in mixin em in the schools either.

Matty: Well, the white people brought this on theirselves.

Elmer: Well, that's true. But I'll tell you what I still believe; they used to be slaves, and they're tryin to get over the whites and make them slaves.

Matty: The whites are the ones who did the wrong when they brought em over here in slave days. They're the only race of people in the United States that's here against their own will. They didn't ask to come here. They went over to those villages and caught em and beat em and brought em here. What can you do with em now that they're here? What can you do but educate em and try to get along with em? What else? You can't kill em. You can't send em back. They tried that. I don't think they oughta make places like Underhill for mixin. They don't get along. In the first place, the colored people wasn't ready for integration. Any darn fool knows that. They weren't ready to be just pushed right up with the white people. And the white people weren't ready to take that either. It should of been done by educatin them first and been done gradually. Back home they have a little place up on a hill called "Africa." They've lived there for years and years, and that's where they stay. They have their own stores and everything.

Elmer: They mind their own business, and the whites mind their own business, too.

Matty: Most of the colored here settled around New York and Chicago and Washington.

Elmer: I work under colored bosses. I've got one on day shift that's just as nice as he can be. And the one on night shift, he's just as nice as he can be. It's just like this; they show me what I gotta do, I do it. They don't bother me; I don't bother them. Less I see somethin go wrong, I don't say anything.

Nancy: When we have complaints or problems, we go to Community Action. We went there last month when we got a nasty letter from the manager. This woman downstairs kept bitchin about my baby, and the manager said if he got one more complaint he was gonna put us out.

Elmer: I went down and I told him, "You cannot put me out till my lease is up."

Nancy: They told us at Community Action, "Don't pay any attention to him. He's upholdin the niggers anyway." So whenever we got a problem, we can always go there.

Elmer: They helped us to get this place. My boss sent us there cause they was helpin the people that needed housing. We thought we'd take it until we found somethin better.

Nancy: We were invited to a meetin of the Tenants Council, but I'll never go to another one. They talked bout the cockroaches, and they blamed me for the cockroaches. Aunt Matty, she made cracks down there. She said, "We feed our cockroaches good, so we know they won't go to any other apartment." I about cracked up when she said that.

Matty: The meetin was about E.J. cryin up here durin the night and the other child runnin on the floors.

Nancy: It was supposed to be about everybody, but all that nigger kept talkin about was E.J.

Matty: She said Nancy should take him out for a walk couple hours every day and maybe he would sleep.

Elmer: My baby don't have to sleep all the time. If my kids want to rip and run and play, I'll let em, is the way I look at it. These people have kids. Do they keep their babies still? I didn't say nothin about their kids ahootin and ahollerin. Children's gotta have their energy to burn up. I have to work at night, but if I'd been there, I'd've told em what I have to say. I wouldn't have been all day either, cause I'm hotheaded. But when they try to rub it in on me, I'm the other way around. I don't understand these goddamn people. I think they just wanna pick. Course it's mostly all goddamn niggers in the stairwell.

Matty: We had a problem with the Corbins upstairs. I didn't care for them at all. I never said nothin to em, but to me they acted very snobbish.

Nancy: That dog would bark all night.

Matty: And you know to this day, they didn't speak to me. I'd go in and out of the buildin and everybody speaks to me or laughs or talks, but they didn't. They turned up their nose. I had no words with em, but I just didn't care for em.

Elmer: Well, I told em to keep the dog still, and they said they didn't have to. The manager said we couldn't have no cats and no dogs, and I said, "Well, how come the people upstairs got a dog?" And he said, "Oh, they ain't gonna be here very long."

Matty: Well, they lost everything in the flood, and he made special arrangements cause they didn't want to lose the dog.

Elmer: They told us we couldn't have any cats or dogs here, but that didn't bother us cause we didn't have none.

Nancy: But the colored lady overhead, she's got two cats and he don't say nothin to her.

Elmer: The damn cats and dogs don't bother me, but in my opinion, if he says there's no cats and dogs allowed, why does he let em in here? Another thing, if your wife's gonna have a baby, you gotta tell him ahead of time. I figure that's none of his business. What is that to him?

Nancy: One day we had an old marriage counselor around here. We didn't even need one.

Elmer: Who in the hell sent her?

Nancy: She knocked on the door and I asked her in, and she asked us what kind of marital problem we had. Only we hardly ever fight. My aunt, she calls us lovers all the time. I told her we didn't need no damn marriage counselor. She wouldn't tell us who sent her here, but she said that she heard we fighted all the time.

Elmer: I told her I didn't need her and I didn't want her to come back around. And I meant it. Who in the hell would want a marriage counselor messin in their life? It's alright if somebody's fightin all the time. But if we had a real problem, I don't know who you'd get to help around here, maybe May and Wally. They seemed to be damn good neighbors when I first moved here. Then, towards the last, he got wild like. I don't know what in hell happened to him. There was some kinda fight, and he knocked the damn door off the hinges. It was a metal door, and I heard him hit it. I don't know how in the hell he ever done it. And then I heard ascreamin and ahowlin with him and May. He was supposed to buy my truck, but he never paid for it. They come and took it back; they repossessed it. I told him I'd pay for the goddamn bill for the truck.

Nancy: Nine hundred and somethin dollars, boy.

Elmer: We was rentin a house before we come here.

Nancy: It looked like a dump.

Matty: I wouldn't have lived in it. My father's hog pen was better than that. I don't see how they charged em the money they charged.

Nancy: The basement stunk so damn bad it looked like somebody just pissed in it.

Matty: For $125 a month, and it didn't even have paneling or nothin up but the plaster. Elmer did all the paneling. I said, "Well, I wouldn't rent this to hogs."

Nancy: We were there from May until they tore it down in July.

Elmer: Before that, we was in Andover for about nine years. I loved that place. We had a big house up on a hill and nobody to bother me. We had 46 acres; we rented it and paid $35 for eight rooms. It only took me five minutes to go to work.

Matty: They commercially zoned it, and they had to move. That house was all they could find in the length of time they had to find it.

Nancy: They wanted to build factories and things.

Elmer: Before that we lived in Baltimore, but I didn't like the city. I walked across the street to work in a junkyard, but we lived in a pretty good place.

Matty: That was a big house. You know that's all nailed up there now. They're gonna tear ail them down, and they're gonna build a road or somethin. They had a whole big six room house.

Elmer: We had a basement, too.

Matty: I used to live with them. It was near a big tavern and a Montgomery Ward; it was nice.

Elmer: Then the man died, and they sold it and ran us out. I've lived around here since I was 18 years old. Come up from West Virginia. I don't like it right in the city; I like it on the outskirts.

Matty: Well, I think the majority likes it on the outskirts.

Elmer: I never was without a job.

Matty: Elmer's a good worker, and he's got good references.

Elmer: I had a letter here just about two weeks ago wantin me to come back to the company I worked for. They had a layoff over there and I didn't have enough of seniority, so I got laid off. I'm what they call a all-around man, janitor, driver, work on the refrigerators. I work with some black people. I talk to em, and they treat me good.

Matty: Well, that's a nice job you have. I'd like that job if I were a man, breaks up the monotony of doin the same thing.

Elmer: I like the job because it only takes me 15 minutes to go to work.

Nancy: He don't work Saturdays and Sundays.

Elmer: But we're thinkin of movin to the same place as my mother in Maryland. I already got a job drivin a dump truck, haulin black top and gravel.

Nancy: I'd like to move back to West Virginia where the houses are cheap. I don't like Maryland; I didn't even like it when I got married. We're all three from West Virginia, and you better believe we miss it. I miss the whole place; I just liked it there.

Matty: Back home when we were kids, we used to go fishin and huntin, play horseshoe, go to school, fight with the schoolkids, get put off the bus.

Nancy: Get expelled for three days.

Elmer: I went to school till the eighth grade, and I know more'n what they know today.

Matty: And you had your big garden and your flowers and you had horses. I lived in a big farmhouse and all of us worked on the farm, but daddy worked in the big limestone quarry. It was our farm.

Elmer: I wasn't no farmer, hell no. If you're gonna move back to the farm, goodbye. I didn't like no farm work. That's for the horses and mules.

Matty: My mama made bloomers for the girls, and I got all these hornets caught in my legs.

Elmer: I was workin in the sand mines back home since I was 14.

Matty: Berkeley Springs, that's where I'm goin on my vacation. Boy, that's the place for me. If it was good enough for Roosevelt, it's good enough for me. That's where he lived, where he went to take his baths when he had paralysis.

Elmer: I wouldn't wanna go back; there ain't no work up there. That's the reason I left the damn place.

Matty: Well, there's plenty of work up there now.

Elmer: They don't pay nothin.

Matty: Well, I think it pays to have fun than to have money.

Elmer: About the only thing up there most of em does is to work in the orchards pickin. People gettin fed up; there's no way to hire nobody to pick anything.

Matty: They bring em in from Cuba.

Elmer: There's a man up there now, he has a big cherry orchard and he says, "Y'all wanna pick cherries?" You pick your own cherries for a dollar a gallon. They only pay the regular people ten cents a gallon to pick the damn things.

Matty: When you have your own home and you're raisin a child, it's different up there. When I first came to Baltimore after my husband died, I just stayed here because you could get one job after another. It was durin the depression and it was always seasonal work, but I could get it. I've often wanted to go back home, but I'm stuck here now. Till recently, there just wasn't any place to work there. If I could find a good job, I'd think about goin back there. I think havin a house there you have more freedom.

Elmer: I wouldn't want to live back in West Virginia. I just don't like it; the place is just dead. There ain't nothin there. They got hippies on dope and drinkin all the time; same as here.

Matty: Well I don't blame you or anybody else for that. I talk to the majority of people where I work, and everybody's tryin to get away from the rat-race. But when I go up home, I think it's where you want to go. I don't find the hippies and things. We go to the Moose Hall, the VFW Club, and places like that. And they're pretty nice people. But it's not so bad here. I was visitin my daughter just the other day, and we had a lovely time.

Elmer: I was married before, and our children was adopted. I was married 20 years. She died of cancer and heart trouble. Nancy and I have been married four years now.

Matty: Elmer has lots of daughters.

Elmer: I see my kids once in a while.

Nancy: My daddy ran a junkyard.

Elmer: My father used to work for the WPA on a shovel handle, diggin ditches along the highway. When the WPA went out of business, he got a job in the sand mines. Hell, I was workin in the sand mines when I was 12. Worked on the railroad, too.

Nancy: I liked my father the best. He died in an accident. I guess my mama's alright, but I can't remember much when I was a little girl.

Elmer: I remember when you was a baby.

Nancy: I have lots of bad memories. I tied my brother in a tree one day and I got whipped. I did it because he took my monkey. Dad laughed about it cause he wasn't hurt. There was eight children in my family.

Elmer: There was five children in my family; I'm the oldest one. My father died of cancer and my mother took it real hard. She's 83 years old. My mother was a good mother.

Nancy: My brother and me went to town with my father when I was six years old. And there was this dollbaby I wanted, so I told my brother, "Steal me that baby." So he goes and takes it and, when we got home, I told daddy, "Look what he done." He got the beatin of his life. I didn't feel bad about it; I laughed. I had a ball when I was little.

Matty: She was daddy's little girl.

Elmer: They want to raise the rent on these places in Underhill, and if you're late on your goddamn rent, they charge you $10. It's gettin just a goddamn shit ass deal. And another thing, ain't no good what you bring home, ain't gonna buy you food and shelter before anything's taken off, income tx or no. How in the hell can you live on $100 and pay your rent and have somethin to eat here?

Matty: They can't raise the rent because the government controls it; it's low income housing. But we don't get to use any of the recreation of the town; you've got to pay for all that. They have a lot of nice activities up here, but I don't go to any of em. We go to shores; there's nothin like the shores.

Elmer: I ain't gonna pay no $300 to join every year.

Nancy: You gotta pay to swim in the damn pool. You just go to a little creek and swim all you want.

Matty: Well, I tried the pool and that done it. There's nothin you smell but that damn chlorine. Last Sunday, we went down to the Potomac river, and we were dirty as pigs from that water. They got pretty beaches near here, but there's nothin like smellin dirty river water. You can't beat it. It's better'n smellin that stinkin chlorine. The way I look at it, that stuff like to kill you there. Oh, Jesus, I was drinkin it.

Nancy: We go away on weekends, go out for a drive.

Matty: We go to the county mall and have lunch; it's beautiful there.

Elmer: Shoppin ain't bad there.

Matty: We have stores and everything.

Nancy: It's beautiful over at the mall, all except the damn niggers.

Elmer: I don't think there's any good doctor here; they don't help you. If you got a bad back, you lay right on the floor. The next mornin you get up and you're okay. I do that once in awhile.

Nancy: Now that I'm gonna have a baby, I go to the doctor I went to before in Baltimore. My husband takes me in the car oncet a month. I don't want to go to no one but him. I have to have a Caesarian and he knows all about what he's doin.

Elmer: The doctors wasn't as high as they are now. And the medicine you bought, it's now ten, fifteen, twenty dollars just to look at you. I went to a doctor here in Columbia with a hurtin in my side, and he told me I was an alcoholic. I don't even drink. I say how in the hell can you be an alcoholic and don't drink? And he said I was depressd after he said I was an alcoholic. I ain't depressed about nothin. All he wanted was to get my money and just tell me somethin. I know one damn thing, he'll never get no more damn $8 offa me. I told him he was a goddamn quack and walked out. I wanted to take his damn license away from him.

Nancy: We tried to get food stamps one time, and they wanted to charge us $19 for $45 worth of food.

Matty: That's not right; I know a woman that pays $12 and gets $45 worth.

Elmer: When I moved here, I was down and could hardly make ends meet.

Nancy: We tried to get that Medical Assistance and he only made $72 a week, and they said that was too much.

Elmer: After I got this job over here, I didn't even go back. I said to hell with em. I don't get any help from the government or anybody; I work for everything. But why should I work and help to pay for keepin somebody else who's more able to work than I was. That's the only thing I got agin it. There's some of these people runnin around in this neighborhood who's livin right off'n welfare that's able to work as well as I am.

Matty: There's a difference livin in an apartment. If you live in a town house with patios in the front and back, there's that feelin you aren't cooped in.

Elmer: An apartment is alright for people who have no kids. E.J. and Walter can't play outside because the kids will throw rocks at em. And my kids can't even go out on that porch, cause if some damn nigger sees em, they gonna try to hit em with a rock. I'll tell you, if one of em ever hits my kids with a rock, God help him. I like all kids. I'd do anything in the world for em. But if they're mean to my kids, I'd pick em up and smack em. But some parents won't agree to that.

Matty: The nigger kids do it cause they're white.

Elmer: My ambition for E.J. and Walter is to send em to school, all through college and everything. After that, they can make their own mind up what they want to do. I don't believe in tellin kids what to do. When they get to a certain age, if they want a desk job, or any job, or travel, that's their business. I want em to have their own chance, and I think they will.

Nancy: I don't really care about that.

Elmer: I wish somebody did that for me. I come from a poor family, and I been workin since I was a kid cuttin timber with a cross-cut saw. And when you went to the store, you bought more stuff and you still had more in your pocket. Now, you go to the store, you go in with a hundred dollar check, and you come back you might have five or ten dollars left. It was happier then than it is now.

Nancy: If you got money, you got bills.

Elmer: If you got money around the house, they'll rob you. And the more money you make, the more the government takes off of you.

Nancy: If you have jewelry and fur coats, you'll just have jewel thieves around here.

Matty: There's a lot of crime in Columbia, and they don't have no police force down here. They're the highest in crime, like rape, dope, robbery, especially in dope. They specialize in it. It's mostly the colored that take the dope. Of course, there's a lot of white people, too.

Elmer: Still, I like this apartment and all like that. It's just the kind of people they got here up overhead and downstairs. You can't walk out; you can't even get in and off of the steps at night. Ain't no children wanna move. And they don't keep the place up. I think they should check these houses every month. They should check the electricity and do somethin about the noise in the walls. I think the project is nice and the town's alright; it's just some of the people that lives in the thing. I want a little house out where they're real far apart, where my kids can get out and run around the yard.

Nancy: Where there ain't nobody fussin about them.

Matty: Where you can have a flower garden.

AUNT MATTY

Elmer always says, "If God Almighty wants it to be, that's the way it's gonna be." Well, he married Nancy even though she was just a kid, but she seems happy enough now. She's 23 and he's 48, and we thought the age difference might be too much. We didn't want her to do it, but what could you do? Besides, Nancy is his cousin by marriage. But they do seem very, very devoted. He gives in to her all the time because he's afraid he'll lose her.

Nancy only went to the sixth grade, but I think you learned a lot more in country schools than you did here in the city schools. And then you learned a lot more out of school which they didn't have the privilege to do in the city. You learned about life and bein out in the woods and gardens. I think kids just had a lot more common sense out there.

My sister met Elmer when she was workin as a nurse in the hospital. He had this big cyst on his eye and they took it out. She kind of did take a likin to him, and when he got out of the hospital she started datin him. He was just wonderful to her, very considerate. She died of cancer and so did my mama.

My sister was like my mother, very religious. She sent her kids to school; she sent em to Bible classs; she sent em to church. Those kids went to every activity in the church. Elmer didn't go to church, but once in a great while they'd go to some affair. Elmer and Nancy aren't churchgoers; Nancy's folks didn't bother to send her to church.

When I was little, we had to go to Sunday School; we had to go to prayer meetin; we had to go to church. My sister in the city, she still goes to church; there's nothin like church to her. We went to church every Sunday; mother seen to that. And we went to Christian Endeavor about four o'clock on Sunday evenin. Christian Endeavor's like you go there and all the ladies bring potato salad, cole slaw, baked beans, hot buns, and somebody bakes a cake. You play all kinds of games and have classes. And I liked that.

My childhood was wonderful till my mother got sick when I was only 11. I took care of her for eight or nine months before she died; she was a bed patient all that time. We had a good life before then; we rode on horses and hoed the corn, if you liked that sort of thing, which I did. She taught me how to bake bread, how to set yeast, and how to can and make peach butter. She was a beautiful seamstress, and she made most of our clothes. I made all my brothers' and sisters' clothes after she died.

That was when the Depression first started, in 1930. They closed the quarry, and my daddy lost his job. Then the house burned down. There was seven of us livin and four dead, and we got strung around quite a bit, here, there, and everywhere. But for quite awhile I kept the routine agoin.

My mother made us go to school, but I had to stop when she got sick. Then after she died, I went back. I would get all the kids ready for school, and I would take my three-year-old sister along with me. My greatest ambition was to finish school, but I only went through the ninth grade. I think I'd love to have been a doctor, but I had to help with the kids. My father drank a lot after mother died, and I had to help support the family.

Our first place was in Foster's Quarry, way down by the shore of the river. In those days, they had houses on wheels and horses pulled them. I was born in a house that was pulled by a horse; it was a little tiny old house that had three rooms. My father had so many kids he had to sell the home, and this is when he bought the farm. He used to be a contractor travelin around helpin to build big tunnels that go through mountains. He was from Pennsylvania and my mother was from Virginia. We've always been American, English on both sides.

Every time we had a heavy rain, we had a flood and we had to move. I can see my mother yet, one of the kids in her arms and leadin one of us by the hand. The water it went quite a distance from where the house was.

But every time they had a flood, it would come up to our house. When it got to our porch, we would leave until it went down, and then we'd come back and live there again.

You could walk right down to where my daddy worked at the quarry. He used to take me down every evenin so I could ride the "dinky"; it's the little train that pulls the trucks out of the mines. It pulls the coal, the gold, the limestone, and the silver, but this was a limestone quarry. Daddy used to go back for overtime in the evenin cause we lived so close. The more of these little trucks that he filled with limestone, the more he got paid.

I got married in Baltimore when I was 20, and I was widowed about a year after. I had one child, a daughter. I was sad then, but I got married again. It lasted ten years, but we were separated more than we were together; oh, he was a pill.

I first went up North when I was about 18, and stayed a couple of weeks lookin for a job. Then I came back down to Baltimore and got part time work; it was just seasonal work at the distillery. I'd strike out in summertime and go to the ice cream company or to the cannin factory and go back to the distillery in the wintertime. When the war broke out, I got a job in the shipyard and I was weldin.

Durin the war, there wasn't much excitement outside of girls and things goin out. I used to belong to the Circular Club. You went there and a lot of the boys from the service came and you left them there. You danced and played cards and you drank, but if you didn't drink you'd have a coke; that was up to you. None of us in the family drink, no religious reasons, just don't like it.

After the war was over, I went into waitress work and I just stayed with that. I'd never done any waitress work before, but I made pretty good money, very good tips in Baltimore. And then I used to cook in a restaurant; I love to cook. I used to cook all the time and give it to the neighbors.

I always liked Baltimore; it was very excitin. When I first came there with my husband, I lived in a lovely neighborhood with my sister. Her husband had a big poolroom there and a big restaurant. She had a couple of boarders and we stayed there with them. She just treated me lovely and we went all over Baltimore. In those days, they had streetcars for the colored and streetcars for the white. You never even seen a colored person then; I don't remember even seein one. Then they stopped that and the white people got on the colored people's streetcars.

I boarded my daughter out to this lady in the suburbs that's raised about 40 children. She loved kids and every one of em's turned out beautiful. Any age, any kind, usually small kids, and she'd raise em up. She gave every one of em a weddin. My daughter was about 12 years old when she went there, and she was there till she was twenty and a half years old, up until the day she was married. It was better than draggin her around an apartment, havin babysitters.

I got up there whenever I wanted; after all I was payin for it. I'd pay for her clothin, bicycles, things like that, but they'd buy a lot of things, too. My daughter felt more like a real child to her. I lived in the city then. I'd bring her home on weekends and on vacations we'd go somewhere. We're very close now, we're the only two close mother and daughters in the family. I have friends who are very wealthy and you wouldn't think they had a dime. They can just mix with anybody and get along fine. Then I have friends that I know don't have a dime, and they think they're better than anybody else. They don't wanna mix; they're just a pain in the neck. I really think bein able to mix people with different incomes depends on the person.

I don't think it makes any difference how much money you make as far as your neighbors is concerned. I have friends who are very wealthy and you wouldn't think they had a dime. They can just mix with anybody and get along fine. Then I have friends that I know don't have a dime, and they think they're better than anybody else. They don't wanna mix; they're just a pain in the neck. I really think bein able to mix people with different incomes depends on the person.

I ride the bus with a lot of people but I don't go to their homes. I like all of them; they're very nice people and we talk to each other. But I think when a person's from a small town they'd rather go to their own friends. I talk a lot to May, the girl next door, and I talk with the colored girl upstairs. Oftentimes I meet em at the door, and they brung me home in their car one time. But they don't seem to be as friendly here as some of the neighborhoods I've lived in.

I think it makes a difference when people live in town houses, where the houses are right beside of each other. Once I had this big patio flat on the ground with nothin but glass in the back. Out front it was the same way, and my kitchen had three windows. I could just sit at the table and look out the window and see if there was anybody at the door. People are more neighborly in a town house because they come out the door and talk to each other; they look out on the street. In apartment houses, they're just put together in separate apartments.

I'm workin now at a coffee shop in Baltimore. It's very busy work but I like it; it keeps you active all the time. All these people from the big office buildins come in there to get stuff five days a week.

The problem is gettin to work in the city and back home to Columbia. At first there was a bus goin down there, but they went out on strike. After that the Columbia Association had a bus, but there wasn't enough riders. The C.A. had a meetin and they were goin to raise our rate. They said there was nothin to discuss, and they didn't even want to talk to us. So everyone in Columbia pulled out.

Next they said the best thing was to have one bus in the mornin and one bus in the evenin, but that wasn't any good because I wasted a whole hour waitin. So we decided to go to the developer to ask why couldn't he help us to get transportation. When we come here, the people said for sure this bus was goin to run. If I can't get a bus, I'll have to change jobs, and I've been there four years.

You've got to have transportation. Where I used to live, they had what's called a jerkwater bus; we called it a jerkwater bus because everybody got on it and it jerked you around. Why can't we have a little jerkwater bus like a minibus to run us over to the main bus that'll take you to town?

This man he keeps on buildin cities but his transportation here is terrible; you've got to have transportation. He's an intelligent man; he's a multi-millionaire. You don't build cities with no transportation. It's not gonna cost him so terrible much money cause we'd be payin for it. Even in Biblical times they at least had a jackass to ride.

I've always wanted to go back home and live on a farm, a place with quite a bit of ground, but I just never got around to it. I think life on the farm to this day is better for bringin up your children. I'd be content to go back now and live on a farm. You sleep so good and you feel so peaceful. In the country, you don't hear all this talk and gossip about murders and killins and the racial problems, the robberies and the Watergate. You just don't hear that.

I can remember one thing my daddy told me when we were goin down to the quarry one evenin. I don't know why he ever told me this cause I was only about ten years old. We seen a colored man walkin by; I can always remember they stunk. He said to me, "My dear daughter, see that Negro? They were once our slaves, and one day we're gonna be their slaves." I don't know how come he said that, but it come true.

I can faintly remember a rape case; this little girl was five years old. My mother took me in town with her and I was so little. They lynched him in the square. I can remember them sayin that when they found him he was hid someplace up in a cabin under a mattress with a gun in his hand. But as far as fightin or arguin with em, we didn't have any of em around. Even livin in the country, you'd see a few on the mountain, you'd see em work at the quarry and you'd see em walk by. I guess they knew better than to bother anybody; they'd kill em, especially the Ku Klux Klan. None of em lived in the town, and I never seen none where you buy clothes or in the grocery stores.

I didn't know much about em till I moved to Baltimore. God, they were plentiful then. Whew. But they never bothered me there in Baltimore or here, yet. They all carried on there when they shot King. I was livin there by myself; I didn't even have a television, and my daughter she come in yellin. But I have no fear of em. I'm not saying they wouldn't bother me, but I just don't have no fear. I was never around em that much. The colored office people where I work, they always seemed to be pretty nice.

But I don't believe in this mixin because I think they're a lower class people than we are. And I resent that they should teach our white children, that our white children should look up to em. I think it makes a white child look like they're dumb and the colored person's so smart. I don't go for that and if I had a child I'd work my fingers to the bone to send him to private school. They don't talk the same; they don't talk like white people. They dress different and they talk different.

To be right down to the heart, I doubt we could ever be friends with em. Maybe we'll be forced into it, but deep inside, I'd say no. I invited some neighbors once, and we spoke to each other and we drank coffee. But that's as far as it went; inside I wasn't friends with em.

They cut people up and they rape. You get in with the nice ones, they're gonna lead you in with the bad ones. They think you're friends with this colored family, so why can't we be friends with you? First thing you know, you hear of some nice white girl gettin strangled or killed. I wouldn't want to be friends with em, like the colored lady upstairs, cause her friends would come in and first thing you know you hear somebody bein murdered. They don't have a respect for nobody; maybe a few does, but not all of em.

As far as I'm concerned, this is not the best place in the world to live. I think this would be a nice life for people if this is the way they wanted to live. They try to make everything around here as convenient as they possibly can; they have lovely shoppin areas and that big mall, and they're always cookin up some amusement for you. But it's not like livin in the country.

It was better the old way; you just felt proud that you had aunts and uncles. They gave you things and you went to visit em. And you had lots of friends; I think I had more friends in the country than I do in the city. You had more time and it was more peaceful. Now you just feel all alone.

COMMENT

Like the Bonnolis, the Turnfinders remember "better times." Indeed, the recollection of their regional subculture so dominates their view of the present that they make practically no effort to adapt to it. Unlike the Bonnolis, the Turnfinders find no precedent or justification for Columbia's racial and ethnic heterogeneity in their more homogeneous, rural background. Thus their view of the Columbia community and their adaptation to it are marked by unyielding hatred of blacks and stubborn adherence to their own distinctive cultural norms.

The Turnfinders do not so much represent a regional culture or subculture of poverty as they exemplify a sort of compulsive defense of the self against a new and threatening world. By adhering to what they conceive of as their past cultural origins, they close themselves to the possibility of making relations with their contemporaries more pleasant and forgiving. Since their rememberance of "better times" provides so few bridges to groups other than their own, they make as many enemies as they see. Eventually, Underhill's management moves them to the ground level of another stairwell in the hope that this will reduce the noise problem for their neighbors. Aunt Matty, the one most liked by neighbors, is forced to leave for another town where commuting to Baltimore is more convenient. Elmer and Nancy continue to be angry at the welfare state that denies them help.

It is easy to dismiss Nancy and Elmer's objections as racism or compulsive self defense. But their objections find a vulnerable institution. As they encounter it, the welfare state is extraordinarily uneven, full of opportunities for discretion and replete with examples of "bending the rules." The fragmentation of the system, its extreme complexity, and its mandate to both control and help clients leave the welfare system open to ambiguous, hopeless red tape. This corrupts the welfare state whether or not its intent is actually well-meaning. It leads Nancy and Elmer to a venomous racial interpretation of their own predicament and of the shortcomings of the welfare state.

Chapter 5

ADA HARRIS
Isolation and Fear Among Seniors

I never thought I'd live in this kind of housing, but it's comfortable and clean, according to how you take care of the house. But there are others right here that you wouldn't want to step in the door, they're so dirty. There's a case right next door, the Smiths; they never had anything decent to live in, don't know how to keep it clean. I don't know whether in your heart you should down those people or whether you should feel deeply sorry for em.

But mommie used to say, "Water is free, and soap really doesn't cost very much." Oh, she kept us busy; we didn't have much time for devilment. And people, white and colored, they'd scrub their kitchen floors. I have learned that if people grow up mistreated and you work em to death and pay em nothin, they live in a dirty fashion. So when the government helps to build homes for em, they don't know how to live in em. Some of em never saw a bath in their lives.

Like the people upstairs, the Turnfinders. One mornin I had started for the door to shake the bathroom rug. I looked up and saw water comin down, dirty, filthy water. I said to them, "How come you have to throw water down there? We have a bathroom; we have a sink; why?" It must have been dish water or somethin. What else could it be with all that grease in it? So I said to Archie, "Look here, those people aren't used to livin in decent places; they must've lived in a shed or somethin. Now I'm not belittlin em because some of us are lucky and others are not, but they don't know what they're doin. Why did you put those people up over me and those people next to me knowin the problems I've got? You made how you were goin to try to look after us." He looked so shocked and I was so sorry. But I said, "Those people are gonna mess up these apartments like you never saw. There's seven children next door, but there's no excuse for all this."

And then the roaches started; I saw one comin down the side of my refrigerator. I never had roaches in my dinin room set that my husband made; it's cedar. But this place is alive with em; they'll bother anything. Sally, a friend of mine who lived on the third floor, told me they also occurred upstairs. So they sent the exterminator man here, and he came downstairs and he shot his little gun all around. He said, "You know Mrs. Harris, you aren't never goin to get rid of roaches." I said, "What do you mean; I never had em before." He said, "Well, you're gonna have em now." And he told us that upstairs at the Turnfinders he'd never seen such a dirty place in his life. And I said, "It couldn't be; they just moved in and haven't been there long enough to unpack."

Another maintenance man came in, a nice fellow who puts the bulbs up in the hallway. He said, "You ought to see next door; it's so awful." Now Archie always said that this woman was so clean over there. The man was here again about a month ago, and I said, "How is it now?" And he said, "Not as bad as it was, but it's bad enough."

I hate to talk about it, but I'm afraid of one of those children next door. This one must be six feet somethin or seven feet; he's very tall. A neighbor told me he refused to go to school and he refused to work. One day I was at my letter box, and I thought I heard a doorknob turn and a door open. I looked up the steps at May Bonnoli's apartment, and I was surprised that her door was closed. That's when I heard the sound, and I dropped all my mail. All of a sudden, I had the most peculiar feelin and I whirled around. He was standin that close to me; all he had to do was breathe down my neck and I would've felt it. Now I'm a scary woman. I mean I'm nervous, and I don't like to be alone in a house at night. I'm afraid of men unless I know em because there's too much in the paper. I think almost all women are frightened to death.

I just looked up at him and I said, "How dare you do that to me, steal up here behind me and stand that close to me. Why didn't you make a noise?" If I had a bad heart, I could fall dead at your feet." And he just stood there and looked at me; I think I shocked him. I said, "Don't you ever do that to me again, and don't you ever do another woman like that." And he said to me, "I'm sorry; I'm sorry." I said, "You are not sorry because if you were sorry, you wouldn't have done it." I happened to look down and he had on those sneakers. I think he wanted to see what I would do; he probably thought I would scream. They know I'm nervous because I have so many locks on the door. But I didn't scream; I acted just the opposite.

It's somethin funny goin on in that house next door; I know it. But I don't dare open my mouth because I think it's dope. All night long somebody's, "Bam, bam, bam, open this door." The door gets open finally, and they stay in there maybe about five or eight minutes. Then they come out, and maybe about three or four o'clock somebody else comes and bangs. Some nights, Saturday nights especially, they're bangin, bangin, bangin all night long. You don't get any sleep hardly. I hear it because my bed is up against the wall, but I don't know what to do about it. I better keep quiet because I have no one to protect me. Once I wasn't afraid of much because my husband watched over me. Now I have to watch over myself and over him, so I have to be careful. But I really think that there's somethin goin on over there that is illegal.

Early one mornin about six o'clock, I heard someone comin down those stairs. He kept knockin on their door; he'd knock and he'd knock but they wouldn't let him in. Finally, I peeped through the peephole and it was a little white boy about ten. He had taken off his sneakers and he was barefoot. He was sittin on the bottom step and he looked funny. Then he got up and started walkin around in circles. It looked to me like maybe somebody gave him somethin; I don't know. He would lean up against the wall on his side, and then he'd go around the other side of the door and lean back. The child looked sick, and I started to call the police. And then I said, "I'd better not; I don't have a soul to protect me." Now isn't that awful? I always said, "I'm not goin to be one of these people who don't want to be involved." That child stayed out there for about two hours, and finally he went away. Since then I've seen white boys come in there, and then I've seen Negro boys come in there.

Now that large boy that I'm afraid of was away for about two weeks. I saw the youngest boy the other day out back, and I said, "Hi there, have you been to camp?" He said, "No, I've been away with my big brother." Then business began to pick up again right away. Boys knockin, boys comin, all day sometimes, but mostly at night. They slam that door so much; I don't know why it stays on the hinges.

But the children in there are better with a deaf mother than many children who have a mother and a father. She doesn't have too much trouble with the smaller ones. I don't hear them fightin much, and they don't stay out when it gets dark. I understand those two older boys are a problem. Last summer, she was almost out of her mind. She couldn't manage em, and they were gettin clear out of hand. I heard that Archie's wife had gotten her a job to be trained for some sort of work for the deaf. But I wondered, why they would give her a job when she has all those kids there and anything can happen. They're real sad people; I think they come from a ghetto.

I don't think the Turnfinders are used to livin decently. They're dirty and I hate to think how they must have lived. She's a big woman, and he's all sloppy lookin, dirty lookin; it would make you ill to look at him. This man works at night, and he comes home about one o'clock. Then he goes to bed and he wants to stay in bed all day long. Any noise down here annoys him. She likes to stay in bed with him much of the time; I guess she's lazy. If they talk loud enough, you can hear everything that goes on upstairs. I can lie on my bed and I've heard plenty.

She sits in that rockin chair; it must be a big one. She rocks back and

forth and it screeches. You know how annoyin that can be all day long. I had
gotten so nervous that the doctor put me on valium to sort of quiet me down.
I didn't know I was so nervous, but he said, "I'll never get your pressure
down." He thought it was the care of my husband. I said, "We all know
that's strenuous, but this noise, I have to hear that all day."

Then she started movin the rockin chair around. She put it in the bedroom one night after I went to sleep, and she was right over my head. It was
horrible. Finally, I had to report it to Archie. "You've got to do somethin."
He'd call em and they would behave for about two weeks. And then they'd
do somethin else.

Their aunt would come and take her shoes off and put on high heels.
She'd walk right over my head from her room across to that glass door, and
she'd turn around. She doesn't walk like people; she walks like a duck. I
said, "Oh, Jesus; this is deliberate." I'm not a bad person and I didn't want
to do it, but I had to report it to save my own self. Sally kept sayin she didn't
hear it, and I said, "Sally, I can't understand that you can't hear all this
noise that's drivin me out of my mind." It finally got so bad Sally admitted
that she did hear it. She said, "Well, you know, I'm like you. I didn't want
to get into anything. But if you don't tell him, I will."

Sally is lovely. She's white and she became one of my very best friends.
She'd come here before eight o'clock in the mornin and help me to lift my
big husband out of the bed into his chair. And then when she came back
in the evenin after dinner, she'd help me to get him out of the chair into
the bed. So I think a lot of her.

But the noise kept up and it got worse. A few weeks ago, Mrs. Turnfinder
put the chair into the kitchen, and then she rocked real hard. I said, "They're
tryin to drive me out of my mind. Now I've got to do somethin, but tellin
Archie isn't doin any good." I had a radio in the kitchen that a dear friend
gave me for sewin for her, but I seldom use it. All of a sudden I said, "I know
what I'll do." I went over there and I turned it on, and she kept rockin. So I
turned it real high, and she kept rockin. Then I turned it as high as I could
get it, and it went on for a few more minutes. Then all of a sudden it stopped,
and I said, "Maybe she's gettin the message." Well, next couple of days it
was reasonably quiet; she rocked a little, nothin much. Then she started up
again one mornin, and I just put the radio up again as high as I could. It
was the only thing I knew how to do. Archie told me to take down notes
when it happened, the time it happened, how long it lasted, and to write him
a letter. I told him I didn't want to have anybody put out, but he said he
was gonna put em out. I said, "I just don't feel I want to do that to anybody,
but they're drivin me crazy. Let's give em a little longer."

Then I got so bad I was staggerin around. My husband called me one
mornin at four o'clock and I nearly fell. I was grabbin the furniture and I
was frightened because I didn't know what had happened. I just threw up
my hands and said, "Ooooh! I got to go to the doctor right away." The doctor
said that my pressure was way up and he didn't understand it. I said, "The
only thing I can tell you is that I wanted to climb the wall, and the next

thing, it completely tore me up inside." I'd been on the fringe of this for years, and all of a sudden it felt to me like everything in me was tearing apart just like that. He said, "This is bad; this is very bad for you."

Now I'm goin to have to move because things aren't goin to work out. Well, I hated to move, so I wrote a second letter to Achie. I said, "I was a little premature when I sent you the letter the other day. Now it's up to you; do what you must." We'll have to wait and see what's gonna happen.

I want to move, but you know rents in Columbia are ridiculously high. My daughter and son said they would try to help me some, and I can get a decent place. In fact, I went to look at one and it's beautiful. But then I said, "I don't know; every day you read in the paper there's somethin in it that'd frighten you half to death." This morning I saw in the paper that food was goin up probably double to what it is now. Gosh, we're gonna need every penny to eat, and my husband has to have good food. The doctor says that I must also have good food and plenty of fruit. But grapefruit that I had been buyin all winter are now two for 45 cents and prices are still goin up.

I was nervous, upset, and excited when I first moved in. Two of my friends came with their station wagon, and they brought my clothes, my plants, that clock out there, which is very old, and my lamps that I didn't want to trust to the movers. My husband was in a nursin home, and when they all left that evenin, I was alone. I checked the door, and it didn't look to me as though the lock was right. Later I found out it wasn't, so I didn't sleep much. You can't even lock the bedroom doors, so I kept the hall light on all the time. This is the way these places have been built; they just slapped em up vey quickly.

But I was glad that I had found this place and that the manager seemed to be so understandin. The woods are beautiful here and I love nature, but I felt I had to get these draperies up right away because I'm on the ground floor. I called the maintenance man from where I lived before, and he came over here and put the rods up. I got the draperies up because anyone could be standin in the woods and look right through here, and they'd see after awhile that I'm in here alone.

I don't know where this man came from; I think he still lives in Underhill, but he and a friend of his would stand right in front of that door and look right in here three or four times every day. It almost gave me a nervous breakdown. My daughter and her husband were here one Sunday, and my daughter said, "Oh, mama, look at that man out there exposin himself." I whirled around and he whirled around so I saw nothin, and I said, 'You must have imagined that." She said, "Mama, do you think I am crazy? I was lookin right at him." He walked on toward the woods, and he stood there awhile with his back to us. He kept on fumblin, but he never let his face around. I told Archie that I had a gun my husband bought for my protection years ago, when we lived in the country. He took me outdoors and taught me to shoot it. Now I'm scared of that gun, but I said, "I will shoot it if I get that frightened." Archie looked as though he was goin through the floor. Anyhow, they never bothered me, but they walked until fall came. Sometimes I would close the draperies, but it made it so dark in here, I had to keep em open.

The doctor said I was supposed to have six months so I could rest while they put my husband in a veteran's nursin home. He said, "rest, my dear, rest; then pack; then move." It didn't quite work that way. I didn't get the apartment right away, and after packin and movin, I was dead tired.

My husband was here when they finally put the chain on the door. Then I went up here and bought this little lock that you slide the bolt and push it down. My husband had told me, "Nobody could get in here because they couldn't get that bolt open to save their life." Well, I felt better than, but I'm told you can just lift those screen doors up and take em out. And a lot of women in here are afraid of this. I know my husband can't help me, him bein crippled, so I don't feel pefectly safe.

Archie told me if I needed help badly always call on him. He told every neighbor in this buildin from the top floor to the bottom floor to come to see me, knock on my door, and see if there was anything they could do for me. Sally came down one mornin and knocked and introduced herself. She said, "The manager told me to come down and offer my services and talk with you when I could, because you were alone and you were a very fine person." He also told her about my husband. The next mornin Sally was knockin on my door again. We just sat down and we talked, and then finally she had to go. She stopped to see me almost every day, and she helped me when my husband came home. She told me later that she liked me so well that first time talkin to me.

Then Mrs. Bonnoli came down to the door, and she said Archie had told em to sort of look after me. Mr. Bonnoli's a big man; he's young and tall. So when my husband came home, May called me and said, "Mrs. Harris, if you need Wally to come down and lift Mr. Harris sometimes, he'll be glad to." He came two or three times and lifted him for me; he could just lift him as you would a baby. Well, he started workin at night for awhile, and I didn't call him any more. I went up once or twice and she said, "He just can't come right now," so I stopped askin.

I kept hearin somethin from up there; I thought it was thunder and that a storm was comin in. Finally, Sally said to me, "Did you hear the Bonnolis fight last night?" And I said, "What fight?" So the next time she came down she said, "Well, I know you heard a fight last night." I said, "No, I didn't hear any fight." I think she thought I was lyin and didn't want to get involved. So finally, one night I did hear it. I heard the little boy cryin; he run in there to the door. He sounded as though he was in my bed because it's against the wall as you go up the steps. He was just screamin; I think he wanted to get to some of us for help. I don't know why they fight. Someone told me he goes out and stays late. When he gets back, she thinks he's out with some girl and she says somethin and they start this fight. We have been lookin for somethin dreadful to happen but it hasn't.

Then Mrs. Turnfinder came. She's really young, I guess about 25 or 28 or somethin. She looked at me sort of funny and she said, "The manager told me to come down and see if we could do anything for you." She looked so queer, and she looked directly at me. And then she said, "If we make too much noise, tell me, not him." I said, "Alright." Then she said it again and she stretched it out, "Tell me." I got my dandy up, so I just said, "I will do that." Then I said, "Will you come in?" And she said, "No, thank you," and she went on upstairs. She's never been down here any more.

May came down once and Mrs. Hunt came once. She's the colored woman from the third floor. Mrs. Hunt never came back until one time she was pickin up money to help to pay somebody's rent. I heard that she got $60, and then I heard again that they bought $40 worth of food with it. I don't know what it was, but I believed the person who told me.

I think her husband's in the service, and she has four children. She has a big boy; he's a nice boy and he's gentle. He came down once and helped me dress my husband. It's very difficult to get his clothes on him, pants and all. He lifted him so tenderly. I had hopes of gettin him to help me all the time with him. One day I asked him, "Could I get you to help me with my husband, take him out for walks and get him to the barber?" And he said, "I can't for a long time because we have band now and we're practicin." I thought this would be perfect and I would pay him somethin, but he never come to do anything.

But what they would come to do made my angry, and it made Sally so mad. She would send the children to your door and ask you for milk, four or five slices of bread, butter, anything that came in their minds. They said their mother sent them. They got Sally first; she didn't know how to say no. She hadn't worked with a group of people like this. I've worked with all that group before I moved here, and I don't believe that you can help em too much. They learn if you give it to em once, you are goin to give it to em every time they want it.

If somebody got sick or if I thought they were hungry, they could have almost anything I have. But I still have to take care of my husband. Sally and I both agreed we would give em anything if they needed. But they wore her out, and finally her husband got angry. If those people were starvin and he knew it, he'd go down in his pocket. He told her, "Don't give em another thing and I mean it! I don't mind givin, but these people are tryin to live off of the others in this buildin. Nobody's givin us anything." Finally, they got on her nerves, and one day she said to the little girl, "I never saw people bum food so much in my life; I'm sick of it." This wasn't Sally at all, and I knew she had reached her limit. I said, "I thought you had to learn for yourself."

The little girl came here first. They didn't bring a little cup or saucer; they brought somethin large. She'd say, "Clara wants some milk, fresh or canned, whatever you have." So I said, "Listen dear, you tell Mrs. Hunt that I don't have any milk; the only milk I have is what my husband has to have for his supper." So she looked at me and went on away. She came back another time for somethin, and I said I didn't have it. I acted just as nice as possible. I got so I would tip to that door and peep through that keyhole. If I couldn't see anybody from that peephole, I'd kind of try to look down and you could see a child's head.

It's probably the way they grew up. I remember we had a neighbor when I was a small child. She was forever sendin her child over to my mother for a cup of sugar, a cup of flour, or three eggs, and my mother would give it to her. I said to her one day, "Mama, why do you always give her your food?" And mama said, "Well, we live in the country; country people never refuse each other." Then she said, "They have the same privilege of buyin what they want when they go to the store on Saturday as we do, but they know they can borrow it from me." That woman wasn't any poorer than we were.

Mrs. Hunt does some sort of work in a lab and, if her husband's in the service, she gets money for those four children. They get everything they need. Sally told me she had her apartment completely furnished this spring. She said, "Ada, you should see her house; it's perfectly beautiful inside. Everything is new and beautiful." Then she said, "Now I see what my husband means. They are takin their money, dressin, makin a beautiful home and borrowin from the neighbors. They don't care whether you like it or not, as long as they get it."

The Bonnolis also began to borrow from me. They wanted powdered sugar to make a cake, or they wanted bakin powder, or they wanted vanilla. Whatever they needed when they wanted to make somethin special, they'd call me and I gave it to em. I couldn't refuse em because he had come down and helped me out.

She and the Hunts upstairs have a problem. The boy has a whole set of instruments, drums, and and electric guitar, and that thing booms. May has four little children, and she told me, "There's no way in this world these kids can take a nap; I'm havin a fit." That woman called the police every day for about two or three months tryin to make em stop this noise. Mrs. Hunt was at work, and she said they didn't do it. Finally, May said, "Well, if you can't stop em, I'm gonna stop em." She thought she could. The police would drive up every day and sometimes twice a day and go up there and knock on the door. They could see the police comin, probably watchin out of the window. Finally, the policeman said that the only way he could do anything was, "If it's just five minutes after midnight, call us, and we'll come; then we can do somethin." I saw em in there last week; maybe she was callin em again. I said to her, "Well, why keep the police comin if they aren't going to help you? It looks so bad." She said, "I'm goin to do it anyhow; I'm just goin to keep on doin it." She's just that type.

Then May called a meetin, and Mrs. Hunt came to my door. She told me that there was gonna be a meetin up in her apartment. I said, "What's the meetin for?" And she said, "The meetin is for all of us to get together in here." Now Archie had already had a meetin in his office when May was complainin about all those others, but nothin came of it. So I said to Mrs. Hunt real nice, "I don't thing I can make the meetin; I gotta be down here with my husband." So she looked at me and she said, "Well, they want you to come so everybody can get together and talk about it, and maybe we can stop some of this noise." I said, "Do you remember the night Archie had us all down there for this same thing, all the noise in the stairway? Well, this is the way I look at it; if he can't stop it, nobody else can. You'll only maybe get to arguin, and then there'll be hard feelins."

Sally came down here later and she said, "I'm stayin home; I'm not thinkin about goin to any meetin because I'm gettin ready to move out of here. I only wish you could move, too." Sally said she thought the Turnfinders didn't go because they were thinkin maybe that I was gonna jump em about the noise. But I wasn't goin to say any more to em.

I heard the meetin sort of split in half. The Bonnolis went up to the Hunts and later the Hunts came down. They had invited some other people in, and it became some sort of a beer party. Sally said beer was just flowin; you could smell it out in the hall. I said, "What? And you mean they wanted to get me into somethin like that?" She said, "And me, too." So we sat here and laughed. I said, "I'm not goin to any meetin unless Archie calls it." Anyhow, nothin has ever been done.

May and I never got any closer together because she cooled it right then. Sally said, "I'll tell you why she doesn't call you any more. She got real mad cause we didn't come to the meetin, and she won't speak to us right now. By the time she gets over it, I'll be gone." Sure enough, by the time May got over it, Sally had moved.

My husband had been ailin with rheumatoid arthritis for years, and he seemed to have gotten worse. So I had to take him to a veteran's hospital, and then they put him in a nursin home because he couldn't walk. It's very sad. They took care of him until I could find a place where I'd be on a lower level; that's why I came over here. Someone gave some money to Archie to cut this door through a solid wall. Archie's very compassionate, and he made them cut the wall because the other one wasn't wide enough to get the wheelchair through it.

The visiting nurse comes twice a week, just for a few minutes. I think she comes out of the County Health Department. I couldn't get anybody outside of that because Medicare will only pay a nurse from the Health Department. They are not allowed to give medication or anything like that, so I had to take his pulse and give him all of his medication. They will bathe him and make his bed and that's all. I used to say, "Well, that isn't very much," but the way I've been feelin lately, that's an awful lot. Because while she's doin that, I can wash the breakfast dishes and maybe get dusted out here or somethin. On the other days, I give him his bath right in bed.

I had wanted him to have therapy so badly, but when he was in the nursin home, they didn't seem to be equipped for it. The social worker told em that he was supposed to have all these things, but when I dared to ask about it once, they didn't seem to like it at all. I've never asked for it here, so I don't know if I could get it or not.

The doctor's been insistin ever since he started comin over here that I get out. I was foolish enough to think that I could nurse him, and I thought, "Why do I have to get out? I'm used to bein alone with him all the time."

But the doctor said, "You must get out of here because to be nursin him all the time, never gettin out or associatin with other people, that's goin to be hard on you and you aren't goin to make it." The Commission on Aging tried to find someone to sit with my husband, but people just didn't seem to want to do it. And I've talked to many people from the Association of Retired People; they'd tell me they didn't have a car or make some other excuse. Finally, I found two men who came over here to sit with him so I could go out. One of em is a letter carrier; he's the nicest man and so compassionate that you can almost see into his heart. When he came the other day, I was so sick that I went into my room to lie down. The other one lives down this road somewhere; he'll come if I call him, but this week he couldn't because he was goin on his vacation. Sometimes these various women come and sit with him, or one would sit and another one would take me out. But I don't know how long it'll last.

It had gotten around that they wanted me to put my husband back in a nursin home, and I wouldn't do it. I know I should but I just can't. But I think I'm comin closer and closer. You see, I have had an operation and I have hypertension and high blood pressure. The doctor has begged me. He said, "You'll just be killin yourself." Archie talks to people and he said, "She's a marvelous woman. She's the best person I've ever known, but she's stubborn and she's hard-headed." So then I knew somebody had told him they couldn't get me to do what I should do. I must be stubborn and hard-headed, but I said to him, "I'm just tryin to do what I think is best. You've got to have compassion; put yourself in my place. How would you be if this had happened to you?"

The doctor tells my husband he is a lucky man. He said to me one day, "Mrs. Harris, my only hope is that if this ever comes to me, anything like this, that somebody will take care of me like you're takin care of your husband."

The nurse told me he never leaves here that he doesn't start talkin about me sayin, "I never seen anything like her in my life." Well, how would any man feel if he got sick and his wife said, "You have to go; I'm not goin to take care of you." People tell me that this is what happens most of the time when you're helpless.

Wherever he did his work, my husband has always been with young men. He was a Boy Scoutmaster in Washington; I've never known anyone who could manage em so well. He was friendly but he was hard with em. They didn't like him at first. But after awhile, they found that he wasn't so bad, and they would do whatever he asked em to do. He also worked in an orphan home where he was assistant to the director. He'd come home sometimes, and he'd be sort of cross or he wouldn't talk. I'd say, "What's wrong with you? I been waitin for you to come home and talk to me." And he said, "Sometimes I feel that I'd like to ask God to come down and have a word with me." Never havin worked with people, I didn't understand this. I thought, "It must be marvelous to be out there workin with a lot of people." When I finally went to work, I found that people you work with sometimes can be an awful lot of trouble to you. They have jealousies if you're a good worker, and they're afraid you might get their job. My husband has often told me, "You lived in a dream world until you married me. You have to stand on your own two feet in this world; you've got to learn to defend yourself and not let people run over you." I was a very timid woman, but I began to learn that I did have to defend myself. Oh, he was always there to defend me; he'd never allow anybody to say a dirty thing to me if he knew it.

I was married to this husband for 35 years, and most of the time we lived in the city. But then he decided he wanted to go back to his home in North Carolina. For years, I had every excuse in the world, but finally we went and we lived there 12 years.

We came back to the city when the Second World War was goin on, and we both got government jobs. Then he was offered a job helpin servicemen, and before that, he was educational director for a government agency. Life with him had been from one place to another, but I did like to travel. It was excitin and I loved meetin people.

I first started workin for the government in 1942. A woman from Georgia came up to me and said her relatives had written to her that gold was actually lyin in the streets of Washington. All you had to do was come and get it. I said, "What are you talkin about?" And she said, "Oh, they meant you could walk right in and get a job."

I remember the first time they took a great big hunk of money out of my check, I nearly had hysterics. I went home and showed it to him and cried. He sat there and looked at me and started laughin, and I got mad with him. I didn't see anything to laugh about. So he said, "Well, this is what they been doin to me all these years." I never knew they took money out for retirement and things because he'd come home after he'd cashed his check. Well, I got used to it and accepted it because you get it back when you retire.

Now both of us have retirement pensions. I get Social Security because I didn't work for the government long enough, and my husband has what is called a nonservice connected disability. I have heard people criticize the government, and I am sure that there must be some reason. But they have been very good to my husband; I could never stop praisin that Veterans Hospital.

But my husband's pension is not what he should have because just about the time he couldn't walk any more, they were takin it away from the veterans again. When the Social Security gave all of the people a raise, the government immediately cut the veteran's pensions. He should be gettin twice or three times what he does. The government representative over here talked to me, and she said, "I'm goin to do evrything I can for you; I'm goin to get him some more pension." I said, "I bet you don't because I read in the paper that they're cuttin pensions." She said, "Oh, it's different because he's crippled." Then she came back and she said, "Mrs. Harris, they are gettin ready to cut em." I said, "As high as everything is, what are people goin to do?" And she said, "I don't know; I have talked until

I'm breathless." Every time *Stars and Stripes* comes, there're letters in there that they've begged Congress, but they haven't done anything.

I used to work on my husband and say, "Let's always try to save as much as we can." He listened to me, so that was a big help. We saved what we could, but it wasn't a great deal because things were high. While he was in the hospital, I saved every penny I could get. I still do and we live comfortably.

I was born on a farm in northwestern Maryland, a day's ride from the nearest town. They had schools and churches there, a post office, and an old fashioned general store with everything it it. It was just a nice place where everybody seemed to get along; everybody liked each other. That stuck with me all down through the years, how lovely people were then.

It was a good life and people knew it; we never wanted for anything. We always had plenty to eat and we had a nice house. Of course my mother was forever cleanin; everything was always clean. They'd use feather beds; I used to love to beat on em.

Every summer, there was what they called camp meetin; churches in the country had em. My mother would be sewin so much making clothes for us. I think we each had three dresses for that day. One you wore, and when you got there, you'd take that off and change. She'd wash you up and then like in the evenin service, dress you again for camp meetin. And then, also, there was a fair in the country. We'd go to that, and the family would get so excited because that happened only once a year. I remember that so well.

Way across the field from our house was a railroad track that came from Washington. My one dream was that, "Someday I'm gonna get on that train, and I'm goin away from here and never come back." I used to go there and stand and wait; I almost knew when that train was goin down that track. I'd stand out there by myself on the other side and I would wave and wave and the people would wave back at me. And then I'd feel so sad. I didn't like the country; to me the country was a lonesome place.

My mother was very strict and very wise. She was a woman with a kind heart. She had lots and lots of friends, but I never knew how many friends she had until her death. People came from everywhere; it was just marvelous to see the people who would come to the house and talk a few minutes and go. She was kind to the neighbors, and when someone got sick she would bake somethin or make soup. We'd see her goin down the street with a little basket and a napkin over it.

My father worked for farmers, but the house was our own and the garden was ours. He was both very kind and very stubborn. I can remember when my mother would say, "You shouldn't do such and such a thing," and he would say, "I'm goin to do it." I don't remember him ever puttin a hand on me but twice.

My great grandmother was pure Indian, and my grandfather was the proudest man I've ever seen in my life. I've never seen people walk as my people walked, just light and very proud with their heads high. It was a walk that you don't see. They were all mostly tall and they were dark, but very good lookin people, very handsome. They lived proudly all their lives, and every one of em had beautiful thoughts. They could sing so beautifully.

Lord, there was large families on both sides. My parents had nine children, but they one by one dropped off. Our relatives didn't live too close but they would come for visits, maybe every two weeks, and then they'd go home. It was nice for me because I was the family pet, and everybody seemed to love me so much. My grandmother lived a long way off from our farm, but you could drive down in a day. They didn't leave there until I was grown and married and had two boys.

I was 12 years old when my mother and father separated, and my mother moved to Washington with the children. We lived with my grandmother and my aunts for awhile, and after a time she remarried. She had to go to work because there were so many of us, but we always had plenty of everything. We didn't have television and those things to worry about; we were satisfied with our dollbabies.

When we moved there, Washington was a lovely place. We always lived in nice neighborhoods and had nice friends. You could associate with practically everybody on the street you lived on because they were nice people. This was in the Southwest, where they built large houses and some of the oldest families lived there at one time. The government and everything was supposed to have gone Southwest and Southeast. Instead it went the other say; it went Northwest. And then Southwest became the worst part of the town, and the people we know as the bad people lived there.

Mama didn't tell us not to speak to people, but she said, "No trash comes in this house." She wanted us to grow up to be good. But she said, "If you're not goin to associate with other people, speak to em nicely and treat em right." One time we decided that we weren't goin to speak to some people over there, and she happened to hear us. She came in the livin room and she said, "You're goin to speak to everybody. Because those people don't have anything and don't keep their place up doesn't mean that they aren't as good as you are. You're goin to speak to everybody, and I better not ever hear of your not speakin to em."

As children we knew nothin about interracial feelins. In the country, everybody was good to each other, and the white children and the colored children played together, if you were close enough or they went to the farm for somethin. I don't remember any violence anywhere near home. The people who lived on our block in Washington were lovely. Right across from us it was a German family, man and wife. On our side, there were about seven or eight colored families, all lovely homes and lovely people. There was one huge house that was white and, on the other side, they were all white. Everybody spoke and everybody was nice to each other. We didn't visit but it was nice.

One day we wanted to go to the movies. We'd heard about the movies, but we'd never been to one. And mommie said, "You can't go." We wanted to know why and she looked at us. She hated to tell us, I guess, but she said,

"Well, they won't let you come in. That's a white movie and they don't want colored people in there." I remember we sat down and we were hurt to our hearts; I think we cried. And then we wanted to go to the drugstore to get a soda, and she said we couldn't do that either. All these things were goin on that we had never known about in the country, and we were very hurt about all this. But still everybody got along; there was no meanness. If people said anything, they said it in their own homes. That's my remembrance of Washington.

I married at 16 the first time. I was very much in love, but my mother said I couldn't marry yet. He went to Mexico, and she said if you still feel this way when he comes back, I might say yes. So she said yes, and we were married and had a beautiful son. My husband found out that I wanted to go to work because there were things I wanted for the boy, things that I wanted in the house. He'd say, "You can only have what I can afford to pay for. I don't believe in this payin on time." Now unless you were a teacher or a nurse or maybe a social worker, there wasn't any other work but domestic work. He said that was silly; I wasn't goin to be doin that because I could do it at home.

The next good job there was for young colored women then was in doctors' offices; they wanted the best and the nicest lookin ones. The girls who worked in the doctors' offices would go on vacation, and they would call and say, "Will you take my job for me while I'm gone?" Then there was a large Negro store on the corner of 11th and U in Washington; the owner was a West Indian. I had a friend workin there who used to call me at Christmas or Easter time and ask me to help out. So I learned how to be a saleslady. My mother used to say, "Any time you can learn anything do it, because you never know when it's comin in handy."

I wanted to work to send my son to summer camp and buy him clothes or whatever he needed. The way I saw it, this had to be done to rear him up nicely. My husband was a substitute letter carrier at this time, and they didn't earn as much as when they were finally regular. I also took a course in Red Cross nursin that taught you how to take care of your children and your husband if they were sick in bed. By that time, I realized that the best place for me to rear my child was at home, the way my mother reared me.

I was divorced after 15 years and remarried seven years later. When we came back to Washington in 1942, things were gettin a little rough. The city was crowded and you just rubbed against people. I remember gettin on the bus how rough people would push you. This was new to me because I'd been away for awhile. One mornin I was on the bus to go to work, and I had bent my body to slide into a seat when a man slipped right behind me and took the seat. Well, this shocked me to death. So then I talked to friends, and they said, "I'll tell you right now; it's not the same." But this was what he did, and he was of my race, too.

I remember goin down 16th Street one day; it was one of the most beautiful streets in Washington. And right on 16th Street, somebody had their clothes hangin out on the front of this balcony. I looked up and I just couldn't believe my eyes. I said to my husband, "There's men's shirts and underwear hangin there on the balcony. This is 16th Street and they're destroyin it."

Once I was goin to work and I saw these little children with great big tablespoons in their hands. They probably had never had grass around their homes in the South, and they never stopped until they dug up every blade of grass in their yards. That used to be a beautiful block, and I almost had a fit. You see I loved Washington; that's the only place I'll call home. I'd sit there and I'd say, "Oh, Washington, beautiful Washington; they're tearin it up."

At this time, my husband's health was off, and my daughter and her husband found Columbia for us. I wanted to go to Washington, but the children said "No, it isn't like you knew it. You will be afraid to go to the store to get a loaf of bread, and we would be afraid to have you do it." I had a friend from Charlottesville who moved to Washington and bought a home. She wrote me and said, "I am so sick. In Charlottesville, we went anywhere we wanted to go. Here, my children don't allow us to go out of the door. This is a terible life to be here in this beautiful city and be afraid to take a walk."

It's just been horrible to see Washington destroyed as it has been. It's because the people had nothin in the South, and they left for a better life where all these jobs were. But they didn't know how to live after they got there. And some of these people in Underhill don't know how to live after they get here.

The church is a very important part of my life now. This is strange, because after I was first married, the most important thing to me was my husband. I loved him so much, and when my son came, I had just everything. And if I wanted somethin and didn't get it, it didn't bother me too much because I knew I had these two people and they were mine. Well, when my marriage went to pot, I nearly died. I used to say, "Why did this have to happen? Oh Lord, help me." And I'd say, "I don't understand why You would do this to me." I couldn't stop cryin. My mother used to say, "Life isn't all happiness; everybody has to suffer. It's a vale of tears, and you might just as well know it because it's comin." And so it does.

I really do believe if you get so caught up that you don't know what to do or which way to go, you just pray to God and then forget it. This is what it says in the Bible. I can't tell you where it says it, but it's in there because I've read it. I found it one day, and it said, "Pray and tell Him what you want and then you forget it." And if it's for you, when you least expect, everything clears up. This is what I believe.

I'd always gone to church, but then I began to get closer to the religion. In later years, especially since my husband got sick, and he's been sick about 15 years, I began to get closer and closer. When we came here, I wanted to bring our membership to the Interfaith Center but he didn't. You see, Interfaith is different from other churches. The Episcopalians and the Methodists are combined, and we have one service in a section of the church. Then it has the Catholics, the Jewish, and the Baptist. Most churches are changin somewhat, but Interfaith is different from any church we ever been in. Somehow it just didn't give you what you were lookin for.

When we came to Columbia, I sat down and I thought, "He's gettin worse and worse. I have got to pray; I've got to have somethin to hold to." So we went up to a meetin at the Interfaith Church, and nobody talked to us. My husband told me before he went he wasn't gonna join. I begged him but he wouldn't. But what do you think would have happened to me if I had not carried my membership up there, with all this trouble that struck me the next year? There would have been no minister to come to see me; there would have been perhaps no one interested in us. People were very distant out here at that time because nobody knew each other. I knew I must be affiliated with some church. And that was the only church that was out here. I joined and I have ever been grateful.

The pastor is a man who could walk into the room this minute, and I think he could take a hold of any situation. He's gentle and kind and we know he means it. When I learned my husband couldn't walk any more, I told him what happened and he said, "Don't worry." Right after that he set up a "carin group," and people would take me to see him every Sunday. They would leave me at a motel outside of the gates of the hospital, and I'd stay three days every time I went. Then I would call a taxi to take me to the station, and I'd get the train back. My son would meet me at the train, and I'd spend the night with him before comin back here. I learned how wonderful people can be, those who want to be. There're plenty of em who never have been near or called me, but I was surprised that so many people came forward. With what I had to go through, I was able to do it with the kindness of the church.

I read about the Columbia Medical Clinic, and I took my husband up there. We told the man about his Medicare, and he said we could join the plan if we wanted to. It's a private thing and you have to pay. But with Medicare, all we had to pay for both of us was a supplement of $25 a month. What Medicare does for him is wonderful, and there is no reason not to have good medical care. Every time you go and the doctor sees you, he'll give you a bill soon after. You pay $2 for that visit, and you pay $2 for each prescription. At first I said, "Well, my goodness, look at all this money we're payin." Then I stopped and thought, "No, this isn't bad because suppose you had to go to a private doctor outside; they're chargin $12 for a visit." My daughter has one doctor she goes to for $15 a visit, so it really isn't that bad here if you stop to think of it.

Once I was terribly sick with a virus. You were supposed to call em when you got sick and tell em what the trouble was. If they thought it was serious enough, they were supposed to come. Well, this doctor didn't come. He kept sayin, "I don't think I need to come." You really had to talk to get em to come out of there from what I hear. He said, "Well, what are you takin?" I told him I was takin aspirin and some cough medicine. And he said, "Well, you just continue that and let me know if you get better." I didn't get better for over a week, and I was so mad by that time. You know other people had told me this.

I never had the necessity to call em again until my husband came down with a virus this winter. I called and my doctor was away for a week. You pick the doctor you want, and if you don't like him you can change. They have what they call adult medicine, and I asked for this nurse who lives up here not far from me. I told her what had happened and I said, "I think he has pneumonia." She came right over and she said, "Doctor's away." She came back again next day, and she told me to get this contraption that you set on the floor and fill with water, a vaporizer. I had to keep that thing goin night and day into the third week. Finally, I said to him, "Let's try to do without it now because you're improvin." It got so moist in here and I suffered from it. When that third week was over he was doin fine.

I have often worried about somethin happenin to me, such as I was so sick here last week and the week before. I have all this hypertension, and it isn't goin to improve. With the stress and strain here, it can only get worse; that's why I try to take things easy. Still, it's hard for me to go slow because I'm just not made that way. But suppose I fell flat on the floor and my husband couldn't see me. He'd call and call; eventually, after a long time, he would know somethin had happened to me. The only way he could get anyone would be to scream, and maybe they'd say, "Somethin's goin on down there." If I was in my bedroom and I had a phone extension there, I could get a doctor or get help from somebody in the buildin. But suppose I couldn't call?

Archie suggested this little social worker, and he said, "Would you talk with her?" I said, "So many people have been and talked with me to try to help me and they haven't done anything." But I talked with her, and she said, "I am goin to find someone to sit with your husband." I said, "It hasn't been done yet. The Commission on Aging tried and people just don't seem to want to do it." And then she told me she could get us food stamps. I said, "Look, I don't need food stamps; I couldn't look myself in the face if I took food stamps. Our pension is enough for me to pay our rent and our bills and to get the food that we need." And she said, "I know, but that would help you so much more." I said, "I don't need it; that's the way I feel."

Nobody in my family on either side has ever been on welfare or ever had to. We're not rich people, but all of us were taught to work and earn what we needed and wanted. There were no sluggards in our families, so I just couldn't do it. I said if I ever needed it, I would say, "Please, will you help me?" But I don't need it. I said, "Well, now look here; I read the paper every day, and there are people out here starvin, children hungry. I would think that I'm takin somethin that they should have."

I really couldn't truthfully tell my age because my mother and father disagreed. I asked my mother for a birth certificate because I had to register to go to school in Washington, and she didn't have it. Then she explained when children were born in the country, you went by some event that happened at that time to tell about when your child was born. She had me down in the Bible as bein born in 1899, but my father said I was born two years later than that.

A lot of older people look to me to be much older than I. Some of them are decrepit, but I seem to be the same as I've always been. Course I know I'm not; healthwise I'm not. But I feel the same. I'd look at em and some of em seemed very senile. Still, you can join the Association of Retired People from 55 on up, so there were many people that were young enough not to be old. We had potluck luncheons, and you'd make a dish or make a dessert or salad and take it. And then they'd decorate the tables; it was really nice. You could talk to each other and get to know people. Then they had trips, but I only got to go on one trip. I couldn't go because that meant gettin someone to sit with him all day long. They tried to get a sitter at the church; they even put it in the church bulletin, but people didn't respond. I think they felt that somethin might happen, and they wouldn't know how to handle it. Too many people have come and asked what they could do, but nothin came of it. People just didn't seem to want to sit with a sick person.

Sometimes my daughter tells me to put on eye shadow, and I say, "You must have lost your mind; after all, I'm not a young woman like you." She says, "You are not old; you can do all these things. You should see these ladies when I go out someplace touchin their white hair and all made up. Mother, they look beautiful." And I said, "Well, when I dress, I think I look mighty nice." She says, "You do, but you need some eye shadow and it's cute."

Here in Underhill, they don't have no place to sit out in the front there. I had heard that they were goin to make a playground for children, and they were goin to put benches out there for the senior citizens so they could come out and enjoy it. But I haven't seen anything. If we had a bench, I would put my husband in his chair and take him out, so he could sit and watch and talk to people.

I go to the mall sometimes because the doctor said that is one of the things I should do. It's beautiful and they have these blocks that you can sit on. So many women go down there, I guess just to get away from the house. You usually buy an ice cream cone and just sit there and talk. I never go alone so I don't go often; I've done it twice this summer.

There are laundry rooms in each of the buildins here, and they're very convenient. But goin to the laundry room, you have to go down and put things in, come back in 30 minutes and take em out, put em in the dryer, and come back in 30 more minutes and take em out of the dryer. That's three trips.

If I go out the back door, I don't have to go up and down these steps to get to the laundry room. I don't like to go unless I have gotten my husband up and put him in the chair, because that door doesn't lock when you go out of it. Once in awhile I leave him and go out the back door real quick. But I usually don't go to this one because I'm afraid of this big boy next door. I went in there one mornin, and he had gone in there with a mandolin and a radio. He had both of em sittin on the tub with the lid turned down. Well, after he had frightened me so badly. I wasn't about to stay in there with him. So I just took one look and turned around and started away. I heard him say, "There's room, there's room," but I never even looked back. So I've been goin to the other one ever since, and I have to walk the steps.

There are rules that we're not supposed to have pets, but you see cats and dogs all around. There's a couple of cats in this stairway. We used to have pets; we had a beautiful dog and a lovely cat. I would also love to have a freezer, but that's against the rules, too. Still, I knew I had to adjust to these things, and I don't let it upset me.

I don't prefer livin in this kind of housing at all. Now, I'm not sayin this sharply, but I just don't prefer doin it. I know now what apartment life is like; you just can't pick the people who live here. You don't know what they're goin to do when they get in there, and then you can't get em out. I'd like to live in a different settin because I've always been used to that. I would prefer a private house rather than an apartment. But it would be hard for me because a house is goin to have a yard. You would have to mow it, and it would not be good for me.

There's nothin wrong with Underhill; they have built these nice apartments that are very comfortable. Since it is housing, it was built for people who are poor and for people a little better off. And they kind of graded it for retireds and some who they know they're not goin to have but so much money. I won't criticize these places because what would people do if they didn't have em? But I do say that a lot of people get into em who have been very poor, and they don't know how to live in em. I guess you have to be compassionate and accept those who were too poor to have been taught how to live and how to treat people. Still, it's hard to live near em. You either move, or you just stay and put up with it.

I think it's fine to mix different kinds except for people who are older. If you put teenagers in with em, they're goin to make noise. It's terrible with Clara's kids upstairs, but I'm on this side and it doesn't disturb me so much. Some old people are very cross and impatient and some are not, but I think noise might disturb em.

Now as far as how much money they would have, or if they're white or colored, it doesn't matter to me one bit. I'm used to white people, and my husband and I have traveled in different places. I don't see any difference except their skin is white. When my friends come in here, they grab me and hug and kiss me. Most friends that I have in Columbia are white.

People of my race felt that this was the poor area, and they didn't want anything to do with us; they were lookin down on us. You could see the minute we walked in the church that we were people just as good as they were; we weren't trash. They'd come up to us and the first thing they'd ask you, "Where do you live?" I remember I said where we lived to this man, and his wife walked off. I'm very sensitive to knowin what's goin on around me; I catch it right away. And I said, "Oh-oh, somethin's wrong." So then somebody else did the same thing; they just ignored us.

I presume white people will feel the same way, but they never said anything to me about it. Some of em were very friendly, but I was lookin for my own to come and be friendly. See, I had grown up in nice neighborhoods where everybody spoke and everybody became friendly. Maybe you never went in their homes, but everybody would stop and talk. After livin in the country for 12 years, I got so I spoke to everybody. When we walked down the street, everybody, white and colored, would shake your hand and take their hats off. One of the bankers there was one of our best friends. If you have respect, people give you respect; that's the way I looked at it.

When I came here they said, "Everybody speaks to everybody." I walked down the street one day and there was a fine lookin woman comin. I kept lookin at her cause I wanted to say, "Good mornin," but she passed me and kept her head up in the air. There's a whole lot of em livin around here won't speak to you. This is the new Negro. He has had it so hard, that now he's got it, he wants to walk over the top of everybody. He wants nothin to do with people that haven't got it. So I said, "Well, just who do they think they are?" And my husband would just sit in his chair and say, "Nobody ever comes. Why did we ever come to this place?"

COMMENT

Ada's rememberance of "better times" is compounded by an almost hysterical fear for her life among her neighbors. Her identification remains unswervingly with the outside world to which she and Clarence belonged before his illness and retirement. Indeed, Ada and Clarence prove unable to deal with the problems that emege in Underhill and move to a private garden apartment in another part of Columbia. Because it is much more expensive than subsidized housing, their children are helping to pay the costs. Clarence passed away soon after the move. Ada is now living by herself, trying to adjust to the loneliness and marginality of her circumstances.

Although Ada's fear of her neighbors is extreme, such fear is common to almost all the cases presented here. Rather than being bound together by any common "culture of poverty," Underhill residents can only periodically create some common understandings and practices. The value of community is given verbal endorsement, and there is no reason to think this ungenuine. But the obstacles to trust are simply too great and numerous. For the most part, residents glorify past periods of economic stability; present relations are equivocal, temporary, and fragile. This sharply limits the cohesion of residential groups and their capacity to engage in much self-help. The community which results is one in which people look to third parties—the police, housing administrator, doctors, social workers— to carry out much of the negotiation that goes on among the residents.

Of course, the sharply segregated 236 housing makes the economic circumstances of each resident especially visible, thus exacerbating the fears that forstall development of a more genuine community. Food stamps, medical cards, and so on add to the visibility of poverty and inhibit congenial relations. The federal insistence upon a completely "integrated" population seems to reduce possible lines of solidarity to a point where ethnic and racial solidarity are not easily achieved, even when they are available. The heterogeneity of Underhill is exceptional, but it is obvious that the formal aspiration for complete "desegregtion" compounds the isolation of some of the marginal poor.

Under conditions of fear and living together in isolation, illnesses, apprehensions, and mental disorders seem to become exaggerated and to intensify. Illness is a widespread complaint of the near poor; living in isolation together seems to make it such a point of preoccupation that it is even more debilitating.

Chapter 6

CLARA AND KAREN HUNT
The Income, Life-style Gap

CLARA HUNT

I like my apartment here in Underhill, but I could find some things about it I don't like. I don't think they're well built; it's not soundproof or anything. You can hear your neighbors and they can hear you. We're always at each other's throats.

Actually, it got so bad we had to go to court with the neighbors under us, the Bonnolis. I only did it because the police advised me to; Wally and May Bonnoli were out here knockin on my door every weekend or every other night. Shortly after I'd get home from work, I'd turn the record player on or my son, Gary, would decide to pick out a tune on his guitar. It was only six-thirty or seven o'clock. I don't really think it's disturbin the neighborhood unless you're really stompin and jouncin, fightin, or makin noise at two or three o'clock in the mornin. It's not a private home; it's a apartment and you're gonna hear noise. I think it could have been avoided had these floors been better insulated between apartments; it would have cut down on a lot of noise. I can hear them down there, and they can hear me just walkin across the floor.

At first, it wasn't really a argument. May used to call here quite frequently, and she'd say to me, "Please cut the noise out." I'd say, "We're not makin noise. If I cut this record player down any more, I won't be able to hear it." If I had company on a weekend, or if I invited some friends in and they were sittin around, drinkin beer and listenin to records, it was embarrassin to have the police knockin at the door. It got so comical, really, with that same cop comin out. He went downstairs and told em, "I parked the car down the street and walked up, and I couldn't hear Mrs. Hunt's hi fi until I got outside of her apartment door." He said it was gettin to be pretty ridiculous.

Before I went to get the warrant, the police advised me to check with the other neighbors. Mrs. Corbin that lived next door, she said, "No, you don't disturb me." I asked anybody else downstairs and it was just the Bonnolis callin the police. Everybody else in the buildin said, "No, we don't hear anything unusual."

So I complained to the court that they were disturbin my peace by harrassin me and callin the police on me without just cause, without good reason. I had the policeman with me, and he told the judge about the time he walked up and he did not hear a lotta noise goin on. That was the night when she called and said it sounded like we were comin through the ceilin. He found only me and my nine-year-old home, and she was asleep. I was sittin here at the sewin machine sewin about ten-thirty or eleven o'clock, and I had the record player on.

Well, they stopped callin the police, and we stopped speakin to each other for awhile. Actually, we weren't speakin much before we went to court. She might call up here and ask me if I had a cup of sugar; sometimes I sent down there for somethin. But we weren't buddy-buddy before all this happened. Now she'll call up here durin the day when I'm at work and say, "Will you please cut the record player down?" Or she'll ask Gary to stop playin the guitar. We speak to each other sometimes; if she sees me, she might say, "Hi," and if she does, I'll say, "Hi." It's a bad way to live.

She's white and I'm black, but I really don't think it was a racial thing. I think I'm dealin with a young couple that has four small kids. She's a very nervous type person and I guess after she puts the kids to bed, she's hopin and prayin that nothin will wake em up. She's tired, you know.

But she has a baby that I can hear cryin in the middle of the night, and I've gotta go to work the next mornin. I tried to talk to her, and I said, "May, you have small kids and I have big kids. Your babies cry, and my kids like music. And at seven-thirty or nine-thirty or on a weekend after I've worked all week, if I want to have company, I don't think that's bein unfair." She told the judge it was her husband that was callin the police, and the judge said he was very sorry for her.

Before I moved to Columbia, I came out here with a group of friends one Sunday, just ridin around and askin the prices of apartments. A lady mentioned some subsidized housin, and that's how I found out about the projects. After we moved in, I was still workin in the city and commutin. Later, I gave up commutin because of my daughter, Julia, who's been ill. I wanted to be close to her because she got sick in school one day, and a coworker had to drive me back to Columbia. That's when I decided to try and find some employment near here, plus commutin is very expensive.

I was lost when I first moved here, so I inquired about the bus service and schedules. The bus used to go into the city on Saturday, but it doesn't anymore. That's where I used to shop, in town on Saturday when I was off. I'd gather the children up, and we'd get on the bus in the mornin, go spend Saturday in the city shoppin and visit my mother. I have a few friends in Columbia now and some in Underhill. One is a long-time girlfriend of 20 years; our children grew up together in the city. I was very responsible for her comin out here.

I talk to my mother almost every day, but I don't get back there as often as I'd like because I don't have a car. Without the bus, about the only way to get in is to get some friend of mine to take me. Sometimes my father will come out and pick me up and bring me back, but I feel kind of guilty askin him. He doesn't like to drive that well because he's been sick.

I don't think I could afford a apartment in the city like the one I have now. Before comin to Columbia, I lived in public housin but it was not like this. There wasn't a mall and a atmosphere like here; it wasn't as nice. It was a very tough neighborhood like the high rise projects all over; every city has these projects. There were more social problems, robberies, people bein honky and fightin and cuttin and drinkin. I lived there for five years, and I wouldn't like to go back to that.

I was glad to get out of there. My parents were glad to see me get out, too, but they didn't want me to come this far. They still live in a nice residential area where I grew up. It was a all black neighborhood; I never went to a school with white kids. If you crossed the main street, that's when you'd see white kids, but you wouldn't go that way too often. I had a strictly all black upbringin, only white people you saw was the grocery store, bill collectors, somebody like that.

I never thought much about white folks when I was a kid. I didn't think they were any better off; I just didn't know all this that I know now. Black history wasn't as popular when I was goin to school. We had Negro History Week and that was once a year. We'd do all this studyin about famous Negroes, which were very few.

I had a very happy childhood life; there was always plenty to eat and a nice home. There were only two children, me and my sister, and we led a very sheltered life. Durin those times, I guess we were considered the rich kids. We always had plenty of everything and some neighborhood kids didn't. Maybe because they had larger families, they didn't have as much as we did. We went to camp every summer and we had music lessons.

My mother was strictly a housewife, family type woman. She's quiet, obedient, and never does anything without my father. He was the king of the house and always has been ever since I can remember. Whatever you said, it was, "Ask your father." They've been married for 40 years and it's still that way. She's a kind person, very active in the church, and she has a lot of friends. I'm very close to her and my father; I love em both dearly.

My parents had a store which was two blocks from our house. Both of em worked there and my grandmother used to go down sometimes and help out. I helped sometimes after school; it was a family thing. Then urban renewal came through and everything was torn down, the store and the house.

Of course, my family got money for their house, and they bought the one they're in now. My father never reopened another business; he went to work for a shoe company. There had been rumors for years that the neighborhood was gonna be torn down, and he was prepared for it. He said the only way he could stop my mother from workin was to close the store up. She had been ill and even though they had some help, she insisted on still comin to work every day.

The manager here in Underhill is the greatest; I really think he's a heck of a man. I've lived in this type housin before, public housin for five years and another project in Columbia for almost three. Each development has had managers, but I think that this is one of the best. He's a top guy, beyond and above a manager. You can pick up the phone and call him at night and say, "I need a ride to take my child to the hospital." He'll help you even though this is not part of his job. If you got a problem with maintenance and you can't get it solved right away, if he can't help you, he'll refer you to somebody that can or make a phone call for you. I think he's a really good man.

I think people in Underhill get along very well; I really do. I see people babysittin for each other, offerin rides, shoppin for you. And I wouldn't say that our kids have any more disturbances than kids anywhere else. They out there playin on the street; they might have a disturbance or fightin, but no more than anywhere else.

It was worse when we lived on the other side of Columbia, which is rapidly becomin an urban type ghetto place; it's crowded and congested. I think poor management has a lot to do with it, because a lot of people are livin there that are not supposed to be there. Like I might have been fortunate enough to get a house there, and I might bring my sister and her ten children to live with me. And someone has her grandmother there and slips in her children.

I really didn't like the atmosphere. There was a lot of hippies and a lot of disturbances. The police stayed there all the time, and it was one thing after another, really becomin kind of bad. I didn't feel comfortable livin there by myself because they had a few break ins. I couldn't half sleep because I didn't feel safe there. That's one of the reasons I chose a third floor apartment here.

Two weeks ago, the lady downstairs in this buildin claimed that a man was standin on her balcony, and they had a whole bunch of police cars out there. I always make sure that the front door is closed, but I leave my back door open. I just couldn't imagine anybody climbin three flights up to break in. But last couple of weeks, I've been gettin up and lockin it. That's the first incident like that I've heard of since I been in here.

If I could've taken my house in the other project and moved it someplace else, I would have. It was a town house with plenty of room and no neighbors to worry about. I loved the dwellin, but I didn't like the atmosphere. That wasn't my reason for movin; my reason was my little girl, Julia, who's eight. She's been sick with asthma, and the doctor thought maybe she should be on the ground floor, instead of constantly runnin up and down the steps like she had to do in a three story town house. Now she has to come up the steps to come in the apartment, but she's all on one floor.

When we first moved to the other project, I felt comfortable sooner than my kids did. I was very proud and happy that I'd moved out of a bad atmosphere in the ghetto, and I felt safer leavin them when I went to work. But Karen, who's 15, and Gary, who's 17, and Elizabeth, who's 13, were kind of lost and missin their old friends and their grandparents, and it took them awhile. They don't particularly like Underhill and apartment livin. They'd just gotten used to a town house, and movin here to a apartment again was another readjustment for them. It didn't take Julia as long as the others, because little kids make friends quicker than teenagers.

Karen and Gary weren't used to the open school system here; I'm not sure they ever adapted to it. There was too much freedom, and their grades went boom. Gary caught on quicker than Karen; in fact, she's back in a conventional school that uses the old system. I took her out because she wasn't doin nothin. Now she's told, "Go to your classes," and it's the same as the school she was raised up in. Gary did a little better in the open space school because he knew that he had to study on his own. The teacher's not gonna say, "You go to Math at 10:00 and English at 11:00 and Science at 12:00." Karen used to mosey up and down the hall most of the time doin nothin, bringin home no credits. So I took her out last year, and this year she's doin fine.

I transferred her against her wishes. I gave her awhile to shape up but she didn't. She didn't wanna go to another school. But after she got in, she saw the teachers were not goin to play with her, so she buckled down. Part of her problem before was the school group that she was with. They were all doin the same thing she was, doin nothin in class, nothin. I thought if I got her away from them that she would do better and she did. She's made some new friends now.

They have a few racial problems at the old school; I've talked to the principal about it several times. He was sayin to me that a lotta white kids were afraid of some of the black kids for no reason at all. Like I had one problem the first year I was here, when Gary asked this white boy for a quarter. He gave the quarter to him, and then he went in the principal's office and said that Gary took his quarter. Actually, he gave it to him.

We got in the office to discuss it, the boy's parents and myself and the principal and a couple of witnesses. The boy said, "Yeah, I gave it to you, but in a way you took it. I just gave it to you because I was afraid of you." So Gary said, "Why are you afraid of me? Did I ever hit you or demand that you give it to me? I just asked you to loan me a quarter, and you reached in your pocket and gave it to me. If you didn't want to loan it to me, why didn't you say no?" He said, "I gave it to you because I was afraid of you." The principal was sayin they have a lotta problems similar to that one.

Karen's very prejudiced, very. I've tried to talk to her about that, but I can't change her attitude. And Gary's different as day and night. He gets black friends and white friends, but Karen, she don't want anything to do with em. She don't like white people. I think maybe she's experienced some bad things; I don't know. She'd say the white kids get away with more at school and the black kids get expelled for it. She has her own reasons. She has a argument about why she feels that way; there's a lotta little things she's pointed out.

Like this job she wanted right up the street from the house. The man had a "help wanted" sign out on the window, and every day she'd come by there and ask em do they need anybody. She was really lookin for a job; she wanted that job real bad. It was close to home and she wouldn't have to pay carfare.

So one time this white girl that she knew told her in school that she got a job there. Karen had been up there like two days before, and the man told her he didn't need anybody. So Karen called up there that next week because he still had the sign out there he needed help. She came right out and said, "You're prejudiced, aren't you? You don't intend to hire me. Why do you keep tellin me to come back next week, or you gonna call me? You hired a girl that goes to my school. I was in there the day before she was, and you told me you didn't need anybody." He told her to come up he wanted to talk to her, and he hired her. So she's had some little incidents to make her feel very prejudiced.

I had a problem with prejudice once when I should've gotten a promotion in a place I worked in. This white girl got the promotion because she had the paper, but she didn't know how to really do the work. I did everything there; I learned from on the job trainin and from bein there all the time. I had been promised the position that she got, but she had a certificate and got the job. I think that was a form of prejudice.

Karen has told me several other things that happened. There was a whole bunch of girls in the auditorium one day, both black and white, and this girl's pocketbook was missin. The principal called them to say he was determined to find out who took the pocketbook, if he had to stay in school all night. He said he was gonna put an end to that kind of thing, and he sent the whole group of girls back to the home room teacher. He called for em to come into his office one at a time to talk to him. And he finally called for all the black girls sayin that he thought one of em took the pocketbook. That upset her pretty bad.

Now, she just don't have anything to say to white people or wanna be around em. You know I have a lotta mixed friends where I work now, both black and white, and she don't want me to be around em. She says, "Oh, mommy, what're you goin out with her for?" She wouldn't be caught dead doin anything like that, goin out with whites.

She has a strong argument. I can't quote her word for word, but she's pretty heavy on her history. She's read a lotta things and she's seen a lotta things, and she's very proud of her blackness. She's had some things happen to her to make her feel very militant. I know my black history pretty good, too, and we'll be debatin on it. She'll point up instances today where she thinks certain forms of slavery still exist, like blacks in low payin jobs, bad housin. The white kids know how she is; she just tells em. They know her from school and in the neighborhood. Man, they don't bother her. She don't go around pickin on anybody; she's not violent. She'll just let em know she don't like em. She don't wanna get to know em.

I think it's healthy that she's proud of her heritage, but I don't think it's right that she should hate all white people. It's not good for her to feel like she can get along in this world without em, because she's gonna have to deal with this later on, and it's gonna be bad. She's gonna run into a lotta conflicts with that attitude. I can't change her because that's the way she feels. She's almost 16 years old and she's molded. She tried to change me, but I told her she couldn't change mommy. I hope she'll get over it.

Karen's more like her father, and Gary, Elizabeth, and Julia are more like me. Her father is kind of militant, but he's actually a very nice guy. I guess that's why I married him. But we started havin problems, and it got to be too much for both of us copin with bein young and havin children, my parents on one end and his parents on the other. Then his sister moved in with us. He come from a big family and I come from a small family. I just couldn't understand all this togetherness.

The last time we separated was not the first time; we had been separated a couple of times between. I have'nt lived with him for seven years now; Julia was a baby the last time I went back. He lives like three blocks from my mother's house and she sees him all the time. He has another family now, but we're not divorced. He has two kids by the woman he lives with, so I don't bother him and he don't bother me. Every now and then, like every four or five months, he might pick up the phone and call.

I have been datin this guy for about three years now, and I don't know what it's gonna be. I think it's my fault we're not married. He has proposed to me several times, but I just don't feel like at this point we would be together for the rest of our lives. I'm crazy about him and he's shown me that he's crazy about me and my kids. But I just don't think I feel that way about him, that I'd want to live with him till death do us part. I love bein around him, but I think my first marriage made me feel thisaway.

I have some pretty rough times with Julia; she takes a lotta time and I feel guilty because she's been a pretty sick little girl. But she hasn't had a attack for six months, and she's been doin pretty good. She doesn't get sick as often as she used to. I've had a lot of experience in usin the Columbia Medical Plan because Julia needs a doctor quite often. I contacted the Department of Social Service when I first moved here for a Medical Assistance Card for Julia, because I didn't belong to the Plan. I had a Medical Assistance Card which was no good in this county. But it was just a matter of them contactin the city, verifyin, and making me a new card, which I got in the mail a few days after I was here.

I had a emergency one night and I had no way to get to the city. I called over there and said my little girl was sick. I said, "I don't care how much it costs, but she needs to see a doctor." Doctor Cohen said to bring her over right away, and he's been her own physician ever since. At that time, they didn't accept Medical Care Cards; you had to be a member of the Plan, so it was very nice of them to take her. You can pick up the phone and call on Saturdays, Sundays, three o'clock in the mornin; they have a 24 hour answerin service. You tell em your problem, and if it's a emergency, they tell you to get over to the clinic right away. In fact, they come out to your house and visit you. So Julia's doin fine.

I used to go to a lot of meetins of the Tenants Council in Underhill because there were things I thought should be done. But it's not workin because they need stronger leadership than it has at the present. I've heard the same opinion from other people. I think when a family has some tight luck or somethin, they should be able to pick up the phone and say, "We need help." There should be some help from the Tenants Council for this. There're plenty of ways to raise money, bake sales and rummage sales and garage sales. We had a very successful rummage sale at Underhill, and I think we raised like eighty or ninety dollars. There was a lotta stuff left over and they gave it away to thrift shops. There're plenty of people here they don't work and they should be more active.

I don't need a babysitter because my child's in school all day, plus I have three teenagers to watch her. But as many small kids as we have here, it looks like there would be some sort of a nursery to help mothers that work. And car pools would help because there are people that don't have cars. If someone sees you need a ride, they'll offer you one, but it's not a set up type of thing.

If someone dies or has a accident or somethin, someone will come around and collect money for people or for flowers. Each buildin is supposed to have a stairwell representative, and you're supposed to get together with the people and sort of keep up on what's goin on, see that everybody is okay. We don't have a representative now; I was and I was dyin. I was wrapped up in too many things at one time. We got three women in the buildin that are housewives, but one is elderly and she has a sick husband, so I'll excude her. But there are two other women that are home full time who could do it.

One of the problems is that there should be some sort of laundry room schedule, because the women that don't work will wait till Saturday mornin to come wash. That's the only day when all the women that do work have to use the laundry room. But that's when you find all the housewives there that are home from Monday till Friday. I've lived in projects where it was like this: if you were caught in the laundry room and it wasn't your day to wash, you were fined for bein down there, unless it was a emergency.

People don't want to think of a Tenants Council as someone tellin residents what to do. But it could work if they got together and voted, and the members said, "All little kids should be in the house at nine o'clock because there's a whole lot of noise underneath people's windows when they're tryin to sleep. If your kid's caught out there after nine, there's gonna be a big problem, or this is gonna be mentioned to you." Or maybe it's a small fine or somethin. People don't like to think of a Tenants Council as bein that domineerin, but it could work if they had stronger leadership.

Some of the rules we got here are good, but some I think are ridiculous. I don't see why we shouldn't be able to have a small freezer. You can have television, and how much current does a freezer use more than a television or a record player? I'm sure they must have some reason for not wantin you to have one, but I don't understand it.

Pets could be a problem in a crowded atmosphere; you can't have pets around a lotta people. But people here are breakin that rule, too. I love pets and I wish we could have em. Like cats don't bark so they wouldn't be noisy. When I get my own house, I'll have pets because my little girl is crazy about em.

But you need rules for noise, for the laundry room, things like that, because you have a variety of people in here. Sometimes you need somebody to coordinate things. I don't think we've had any real problems from different backgrounds of people here; I don't think that's causin anything. It's people, not just because there's a mixture.

I've heard of some racial problems here, but I haven't experienced it myself. There's a black family, she has a couple of small kids, and she was always gettin letters from the office about things that her two little boys had done. The lady next door to her was a white family, and their kids did not get along together. The black girl seemed to think it was a racial thing, because one day the lady called her kids, "You little black so and so's." This was wrong, if she said it. But whenever the black lady reported anything, there was nothin said about it. So she seemed to think it was racial. Thank heavens the white family's gone now. She was openly prejudiced; she didn't hide it.

And then, Elmer in our stairwell said somethin in the presence of the manager. He was complainin about the kids, and instead of sayin, "Those children," he said, "Those niggers." The manager asked him not to use that word; but that wasn't the first time he had done this. The kids were out on the steps playin when he was tryin to get past, and he said somethin like, "You black so and so's, move." The children were insulted at what he said, but I told them, "Don't pay him any mind. As long as he doesn't hit you, he can say whatever he wants. See, he's very ignorant." He's openly prejudiced, but I can look down at him. It doesn't upset me if he say somethin like that because he's what I call poor white trash, from some hills somewhere in Virginny. I feel sorry for him; I really do. Still, I called the manager and told him that he called my kids niggers. Archie said, "Well, he came down here and used that word in front of me and I wrote him a letter. Just ignore him, Clara." So I said, "Well, I will." And Archie said, "He's to be pitied, really. You know, he's an uneducated man."

For a long time I wanted to be a librarian, but that didn't work out. I used to read, read, read; it came from bein by myself a lot. I've got almost two years of college I've acquired since I was married. I could've gotten a few more credits, but I felt guilty about bein away from the children all day and out at night. And I didn't intend to have another nervous breakdown either. I think the pressure had a lot to do with me gettin sick.

About five or six years ago, I was admitted to the State Hospital. Everything sort of caught up with me, and I had a nervous breakdown. It came from a combination of things, hard work, separation, goin to night school, and workin full time durin the day. I lost a lotta weight and couldn't sleep, nervous like. Three weeks in the hospital and I was released. I went back and forth to the outpatient department for about five months. I've had a few rough periods since, but not bad enough to go to the hospital. They have counseling help here and all kinds of doctors.

Karen has had counseling, but she doesn't go any more. I see a big improvement in her whole outlook. I think she was just goin through a stage with school problems and the wrong type of friends. That was durin the period when I had to have her transferred. She went through this rebellious type stage for six or seven months, maybe a little longer. I'd insist on her goin for counseling and she even rebelled against that, but she did go. She went once a week after school for about three months, and she really calmed down. She was able to open up with them, things which she couldn't talk to me about, things that was botherin her.

Overall, I think the social service here is good, but when you're black, this depends on who you come in contact with. Some social workers, I don't know whether it's part of their job or whether they do it not realizin they're doin it, but sometimes they can make you feel pretty bad, like you're beggin or somethin. I think a lotta people that need help sometimes dread goin to them for help, thinkin they're gonna put them through the third degree or somethin like that. Sometimes it really hurts. And then again, if you contact the same agency and get a different social worker or different person, you can feel that you've really been helped, that this person really went all out to help you. I guess it really depends.

Once I applied for food stamps, but they said I was fifty or sixty dollars over the ceilin which they allow for my size family. I'm the sole source of income for my family, and I think this is ridiculous. Julia gets free lunch at school because of her illness. I think that's how she qualified, because accordin to that pay scale they have on there when you apply for it, I didn't think I was gonna make that either.

Another time I had to contact the Department of Social Service when I was tryin to find a lady to take care of Julia. She was in the hospital and I was expectin her to come home; I wanted somebody to come in and keep her. I was lookin for a nice day care mother that was near my house. But that didn't work out, and I had to find one myself.

I think a lotta mothers do have problems with day care. Half a day nursery schools in Columbia are very expensive. They have one that works on a slidin pay scale accordin to your income, but they have a limit of 40 or 50 children.

Some places here you can go to for help when you need it. Like I lost my paycheck, and I called the Christian Women's Thrift Shop for some assistance, for some food. They came out and took me to the market. I think I bought $30 worth of groceries which I paid back. I heard about them from some people in Underhill.

They have a lotta clubs in Columbia; some of em is activities for singles. They also have big, beautiful teen centers and a lotta teen programs. But most of the time the kids are somewhere else, doin somethin else. The Columbia Association also have a skatin rink and swimmin pools. If you don't have the money to pay for a membership, they have other ways. Karen worked 50 hours and Gary worked 50 hours in the Earn-A-Membership program. Karen went faithfully; this was a challenge to her to get her hours over with so she could get her card. But Gary slacked off a little bit, and he had to go back. The last two years, we didn't have it; they just paid as they went along. Like if they wanted to go skatin, I had to give em money to go skatin with.

I just recently joined a black women's group in Columbia. We're really just gettin off the ground. We're tryin to have some benefits and raise money to do some things, maybe somethin with black teenagers, maybe sponsor some trips or tutorin programs. That's what I think I'd be best suited for, helpin teenagers with tutorin because I do read a lotta books.

Quite a few people here feel very militant, but in a good way. They believe that our children should be pushed to know their black history and have pride. I think what they're preachin and what they're aimin at is not bad; their goals are good. The women wanna deal more with awareness problems, black awareness, maybe in the form of education. One woman is a librarian, and she said she'd like to get some black history books circulatin among the kids, maybe set up a small library with black history books, art, magazines.

But a lotta black people move away from this and don't wanna look back. Some people, when they make it, they forget there are other people back there experiencin this right now and they put all this behind em. We call em black bourgeoisie; they're sort of separate. They're livin the white man's town now, not joinin any black nothin. They don't wanna think about those times or lend a hand or try to help somebody else get up to the point where they are.

A lotta black people out here in Columbia have moved away from the kind of environment that I used to live in, the projects, the ghetto, the rough neighborhoods. But we still have some of the same problems out here in Columbia that we had in the ghetto, namely, drugs. You say to yourself, "I'm gonna get my kids outta here before it's too late and put em in a better atmosphere so things like this won't affect their lives." But it's all around em. Only thing you did was move your kid in a better neighborhood, a better dwellin to live in without the rats. They have a newer school buildin to go to and all the equipment, audiovisual and all this bit. They have a teen center, where in the city they played out in the streets. You gave em all these things but you still facin some of the same problems. I think a lotta parents turn their back and don't wanna admit this. You can go down to that lake front any night in summer and say, "We've got some real problems." We've heard some pretty frightenin experiences that have happened with both black and white teenagers. They've had racial fights, drugs, abortions. This is a city, you know, and where you have a city, you have people and you have problems. So all I did for my kids was struggle and work hard and move em to a better environment. Things that I thought I was gettin em away from, they still exist right here.

You have some black people here that are very militant; you have some whites that are very prejudiced. But on the whole, I think it's controlled. It's not done openly, especially with the adults. But the kids have separated themselves, the black and white kids. You see a group of white kids on this corner, and you go a couple blocks up the street and you see a group of black kids. They've sort of divided themselves like in the teen centers. The Columbia Association don't wanna admit it, but there is a black teen center and a white teen center. The kids have did this to themselves; they've divided theirselves.

Blacks are more powerful now than they were; my parents' generation was not powerful. They had a few fights for the cause, equal rights, but not as many as you have now. They were quiet and they didn't go out and riot. I think the riots did a lot. It was a bad thing, but I think it really brought about a change. Martin Luther King, naturally, was one of the greatest black men that ever lived. I think his way was good, nonviolent. On the other hand, violence rocked cross the nation, and most of your major cities were burned. Now there are blacks in the White House; I think it brought about a change.

There's more racial pride among teenagers than in my age group. Karen, she's more aware of her racial pride at 15 years old than I was, because I didn't experience what she's experiencin. She very seldom goes up the street to this center; she goes to the other one where all the black kids go. I think racial pride is good, their dress, their hair, dashikis, bein more aware of black history, black posters and black music. But some of em run it to an extreme, like in some black movies bein publicized now.

The black group I belong to is a way of showin awareness, but I don't think I need the group to strengthen my pride. I think I've already got my share. I joined the group to do somethin good for my people in a small way, as a mother of teenagers who happen to be black. I would think it was good if it was a white group doin the same thing. I can't see any harm or anything bad comin out of that.

I feel like I really need a home because apartment livin is so cramped. My big boy is interested in music, and he has a room full of amplifiers. We stumble over each other because, when I get home from work, I don't want to hear loud noises. If I had a basement, I think it would be nice for him and the other kids. That's what I'm workin for, a home.

They're buildin some subsidized housin in Columbia for certain income groups and I have a house picked out. It's nothin fancy, just a plain old town house. Only certain people qualify, and there's down payments to meet. Concentratin on gettin the money together for this house is really takin all my spare time. I got two jobs now. I work seven days a week, five days in a lab and part time on weekends in the new hospital that just opened up here. I don't intend to make this a permanent thing. I'm tryin to accomplish somethin right now, tryin to get a home here in Columbia. That's all I can think about now is the house.

I read a article in the paper addressed to the builders of Columbia, this "next America." I don't know if the lady was jokin or not, but it was really puttin em down. She said the laborers constructin the buildins, the people who paved the streets and created the beautiful mall, they come in from the city on trucks to work, because they can't afford to live here. Underhill and the other projects can't hold all of the people, and there's also not enough houses out here for middle incomes. Either you're poor and live here, or you're rich and you live in one of the homes. If I didn't qualify for this housin, I would have to move back to the city to have a place to suit my needs. Anything else in Columbia is more than I could afford; there is no middle housin here.

The thing that worries me most is not bein able to work and havin illnesses. I don't know whether that's a abnormal fear, but I don't have any great favorin to see my mother and father come and get me and take me and the kids back to town to live with em. I couldn't survive without workin. I'd end up on welfare and I couldn't afford to take care of my kids.

I'd like to stay around and see the kids self supportin. My parents, I know they'd take care of em. But Julia, she needs gettin up in the middle of the night sometimes and runnin back and forth to the clinic and the hospital. That would be too much on my mother. I don't think my husband would do anything; he's got his own world now and my kids are not included. It's definitely on my parents if anything happens to me.

Because I'm separated, a lotta people think my kids are burdens to me. But if I didn't have em, then I wouldn't have anybody. I could be home with my parents, but at this age that wouldn't be any good. I think I'm relaxin more now, because my kids are gettin older and they're company for me. They went through some bad times which they have gotten over. They bring me happiness and I'm proud of em. I can't imagine bein without em.

KAREN HUNT

My friends in school is bad because they start racial fights all the time and don't go to class. Like in the bathroom, if a white girl walks in, they just start pickin on her. If she be brushin her hair, they say, "Piece a hair got on me." Then they hit her just because of that. Sometimes, if no white person is in the bathroom, they turn on the fire extinguisher and water come all out. They put a match up to it and start it goin. That's why some of em are out now; they got put out. They made me transfer out, too.

I think I deserved to get away from em because after I left they did even more worser things, like cuttin people's hair and just fightin. I would just mainly write on the wall, somethin like that. There was about nine of us in the group. We never picked on the blacks, only the Toms and the Oreos. Everything that was missin or anything, we would get blamed for it. Half the things, we didn't even know about. We did a lotta things, but some of the stuff wasn't always what we did.

I met em when I lived in the project on the other side of Columbia; they all lived around there. My best girlfriend was in it, so I decided to be in it. I mean, it was a good feelin to be around em while they was doin anything, but when we got in trouble at school, it wasn't a good feelin. The principal was always tellin me, "Why don't you get out of it? Why don't you start goin to class?" I finally had to get out cause all at one time they just jumped on me.

I used to go to the center over here once a week, but I didn't like it because there was nothin to do. I went to the center on the other side for awhile because we had a lotta activities there, trips and fashion shows. At first, the center was mostly white. Then blacks started goin there, and all the whites stopped comin.

The trouble started with the older kids; they come from all over Columbia. Some of em lived in houses and some in apartments. The white kids stopped comin because they was afraid of the blacks. But I thought if they could go to school with em, why couldn't they come to the centers with em?

People from other places come here and cause disturbances, and Columbia teens get blamed for somethin they didn't have anything to do with. Like they're gonna stop havin rock concerts this summer because they say Columbia teens doesn't know how to act. But fights mostly start with people from other places. Columbia teens are involved in it, but they're not the main ones who start trouble. They can't go to the city and get the people who come out here and start it, so they blame it on the teens that's here.

This rock group come out here last summer, and the kids tore down a fence. Then there was fightin with the guards and everything. The guards are mainly white. They're not really policemen; they don't carry a weapon. They're like security, and they don't arrest people too much. They just try to stop it. I think that fight was probably started by the visitors, and then Columbia got involved in it.

I don't think we'd have fights if people didn't come in from the city. When we have parties with just Columbia teens, there's no fightin or nothin cause everybody knows each other and there's no problem. But if some other kids hear about a party and come out here, that's when the trouble starts.

There was a lotta trouble in the teen center that was mainly from Columbia kids, and the man would come and arrest people. Seems like there's a lotta drugs over here because it's a small city. Most of my friends take drugs. That's fine; if they wanna take drugs, they can go ahead.

I tried it myself. I smoked reefers, took pills, but I stopped about a year ago because I took acid and had a bad trip. It scared me, really; it was my first time and I didn't know anything about it. It was like seein colors and just a lotta hallucinatin things, things that aren't really there, but you're seein em. I went to the hospital the next day because I was scared. My mother called over there, and they told her to bring me over and not to give me anything. I don't remember what happened to me in the hospital.

After that, I got very paranoid. It happens real fast when I'm home by myself. If I don't have anything to do, I just start thinkin about my trip and get paranoid. Mainly, that's all I think about. I think it's gonna come back cause people tellin me about flashbacks. I haven't had one yet, and I don't think it'll ever come because it's been a year now. But some people say it could come in two years, in five years.

My girlfriend, she said acid was better than drinkin. Drinkin supposed to do somethin to your insides and mess you up. So she say, "If you take this, it won't hurt you. You'll just feel high like you're drinkin." But it wasn't a high like I was drinkin; it wasn't a sleepy high, nothin like that. I couldn't go to sleep. Seemed like everything was just different, like I was in another world where people were different. They looked strange.

One time I took a downer; that gives you a feelin like you've been drinkin too much. And I used to smoke reefers, but a reefer is not really a drug. It's a natural thing; it grows. Drugs are somethin the doctors have to make; somebody has to make it.

A lotta kids in Columbia are takin acid and stuff; they take it like candy. My girlfriend who gave me the acid started takin heroin. She's on methadone now, and she's goin to the clinic. I hardly see her now.

When I was havin this problem with acid, the hospital thought I should see a counselor. But it was kinda hard to talk to her because I didn't know her. She wasn't a friend. To me, she was just a counselor who tried to convince me that I had a problem. And I couldn't see what my problem was; I didn't think I had a problem. So it didn't help me because I was gonna do what I wanted to do anyway.

My mother, she seems to drink too much. I think she has hypertension, and she fusses all the time. If she's not drinkin, she's fussin, so I'd rather to see her drink than to fuss because when she drinks she's relaxed. We get along right good when she's drinkin.

She can't relax without two or three beers a day, and on weekends I don't know how many beers she has. She doesn't drink whiskey or nothin like that; it's just beer. And she says, "What do you want me to do, go out on the streets like most mothers and stay out all the time?" I say, "Why don't you just live? You can go out sometimes." She says if she doesn't drink beer, then she's gonna go out every night. I say, "Well, you can go out some nights." But I guess she'd rather drink.

Me and Mrs. Bonnoli upstairs talk a lot; I babysit for em. I was tellin her about my mother drinks too much, and she tried to talk to her. They would go out and she'd try to get my mother's mind offa drinkin, go bowlin or go shoppin. It helped me to talk to her, but I don't think it helped my mother any. She told me not to worry about my mother, but it didn't change things. The Bonnolis used to complain about my brother makin noise, but I liked em.

My brother's bass sounds good with all the music, but without the drums or anything, it just rattles the house. We get along very good except we argue about the bass. Also, he was goin with a white girl, and my friends didn't like it too much. There was a few black and white couples in the school goin together. They put him down, called him Tom.

I don't like Verna's children too much because every time they come in my house somethin is missin. One time my little sister saved up $5 for a Christmas present for my mother, and it was gone when one of Verna's children was here. It was the youngest girl that took it; she was friends with my little sister. Her sister told me she was stealin in school. She took the teacher's pocketbook, and she would steal from us a lot.

Verna is nice, but she's more close to my mother than to me. But I'm afraid of Albin because he threatened my brother one time they had an argument. He threatened to kill him. Mostly, I don't associate with people in Underhill because I'm too busy.

I only have one real friend; she's my best friend. She's black but she didn't used to associate with no black people at all. I asked her why did she always be with white people, and she said so that she could get high. She just liked to get high, and they always had somethin for the head. Drugs, you know. She just started hangin with black people all of a sudden, and I didn't know why. She said she didn't need em any more cause she stopped takin drugs.

My friends are black by choice. I wouldn't know how to cope with bein friends with a white person because I never had a white friend. I'd speak to em now and then, talk to em sometimes in school, but not really friends. I figure like I wasn't friends with em before I moved here, so why should I now? White people exist to me, but I just don't like bein around em because I feel strange. It's probably because of our history, black history, and a lotta things that happened before. I would like to see it change, but I couldn't change it. I don't think anybody could change it, not right now, maybe 200 years from now.

Like in my black studies class, we have some white people in it, and we talk to em and everything. One girl said why do I feel the way I do; why do I have to take somethin out on em now for what happened 500 years ago. I just said, "I'm not takin anything out on you. That's the way I feel, and it's still happenin now." Our black studies teacher said that a black man can go to college for four years and a white man can have four years of high school and they both get paid the same. But I didn't need to learn that in my black history course because I've been taught all that by my mother.

A lotta black women work, and a lotta white women don't work. A lot of em stay home. My mother works all the time and she's never home. She has two years of college, but I don't think she gets paid enough. She'll tell me things like white women at her job, half of em can't do anything. She knows how to do it and they always come at her, ask her to do things for em. So if she can do it, how come she's not gettin paid the same money they are?

I figure we're free, but not really free. We can go anywhere we want or do anything we want, but not for job opportunities. The history of slavery doesn't bother me really, because that's the past. What bothers me is today, what's happenin today.

I put in an application at this restaurant near where I live, and this man kept on saying. "Come back this week; come back next week." That's how it went for a while, and then I finally told him, "Look, I really need a job; I'm tired of waitin." I told him I thought he was prejudiced. He said, "No, that isn't true." I guess after me tellin him how I really felt he just hired me. He called me the next day and hired me. I was the first black girl that started in, so I guess there was prejudice. But that's everywhere in Columbia.

I don't know how people can go around sayin "black power" and then rob you in the next five minutes. Black people don't stick together. They just stick together when it comes to fightin. But why do they kill each other all the time, break in each other's houses all the time? Black power is just a word; we have no power. You never heard of a black president or anything like that. Then maybe you could say, "black power."

I figure like if the white man wants to wipe us out, he could right now. Because half of us are on drugs. A lotta white people are on drugs, too. But if they wanted to wipe out half the blacks, the only thing they'd have to do is put pure heroin in the heart of the city. A lotta blacks would die because heroin is not pure on the streets. It's cut with somethin else.

A lotta white people would like this. I mean the other day, it was funny. My mother gave me this number to call and this man gets on the phone and says, "Send the niggers back to Africa." Talks about niggers this and niggers that. He said that we are destroyin them, goin out with their women. I guess there's a lotta white people who feel that they'd wanna send us back to Africa. And when we go over there, they don't want us because I guess we're mixed.

In my black studies class the other day, this one guy who spent eight years in Africa said, "There's no prejudice there. They consider white people foreigners and it's a completely different world." He said, "There's no drugs in Africa; the only thing they do is drink." I would like to visit there and maybe after I'd visited and seen how it was, maybe I would like to live there. I'd like to visit all the other countries because the United States is just fallin apart. It's about the only country that really has a lotta drugs.

I wouldn't go out with a white boy because I would feel like I was committin a sin or somethin. The Black Muslims say if a black woman goes out with a white man, it's like committin a sin. The same if a black man goes out with a white woman. I believe in a lotta their rules, like not eatin pork. When we were slaves, they used to take the pig and cut all the good meat off and give us the garbage left. That's what they call soul food, chittlins and stuff. Some of the things the Muslims say is true, like don't eat soul food.

I've been readin a lot about the Muslims; it's just started here in Columbia. This man from the city teaches religion and karate at the center. A lotta my friends are Muslims; it appeals mostly to the younger people. It's not violent; it's like a religion.

I never have believed in violence. I wasn't involved in the riots, but I was livin in the city when it happened there, about Martin Luther King. I didn't know too much about it then cause I was younger, but I don't see what you're gonna prove by violence. I think you should use your brain and you would gain more than by fightin all the time. You would gain more by tryin to talk about things.

Livin in Columbia is better than livin where I used to, in the city, because it's cleaner. You can walk around the streets at night here, but you can't in the city. And livin here in Columbia is more comfortable because it's not as crowded. A lotta people work up to get to a place like this. But for me, it's like a dream world. There's no crime, the school system is different, and it closes at ten o'clock. I wanna live here, but I wanna leave, too.

Right now if we lived in the city, we wouldn't be considered poor. But in Columbia you're considered poor if you live in this kind of housing. Mostly all the blacks live in the projects. It's like there's a lower class black group and a higher class black group. The higher class people, they live in the houses, and the lower income people live in apartments or projects. There's not one group in Columbia. There's the higher class and the lower class.

The higher class blacks don't really put you down; they just speak to you. Half of em drive, and they go out of Columbia with their other friends. They talk about how much good times they have in the city. I've never really tried to associate with em because they've never tried to associate with me. I guess I wouldn't mind livin here if I had a car, so I could get out when I wanted to.

My girlfriend, she lived in a real big house. It was real pretty. I think they lost it, and that's why they moved to the project. But she was still friends with me when she was higher class. She wanted to be with lower class people all the time. She didn't wanna be with higher class people because she felt they were prejudiced against the lower class. They felt they couldn't be with em because they lived in big houses, and we lived in little ones. But she was different than the others.

I don't think about friendships right now because I don't wanna get involved with a boyfriend. That's somethin I wanna do when I get older, have a boyfriend. This place is so small mostly all of the girls have boyfriends they've been goin with for two years. I have a boyfriend in the city who comes out weekends, but not like my other girlfriends. They have babies, and I don't wanna have any, not right now. I wanna meet all kinds of boys so I can choose the best.

None of my friends who have babies are married. There's about five of em, about 16, 17, or 18 years old. I think it was kinda good to have em in a way, and in a way kinda bad because they're not finished school yet. It's beautiful to bring another person into the world, but not when you're 18 and not finished school. But I guess they didn't wanna kill it. I think they should have, though. Because I don't think they're ready for havin babies without bein married. Half of em used birth control for awhile, and half of em has had abortions before. I guess they got tired of havin abortions so they went on and had the babies.

I don't wanna have any children now because I'm not gonna have time. I might have one child, but havin children is too much to me. My mother has children, and it seems like it's hard for her to raise us. I just wanna go places and meet other people and get out of Columbia.

I stay in the house most of the time, but when I go out, it's out of Columbia. I'm tired of seein the same faces; I just wanna go places. Columbia is just like a little city that closes early every night. If you're stranded somewhere, you can't catch the bus, you can't call a cab. You have to call your family to get you.

I feel like when I go back to the city, I'm not gonna be ready for life. It's gonna be a whole new different thing. Because when I go to New York every summer to be with my relatives, it's like a different life; everything is different. It's more interesting because it's different. I just like the city; I don't know why.

They don't have any shows or good movies here. The things that I like is not in Columbia, like black pictures and shows. Black movies, that's the kind I like. But they don't have em here. And I like seein new people. There's more excitement in the city than it is out here. Here it seems like I see the same faces every day, or go to the same mall every day.

Here in Columbia, I only enjoy the swimmin. I tried ice skatin a couple of times, but I didn't know how. Once I worked to earn a membership so I could go to the pool, but I wouldn't do it again. I could be doin somethin else and gettin paid for it. I like money now; I just like to get paid.

I'm tryin to decide what I wanna be or what I wanna do. I know that I don't wanna have any children right now. And I know I won't take drugs. I just like workin in my job. But I can't seem to do anything at school. I didn't learn anything in the open space school. I went to class and everything, but the teachers just gave you a book and said, "Do it." They didn't force you to do anything. It seems like it's takin too long. I might just quit and go and take the high school proficiency test. If I pass it, I will likely get a job durin the day and go to college at night for math. I'm good in math and English.

I guess things have improved for black people; a lot of 'em can go to college now. Maybe it's gonna be better for me, too, because I can do just about anything a white person can. My future is to see my family get up, like havin somethin, a household, just havin things that white people have out here.

I guess I've matured more than I was before. I used to be very prejudiced. I just hated white people, but I didn't know why. My feelins about whites are startin to change a little, probably from me workin with em. I can judge people as people now. And I think I can be friends with a white person, too. Just like I could with a black person. It all depends on the things that I like to do, maybe they'd like to do the same things. But if I had to be around em all the time, I guess I would feel uncomfortable.

COMMENT

The change to "better surroundings" has not substantially improved the lives of Clara and Karen Hunt. In the middle class setting of Columbia, they encounter problems similar to those they faced previously—drugs, community conflict, and rejection. When a new manager evicts them for falling behind in their rent, they are forced to move to a smaller apartment in a less desirable project in Columbia.

The Hunts and others in similar circumstances are brought to places like Columbia in order to counter the trend of urban populations toward racial and socioeconomic separation. It is believed that urban poverty can best be attacked by reducing spatial concentrations of the poor and minorities and increasing their accessibility to suburban job opportunities and housing.

As a matter of public policy, a dispersal strategy has been developed to facilitate the movement of such families to middle class communities. But for people like the Hunts, the loss of the protective environment of family and friends is very threatening and limits the possibilities for success. They are victimized by a process of mobility and work transition that is accompanied by social and friend transition. The social identity that existed with family and neighborhood breaks down as they lose the benefits of a safe home in a secure and stable environment.

Life is also difficult in a community where poor and near-poor people are looked down upon by their neighbors. The experiences of Clara and Karen are especially tragic because they are ostracized by blacks with higher incomes and different life styles. Adding to the problems of adjustment are the interpersonal and intergroup conflicts that stem from their perceptions of racial injustice and inequality. Generational differences underscore the trauma inherent in their situations: Clara deplores the gap between the races, while Karen acts out her hatred of white people.

The difficulties faced by families just above the poverty category are not dealt with effectively by the fragmented mechanisms of government. A welfare apparatus that provides benefits to some of their neighbors is tantalizingly close and often inaccessible. But even when they are receiving help, many of the families living in Underhill look forward to the time when they can be self-sufficient and escape the machinery of the welfare state.

Chapter 7

VERNA SMITH
Bringing Your Problems with You

When I was ten years old, I was sent away to the deaf school. My mother had got on public assistance when she and my father separated, and her social worker told her about this school I could go to. I've been almost deaf since my hearing was damaged by illness when I was six years old.

The social worker and my mother brought me to the school, but I was scared. If you have very little hearing and you go to a strange place, why automatically you're afraid. It's like if you used to be at home with your parent and you go someplace you don't know anything about.

The girls at the school and the teachers were very friendly and helpful. Of course, I got a little homesick cause I was used to bein around my mother. We had a housemother there and she made me feel at home, but she wasn't like bein home with mama.

It was a boardin school and I would come home on holidays. At Christmas or Thanksgivin when it was time to go home, I was happy cause I'd be lookin forward to seein my brothers and sisters. Sometimes my aunt came out there with my mother at Christmas time to bring the kids gifts. Then when I became a teenager, I learned how to come home on the weekends on a bus.

The school taught me home economics, geography, keepin house, cookin, and things like that. I also learned lip readin and sign language. All I can remember about my teen years was goin to school and sometimes goin out on picnics. I went until I was 18 and I was in the eighth grade. You see, I didn't go to no school before I was ten.

After my parents were separated, my mother had to work. She had four boys and three girls to take care of, but we always had food to eat. We probably didn't have the best of clothin, but we had clothes to wear. I was taken care of by my two elder brothers when she went off to work. My mother did domestic work, but now she's not workin because of a heart condition and high blood pressure. She's more concerned about me than she is about the other kids because of my hearin condition. Right now my 14-year-old son is visitin her for the summer.

When I came back to Washington after school, I got married right away. I had known my husband since I was 16. We lived in a lot of places, but I didn't like it too good. There's more crime in Washington, and lots of times kids get kidnapped or someone would pass narcotics around in candy. Although my kids didn't get any of them, I know they were passin narcotics around in the schools.

I always dreamed of bein a teacher and teachin the deaf, but then I got pregnant with my first kid. So I said, "There goes the dream." We had seven kids who are livin and we lost one. There was no happiness when I was with my husband; I was always unhappy. When we were together, I stayed in the house most of the time. I didn't have friends cause I didn't go anywhere. We were married 18 years and I stayed home all that time.

He was irresponsible; that's why we're separated. Like he worked drivin a truck when he wanted to. When you have seven kids and you're raisin a family, you can't work when you want to. I guess we did have some happy times together when he wasn't drinkin. That interfered with his job cause when he would drink a lot, he wouldn't go to work.

Once when I was carryin James, he hit me in the eye and knocked me down the steps. The left eye was completely closed and I couldn't see at all for a whole night and a whole day. Next day my mother took me to the hospital, and they put some medicine in my eye. Slowly my vision started comin back into it. I didn't press any charges against him because I was afraid to.

He would also beat the children with belts. He whipped Gloria with a cord when she was about two years old, and she has the mark on her now. I don't think he was drinkin that night; he just had a quick temper. You know how babies keep cryin and whinin, and so she kept on doin it. When she wouldn't stop, he ran in and whipped her.

When James was about ten months old, we separated for a year because of the fact that he wouldn't pay the rent and he wouldn't buy any food. The landlord and his wife was friends of mine so they thought that I would be better without him. They didn't put me out; they told him he had to leave because he didn't pay the rent. So I went down and got Public Assistance, and we stayed separated for a year. He kept comin around beggin me to come back to him and he would do better. We finally got back together, and instead of bein better he was worse. I stayed with him up until six years ago, and that's when he left me. He's somewhere in Washington, I presume, but I haven't heard from him since then.

I worked for awhile near Washington doin assemblin in a factory. Then my son's godfather told me about a new community in Maryland and we moved. I didn't work there because I didn't have a counselor to help me find a job. I also didn't work because I didn't know how to ride the buses.

We had a nice apartment in a public housin project, except it would get flooded a lot of times. When it rained, the water would come all in the apartment and mess up the furniture and the rug.

After the first year, the people had tore the place down and started havin narcotics in the schools and everything. They had a lot of crime and race in the neighborhood, and you couldn't let the kids outside and play. You had to bring them in the house at nighttime. I talked with my son's godfather, and he told me he knew a friend that was out here in Columbia. He asked me whether I would be interested in movin out here, and I told him I would, because I wanted the kids brought up in a different neighborhood than that.

My seven children are from seven to 17 years old. Gloria is the baby; then there's Shirley, who's eight; Anna, who's ten; Barbara, who's 12; and Ellen is 13. The two boys are older—James is 15 and Albin 17. They seem to be pretty good kids; they're obedient and they get very good report cards. I think they're doin very well. Sometimes you hear fights and things with the other kids, but it's nothin serious.

Ever since she was small, my 13-year-old girl would go with me to the store to help with my shoppin. If she didn't know where a certain kind of food was, she'd ask people in the store and they'd tell her or show her. She's also very helpful with the telephone, like takin messages.

But I have problems with the two oldest boys; they're both in jail right now. The oldest was found guilty of robbery, and the other one is waitin for trial on stealin a car. Albin was accused of holdin up a store at the village center. They said he got angry when they didn't move fast enough and roughed up the clerk. Although he's only 17, he was tried as an adult because armed robbery is considered an adult crime. I've had problems with him before, like not goin to school, gettin into trouble in the schools, breakin and enterin, burglary, things like that. He's been arrested before but this is his first time bein in the jail. They usually sent him to the juvenile halls and the children's center.

I would talk with him but he wouldn't seem to pay any attention. Seems like it went in one ear and out the other. He got along with his brother and sisters up until the point when he would try to boss them around. He and James didn't get along too good. But he seemed to get along with the girls in the neighborhood, except he would try to be bossy like.

When Albin first started to walk, he was real bowlegged. He would walk with his legs open wide, and kids would laugh at him and tease him. His grandmother would get highly upset. He had to wear those corrective shoes; they had them on boards and he had to sleep in them. They wanted to break his legs but I didn't give permission. So instead he wore those corrective shoes for about six months.

He liked to play with the other kids but, when he was a baby, he wasn't very friendly. He would never smile, like when I'd take him to the clinic, the doctor would tell me to try to get him to smile but he never would. His father didn't take any interest in him. You know like fathers would take the boys to a ball game or take them to a movie or somethin like that. But he never did that with them; he never took them anywhere.

James has had more than Albin by him livin with his godparents for four or five years and gettin more clothes and things. His godfather is a social worker and he and his wife didn't have any kids, so they've thought of James as their own. They have been very helpful, like if I have any problems, they'll try to help. They sent James to private schools and camps in the summer and like that. James would always brag about havin more than Albin. That would make Albin angry and they would get into arguments. James also had a higher I.Q. than Albin, and they'd argue all the time about who was smarter.

James has been runnin away from home ever since he was about six or seven. At that time, my husband worked partially. James was in school and he didn't have sufficient clothin to wear, so the kids would make fun of him because of his clothin. He just wouldn't go to school; he'd run away from home, and I would call the police and they would find him asleep in some empty house or sometimes on a curb, anywhere. It got to the point that he kept runnin away and stealin things, so they put him in a junior village when he was around nine and he stayed there till he was about 11 years old.

That's when we met James's godparents. We were livin in a basement apartment in Washington, and they came around and asked us if we would like to move into a house that was larger than the apartment. So we said yes, and they got us a large furnished house. This was where they first took an interest in James. He had started to get in trouble again, and he had to go to court. That's when they said they would take responsibility for him. They've been his legal guardians since then and they still are.

James was in a private school in Ohio when his godfather got us a place out here in Underhill. He thought that by movin him to a new neighborhood James could adjust. They took him out of that school and brought him home and enrolled him in the high school here. He went there a few times, and the times he went he would go in the front door and out the back door. Then he met some boys around here and he started drinkin in places and stealin cars and gettin into trouble.

I don't sleep all through the night, so I'd get up and come out to the kitchen and I'd notice that James' door was open. I would go in his room and I would see the window open where he had climbed through, and he would be gone. The front door would be locked, so I know he couldn't have gone out there. I don't know when he left, and I wouldn't know when he came back.

He's in the county jail now, and I think he is gonna be there for months before trial. He's accused of stealin a car and robbery, and he's gonna be tried as an adult. I talked with him about it, but he doesn't talk much to me. He just seems to clam up, you know. I asked him did he do these things, and he said stealin the car he did, but as far as robbery, he didn't do it.

His godfather had this lawyer workin on this thing and they said they got James mixed up with another boy. The lawyer's gonna try to get his trial earlier, and they're gonna send him to the State Hospital for mental evaluation as soon as they can get an empty room. They sent him to another place before, but he ran away from there over a ten foot wall and barbed wire. They caught him about three weeks later at a friend's house. I didn't hear from him at all durin that time; he didn't contact me.

I was kind of frightened when I found out I was movin to Columbia, because I didn't have much hearin and because I had the kids. I felt like I was alone, and I was nervous. I had got to know the place I was livin in pretty good, and I was kind of frightened about movin away out here with just the kids and myself. But when we moved in, the manager and the people made us feel welcome. You know like he's not only a manager; he's a friend. If I have problems with somethin, I can go and talk with him about them. So I like it out here; it's very nice.

The first day that we moved here, they had a note on the door sayin, "Welcome to Underhill." Then the manager introduced some of the neighbors to me, and eveybody was very nice and helpful. It didn't take me too long at all to settle down here. Once I get in a place and I learn my way around and learn the people and everything, I feel very comfortable like I do here. I was made to feel at home like the first day I moved in.

I love it here because it's so beautiful, and I like the schools that the kids go to. I think the neighborhood is better and the kids have a better chance out here than they would in D.C. They have a lot of opportunities like ice skatin, swimmin pools, miniature golf, and roller skatin. The only problem was that I had to pay for them because I'm not a member of the place. Still, they do different things and they have different activities; they never had those where we used to live.

When we moved in, they explained the rules here like havin no pets. We had a big dog, but we had got rid of it before we moved, so it wasn't a problem. They also told me all about the schools here, how far they were and how they would get free lunches. A little bit before school opened, one of my neighbors took my kids up there to fill out the forms. That's Clara Hunt, who's a very good friend. She was the first one I met when I moved out here and she was very helpful.

I have also had help from some of the organizations in the county, like public assistance for dependent children from the Department of Social Services. Since my kids and I are on welfare, we have a Medical Assistance Card that entitles us to use the clinic here. Once I had to take a physical before I could get a job, and then my little daughter went there for some kind of rash on her head. The doctors were very friendly and we liked the treatment we got.

I had trouble in gettin my food stamp coupons transferred when I first moved here, so Community Action gave us the food. They were also the ones that gave us a basket at Christmas time. Then Archie told someone at the company that's buildin the town about my family. This man called me and asked if one of my kids would be interested in goin to camp for three weeks, and I sent my oldest daughter. I got some of her camp clothes free from the Christian Women's Thrift Shop.

The Department of Social Services said since I wasn't havin any problems, that I didn't need a social worker. But if I did, I could call them. I told the manager I needed some help, so he got in touch with the Children's Aid and Family Service Agency and they sent someone to see me. She comes to visit me approximately once a week, and like if I have any problems with the kids or anything, she'll try and help me solve them. Most of the time she's helpful, but if I can't get in touch with her, I'll talk with my manager and he'll try to help me.

I was havin a lot of problems, like I had developed a nervous condition and I was hysterical. So I would talk with my counselor and tell her my problems and everything. And then when I was havin trouble with my two oldest sons, she would talk to me about them. Like, for instance, when my 17-year-old quit school and he wouldn't get a job, all he'd do was lay around the house and he wouldn't do anything. She advised me that if he wouldn't get a job and he didn't want to go to school, just ask him to leave.

I love my apartment. It's large enough, and I like the air conditionin and the patio outside. I can go and sit outside and it's very nice. And we have good service here, like if there's anything wrong, we call the maintenance man and he'll fix it. When my garbage disposal was leakin, we called the maintenance man and he put in a new one.

Then we had a Tenants Council here and I would go to some of the meetins. There was a problem when the kids would mess up around the buildin, like droppin paper or trash all over the ground. They suggested that instead of the kids puttin trash on the ground, they put it over in the dust bins. The kids around this buildin seem to be pretty helpful about doin it.

Livin down here with just the kids and myself, sometimes I get frightened. Aunt Matty upstairs said last night someone was tryin to get in her apartment right up there on the second floor. So like I think if they'd try to get in her apartment, maybe they'd try to get in my apartment. See there's nobody down here but my kids and myself. We keep the doors locked and the windows locked here. There's a bar on the door in the back, and we have locks on the windows and everything.

Then we had another big problem upstairs with the Bonnolis. It was in the afternoon, and my kids said it sounded like Wally was breakin up tables or somethin. Then he kicked in the front door, plus the door was off in the bedroom. I don't know how he did it, but that heavy metal front door was off. There were holes in the walls and a lot of damage to the apartment.

May sent her little boy down here to tell me that Wally was loadin a gun and she was afraid he was mental. So she asked my kids to call the police because she couldn't get to the phone. I didn't want us to interfere, but she said it was a matter of life or death, so we called the police. Then she grabbed the kids and came runnin out of the apartment. By this time, Gary Hunt upstairs had heard about it, so he pushed them into his apartment. Before the police could get there, Wally had left. The police came and he asked May what happened, and she told him. He had beat her pretty bad, but she was not seriously injured. They went and got him and they found a gun on him. They took the gun, handcuffed him, and took him down to the jail.

The followin day, they went to court for the purpose of havin him committed to the State Hospital for an evaluation. But instead of recommendin that he be committed, they said he needed marital counselin. They were plannin to release him on probation, but May was frightened and didn't feel good about lettin him home.

That night, one of May's friends called and said Wally was tryin to get in their front door. May said it couldn't be Wally because he was still in jail. But it was Wally; someone had paid his bail and they let him out. Later, May said he was home and actin calm, but I was frightened. The next day he committed himself to the State Hospital. They said he did this to show he didn't know what he was doin.

While all this was goin on, May went to Social Services for help because she had no money or food for the kids. They said they couldn't see her for a week or ten days because there were lots of emergencies. But Archie went to them, and they saw her the next day.

Some of the people here heard that Wally had also been havin trouble on the job. The boss was complainin that he was pushin one of the workers too hard. He was afraid he might lose him. They said Wally picked him up and shook him and called him a dirty nigger. The boss told May he wasn't goin to take Wally back until he had some counselin and was ready to work.

May used to complain a lot if the kids would play the record player. She would complain about the bass on it and we would turn it down. We never said anything back to her; we'd just cut it down. People would say that I was stupid, but I didn't want any confusion. I couldn't tell how much noise that thing was makin, so we just cut it down. They made a lot of noise, but we didn't complain about it. The kids heard them arguin and fightin all the time, and him tearin up things and the babies screamin and cryin. That's been a lot of times, but we didn't say anything.

Clara and I didn't get along sometimes. I don't guess you would call them problems, but she used to put my kids down and I didn't like it. You know, like she'd put hers on a pedestal and put mine down. I don't think there are any kids that are perfect, but I didn't say anything to her. When this thing about James happened, she would talk about it, but I told her I didn't want to discuss it. Sometimes I have to keep Clara's little girl, like when she's at work and the school calls and tells her that Julia is sick. I guess she's sick a lot because of the asthma. Clara made an arrangement for me to keep her until she comes back from work.

I had this man livin with me here for awhile, but I found out that he was just a user. So I told him that he would have to leave. I mean he wanted somethin for nothin. And another thing, he reminded me of my husband. He'd drink a lot and he didn't want to half work, so I just told him I couldn't use that.

He wanted to stay, makin different promises that he would stop drinkin and go to AA. He said he would get a steady job, and he would sit down and talk with my counselor and try to solve his problems. I guess he was here on and off for ten or twelve months, but I knew him before I moved here. The kids seemed to like him because he gave them attention, and he would take them places and buy them things. But that's not the same as him not drinkin and half workin; those are different things.

I don't go anywhere too much; I stay around the house. Once in awhile I go out to my friend's house, but otherwise I just stay in the house cause I don't know too many people around here. My friend lives here in Underhill, and a lot of times if I have problems or somethin, I'll walk down the street and talk with her.

I was workin for about four months, and at first I was assemblin things. Then I started makin mops and later we were doin different kinds of boxes. The problem was I made like about $12 a week, and they took that out of my assistance grant. I don't think they should have done that. People in Washington on public assistance are workin and makin lots more money than what I was, and they don't take their money out.

My boss, he wrote them a letter tellin them that I wasn't workin any more, and they're supposed to be addin back on to my grant the money they took out. He told them that when I did come back to work, he would let them know. We didn't make that much for them to take it out of the grant. So I said, "Well, I might as well stay at home."

I would rather work and support my own kids instead of havin public assistance. That would make me feel better. I would also like to have a house of my own instead of an apartment, cause if we were livin in a house, the kids would have their own backyard and their own basement to entertain. Mostly, what I want out of life is my own home and to support my own kids. I don't want to ever marry again. Some people say all marriages are not alike, but even so, I don't want to remarry.

The most important thing for me is to do things by myself, like I do my own laundry and housework and cookin. Some people come in, and they'll be impressed how clean the house is and how good I have it organized. I try to keep it clean because that's the way my mother taught me. I have gotten compliments from a lot of people, and that makes you feel good and try harder.

I guess I'm glad we came here because the kids and I are very happy. They have sports and things and I have my friends I go out with once in awhile. And I've gotten notes from their teachers sayin how well they did in school and how proud they were of them. I have all this and my apartment, so I think my life has improved a lot in Underhill.

COMMENT

Before the advent of the modern welfare state, many of the social services provided for those in need were under the aegis of the family, the church, and voluntary associations. With the burgeoning mobility of millions of people, these institutions are far less able to provide help and to cushion the shock of social disruption and economic distress.

The public sector is increasingly taking over the responsibilities of home and neighborhood, with the result that people like the Smiths are cut off from the support systems of friends and family. For Verna, the situation is exacerbated by her handicapped condition, which adds to the anxiety she feels at living in a new and strange place. The change of managers and Clara's move to another project make Verna more alone and frightened than ever.

Community and neighborhood are closely linked to the family for most Americans. Despite the counterculture and high divorce rates, the family continues to hold a central place in our lives. Individuals need strong families in order to grow up, develop a meaningful sense of identity, and maintain a set of values. For many people, the family is the most valuable thing to which they can attach themselves; it is an institution to which they have made a moral and emotional commitment.

The lack of the sheltered environment usually afforded by home and community is felt most keenly by the poor and near-poor, who are ill equipped to handle the displacement and disruption that are so much a part of contemporary urban culture. This is particularly true for Verna's two sons, who do not have the social and psychological resources needed to overcome the problems they bring with them to Columbia. The inadequate and complex bureaucracies of the welfare state add to the difficulties faced by Verna and her family. Verna's wish to be self-sufficient is frustrated by the rules of the Aid to Dependent Children program, which take away her income as well as her desire to remain employed. This points up the contradictions of a welfare system that seeks to impose vigorous work requirements while at the same time effectively stifling motivation to work.

The assumption that social services delivered by public agencies will improve the lives of those who receive them is challenged by a growing body of data that underscores the inability of government to effectively manage its institutions. Situations such as those facing the families of Underhill indicate that existing programs are fragmented and often not helpful, so that the welfare system offers little promise of improving the lives of its beneficiaries.

Chapter 8

JOE CORBIN
Escaping the Welfare State

We lived up there in Harperville 14 years, and every couple of years we'd get water in the basement. But this last flood that we had from the hurricane come all the way up to the roof, like six inches from touchin the ceilin in the upstairs livin quarters. The flood took both the porches off, the front and the back, and all the furniture and everything in the house was completely lost.

Year before last, we lost what was in the basement and my tool shed. The neighbors next door, their house sits lower, and the water come in on em and ruined their baseboard heatin and their carpets and got up on their furniture. But there never was nothin like this flood; we was completely totalled out.

Actually, this flood here was the river, but the one that we had year before last was from a little stream in the back. We had a bridge that went across the river below us, and they also had a quarry on the other side. This quarry got permission to put piers underneath the bridge. Then all this debris from dead trees and everything that were layin in the river banks come down and hit against the abutments underneath the bridge. It build a barricade which backed the water up to the little stream, and then it backed up into the houses. Three of em was almost total and one partially total.

This time it was all over the place; there was lots of em gone, houses and industries. This cotton mill had gotten completely wiped out which they have no intentions of openin up. And the plant where I used to work, it was just gutted, ripped all apart. It took em approximately a year to reopen.

We was up that night and when this water come up, we expected it. I had some stuff in the shed, a garden tractor, lawn mower, motorcycles, stuff like that which we pushed up to higher ground. We went down there in the basement and stood everything up high because it usually just gets up maybe a foot. But the water was still comin up; I guess it was three or four foot in the backyard.

I seen the water was near to my electric panel in the basement, so I was on the phone tryin to get hold of the electric company. I wanted em to come out and cut the service off, so it wouldn't spark and burn the house down. Meantime, my wife, Sally, and the kids, they was on the way out. The house was on a slope and there was policemen up on the bank yellin, "Get outta there; get outta there." I didn't know it was comin up that fast, but then I looked out and seen it. The only thing I could do was hang the phone up and head for the front road. By that time, it was up to my waist in the front yard. We got into our automobiles and drove to higher ground, hopin that it would diminish. It goes down purty fast when it stops. But we got stuck on the hill in between the flood and the washed out road, which we had to sit there all night in our automobile. We was afraid to go either way. We turned the car motor on to keep warm and turned it off; we like to froze. And the only thing we come out with was what was on us, a pair of boots and clothes; that was the only thing we had.

When we got back into the house, which was on the next day real late, we waded through about 14 or 16 inches of mud. All the doors had swollen, and I had to take and bust em down. Everything was just turned upside down with a curtain of slippery mud all over, just slimey mud. The only thing I could do was start throwin everything in the whole house into a pile. There was a dump truck there that hauled it away. Then we got a big fire pump and a big fire hose and went through the whole house washin it all down. I had to redec the whole house, put new panelin up, rugs, and ceilins. I completely renovated the house to sell it because it wasn't worth anything. It took me about a year to do that.

There was this man down there with people from the Interfaith Center in Columbia helpin us shovel mud. He asked me where I was goin, and I told him I really didn't know. He said, "I'll see if I can help you." After he left, I asked this rabbi there who the gentleman was. He said, "If anybody can help you, he can, because he's a top executive of the company that's developin Columbia." Well, the next day I got a phone call said there was an apartment for us in Columbia. That's where the biggest help come.

Lots of people from the churches come down to help us dig mud, and they gave us food and everything. There was one particular family that stayed with us all the way, helped us locate furniture, and took phone calls from people that wanted to donate things. That's the way we accumulated our furniture and started over.

Help really come through Red Cross which was tremendous; no one'll talk about Red Cross to me. They set up shop down near the high school and I'd go there and see em two or three times a day. Each time I'd go they'd ask me what I lost, and I told em I lost everything completely. They would sit down and ask how many was in the family, and they would write us a check for clothin. I think it was $60 apiece they gave us to replace our clothin. We had to figure it out and they gave us what we said we needed. They also got us green stamps for us to get food, like meat and stuff that we wasn't gettin.

Then we'd go to get beds and beddin from the Thrift Shop. They said they'd rather not for us to sleep on a used mattress, so they gave us all new mattresses, linens, sheets, pillowcases, things like that. They just wrote us out a check for anything else that we could think of. In the meantime, there was used stuff where people was donatin, like toasters, irons, ironin boards, and dishes.

The food come in truckloads, more than we knew what to do with. They had this canned stuff sittin all over the church up there which got a little outta hand because they had more than they could use. They had to turn the trucks around and send em back out because it was just too much. It's just that people was overwillin to help.

No one had any flood insurance, but the federal government they gave us $5,000 clear outright. I imagine it come from the president or someplace because of the disaster. Now I don't know whether people that rented got that much or just the homeowners, but the homeowners I talked to did get the money. They also supplemented that by the money that you needed to repair your house and replace your property. If the $5,000 didn't cover it you could borrow additional money at one percent interest. I borrowed $5,000 and used that to renovate the house and get it into shape. Then, when I sold the house, I paid the government their money back.

Before the flood, I owed $4,000 on my home, and now I'm $13,000 in debt. And there are other things that we haven't replaced yet. I had a swimmin pool, tents, cannin equipment, freezer, things like that. Now I haven't got any of that, and I'm more in debt than I was before.

What happened was one of those things, but it worried Sally a lot. It didn't bother me because I'd get in and dig it out and start all over again. It was just material things which doesn't bother me too much. I considered stayin in the house, but my wife says no and I agreed with her. I didn't need much persuasion because it's gonna come again. If it didn't happen to us, it would happen to one of the kids. So the best thing was to just unload it for what I could get.

We stayed at my sister's for two weeks, and then we moved into the apartment. Actually, there wasn't nothin to it. The way it works is HUD or the federal government rents from Columbia; in other words, we subleased from HUD. The gentlemen from HUD come out to the apartment after we moved in and had us sign the leases and everything like that. I mean they didn't run us here and they didn't run us there.

There was $100 which we was supposed to pay down when we moved in, but we didn't have any money atall. I don't know who he called, but Archie made a phone call and they said, "Forget it." HUD paid for the rent for the year we was there; the only thing I paid was the utilities.

The apartment we moved in was fine, but I couldn't get used to them stair steps. We was on the third floor, and I just don't like movin up and down staircases. It looked real good to us, though. We come out of that flood, and we didn't even care what it was. We could of even laid on the floor if we had a roof over our head.

It's hard for us to say how good apartments is here because we never lived in anything like this before. We was in an apartment the first couple of years of our marriage, but then we moved out in the country and forgot all about how to live in apartments. You can hear everything that goes on; there's a lot of the noise carries down through the floor.

I heard from a neighbor that Elmer Turnfinder, the man under me, would run down to the manager's office sayin that we was makin noise. He didn't complain to me, but Archie did tell me not to worry about it. He said he knew that we're not there all day, and he didn't see how we could be makin noise like Elmer said we was. Archie said he was just complainin because of Mrs. Harris, the lady underneath of him. She went down and complained about them because they'd get up at say two o'clock in the mornin, and they'd wake up everybody in the stairway there. They'd slam the door, go out and slam the car doors, and be ahollerin and ahootin. I don't blame that lady; her husband's sick and you just don't get up at two o'clock in the mornin and make all kinds of noise like that. Well, after she complained, the Turnfinders got mad. They had to have somethin to say, so they complained about us.

Actually, the kids was in school all day, and I left at seven o'clock. Sally, she left at eight, and there was no one home until five o'clock in the evenin. We tiptoed around on our toes and turned the television down low where no one could hear it. We had to sit on top of it to hear our television. I didn't like livin like that.

The reason we was doin that was that the Hunts that lived next door to us was in an argument with the Bonnolis underneath em. I think every couple of days the Bonnolis would call the police to complain about the noise. They squabbled and carried on like that all the time we was there. Like the first day he moved in, I think, I heard Wally come barrelin up the steps bangin on the woman's door. She had a teenage son which does have a guitar amplifyin thing. He come home five o'clock in the evenin, and he wanted to listen to it until nine at night or somethin like this. I think it was the boy's business, you know, playin his instrument. Well, Bonnoli banged on the door and said he'd moved out of one apartment because of this stuff, and he wasn't gonna do it again, stuff like that which he didn't have no right to do. I think you got to approach people the right way. If Bonnoli had small kids sleepin, he could of come up and knocked at the door and asked them to turn it down or somethin like that, instead of gettin mad and hollerin and carryin on. Of course, their kids they'd scream and holler. That's just the way they went on. Anytime you looked out, there was the police knockin on the door. They would make up one week, and the next week the police was bangin on the door again. Once, though, they was mad at each other for a month, wouldn't speak to each other or nothin.

There was a couple of people in our section that would be out in the street late, usin all kinds of language and everything else. When you'd go down in the mornin, there'd be trash all over the staircase, paper, beer cans, just filthy. We had company on a weekend; my wife's sister come and her mother. They said, "Go downstairs and look at that filthy stairway." There was spit all over the mailboxes and clods of bubble gum right in front of the door. It was so awful they said they didn't feel like they even wanted to come in and see nobody. You know, like it made them half sick.

Our stairway was very clean when we just lived here and Mrs. Harris. It was clean until the other parties started movin in. They even had a meetin down in the manager's office about this, how dirty it was. And they was tryin to tell us they didn't think it was dirty. You know, Archie said, "I don't agree on that; it's one of the dirtiest stairways in Underhill." He said if they didn't start pickin up papers and keepin it clean, that he would start raisin their rent. They'd have to pay the maintenance man more money, since it'd take him longer to clean. But they didn't pay any attention to it. It was so filthy they were drawin rats and mice around.

It was a new apartment when we moved in there; we was the first ones to move into the section. But when the others started movin in, them roaches come in and we couldn't get rid of em. We had em crawlin on the walls, and we didn't like that. The exterminator was up twice but said he couldn't do nothin unless the whole section had it. Some of em wouldn't agree to it, and we just couldn't fight em. We'd run around with White Flag and spray the baseboards, but it didn't do any good. When you have filthy people like that, you're not gonna get rid of em.

Then Wally, he worked in construction, he'd come home with mud all over his shoes, which we're not used to. Instead of pullin his boots off down below the steps or somethin, or knockin it off at the job, he'd trot right up to his door and leave mud all the way up the steps. He was the one who said the stairway wasn't dirty.

And carts, they was forever bringin carts up there and pushin em in people's cars. One lady complained and said how much it cost to have a paint job done on her car. The manager sent a notice around that all carts had to be moved because they wasn't supposed to take em up there. Archie said he knew what family done it, and he was gonna make em pay a fine or somethin. But, you know, it's still goin on.

They planted bushes around there, and the kids would just tear em down, dig em up, stomp over the top of em. Then, you'd park your car outside and look out the window, and there'd be two or three kids on top of it, or they got a bicycle leanin up against it. I told one kid, I said, "Boy, you shouldn't do that." The first thing they were usin profanity at it, sayin it was none of your business. Then you'd come out and look your car over, and somebody done run down the side of you with a belt buckle or somethin like that. So you just learned to keep your mouth shut. If they knocked a window out, you turned your head, because if you didn't, you were gonna get it one way or the other. I just ignored the whole thing because I knew I was movin. This apartment livin didn't appeal to me.

And borrow, I never seen people borrow so much, borrow food from you and stuff. It was just from one neighbor, the Hunts. They'd come every day, twice a day, till we got so tired of em, we just kept tellin em we didn't have it. They wasn't poor; that's what got us. She dressed better than we did. She was the one that would go out and buy beer and sit on the porch and drink. And that same evenin or next mornin, she would knock on the door for coffee, or butter and eggs, milk, and things like that. Yet she could go out and buy her beer and stuff. I never saw her husband which he was in the service. I think he made pretty good money and she worked too. If they was depressed for money, I would of give it to em. But they didn't need it.

I was born on a farm near where Columbia is now, and it was a rough life. There was always hard work, seven days a week, not like today where you go out and work eight hours and come home and forget it. Farm life's not like that; it's from daylight to dark. Still, I'd like to live on a farm if I didn't

My father was farm manager for the people that owned it, which was a man in Fenton City. We had a couple of milk cows and you'd have to get up and milk em, go out and feed the rest of the cows and get the hay in. And thrashin time, it wasn't like farmin today where one farmer can take a combine down, chuck the bales up on the wagon, bag his wheat and throw it right into a truck.

My parents was wonderful, but if you done somethin wrong, you'd get the stick. My father, he never beat us; he'd just talk to us. My mother, when we got a beatin, she'd send us out to get the stick. You'd go cut your own stick and you got it, weren't no make believe, you got it. But that didn't come up too often.

Back when I was smaller, every Saturday night we'd go to the movies and go shoppin. Because we lived on a farm, we didn't do too much shoppin, just the things that we couldn't raise on the farm, like pepper, sugar, and salt. We'd put our flour in corn meal sacks and take it right to the mill and grind it.

Mama was always on the go. There was eight of us in the family and we always had a couple of boarders. The house we lived in I think had about 12 rooms. Durin thrashin time, there was always five or six ranch hands around, plus durin the war they would bring out war prisoners to work. She would always fix somethin special for em, you know.

The kitchen back in them days was as big as this whole house. You'd sit down to breakfast, one'd get up, then the other one'd sit down. You'd have a big platter of eggs and a platter of ham and a platter of bacon; then you'd have hot biscuits and gravy. You could come in any time durin the mornin, and over the top of the wood stove there was ham, bacon, and biscuits, and you could fix you a sandwich. They just wasn't runnin to the store and buyin anything because we had our own smokehouse and it was kept full of meat. The man we worked for give us the meat free, the beef, the ham, and all the chickens and eggs that we wanted. He also give us a garden plot and we grew things and canned everything we needed.

I only went to school eight years. At age 16, I quit and went to industry, to the cotton mill. Then I quit there and took care of a store for awhile. After that I become a carpenter; I learned that on the job. I worked durin the day and I'd run around at night just like any other kid, go to the sweet shop and things like that. I bought my own car, had my own motorcycle, and I had a good job.

I always wanted to go into the army, but I was cured soon after I joined. It was the first time I'd ever been away from home. That cured me of a career in the army because I wanted to get back to my hometown, to my friends. It was somethin like livin in an apartment; I was confined and couldn't roam. After that, I just wanted to get a job and raise a family and lead a good life.

My wife is 42, the same age I am, and we have four kids. She was born and raised in a house about ten miles from Fenton City. There was six in her family. She went to school as far as the eighth grade, and then her father was crippled on the job. So then she had to stay home mostly and help her mother take care of the house. They was poor, too. We didn't make this kind of money in them days.

She didn't live too far from where I lived; this was after I had left the farm. I'd go by and blow the horn, and we'd go to the movies and different places. We was 19 when we got married, and we had two boys and two girls. The oldest three are married, so we just have the one boy, 14, with us still goin to school. We've had a happy life and we got nice children.

If I could afford it, I'd love to live in Columbia, but I'd like to move around and find my section. As far as Columbia itself, I think it's wonderful; there's so much to do. My boy misses the recreation because there was always somethin for him to do, to keep busy. I mean you had everything, your swimmin pool, ice skatin in the wintertime, everything which is good for the children. This boy of mine liked it so much, we had to go hunt for him to make him come in.

The kids in Underhill, they have no kicks about playin in the street; there was too many other activities goin on for a kid even to have to get into the street. But they did anyway. They'd roller skate up and down the streets, whip down through there and grab a person's car, lean all over it. I never seen mine do it; if he'd done it, he would of got the stick.

Still, the kids was real nice in Underhill. You could leave him go out and you could trust him with em without gettin into a fight or somethin. But there was one incident happened with my boy that bothered us. He was a little mature for his age, and he didn't want to play in the center they had for them little kids seven and eight. He wanted to join the teen center, but some of the bigger boys wouldn't let him. They was colored boys stopped him in the stairway, so I wouldn't let him go back up there any more.

But he just didn't want to play with them little kids. He wanted to use the table tennis at the teen place, but they wouldn't let him come in. They said he was too young. He stayed home till the director there said he could come, but they still blocked him. So we was afraid to let him go. You get up there with some boys 17 or 18 years old, and if they didn't get him then, they'd get him at night walkin down the street.

Some of em we wouldn't let him go around with because they would hang out in the stores up there, and you could see em pickin candy just like it belonged to em. It wasn't the first time this happened; they just hadn't got caught. See, the parents didn't care; they let em go up there and stay all day Saturday. They'd leave the kids and didn't give em no money or nothin. I told him, "I don't want you up there and don't want you around em." Because he could be the very one who'd be accused. These was colored kids that done it, some of the friends that he played with. They might have blamed him if they seen him there.

Archie had a regulation that a certain age had to be off the street at ten o'clock at night. I didn't see any kids hangin around the streets in Underhill, but up around the village, you'd go up there and it made you a little shaky when you walked through. Because gangs of em would be standin around talkin. Might've been innocent; I didn't know what they was doin. I just felt shaky walkin through em because of things you've read, not what you've seen.

When we first come there, I asked Archie, "Can we have a dog here?" He said, "No. Rules and regulations." Then I said, "I don't want to get rid of my dog," and he said, "I don't know you got it; I haven't seen it." So he was real nice about it, and when we moved in, there was only one person complained about my dog and that was the Turnfinders. All the neighbors in that area said they never heard my dog, didn't know I had him until they used to see us take him out. The only time they ever heard him was when somebody would knock at the door. Well, Archie sent a notice sayin we had to get rid of the dog because the people was complainin about him. So we took him down to Sally's mother and let him stay there for about two weeks. But he got sick and wouldn't eat or anything, so we went down to see Archie and he said, "Bring him back."

They called a meetin to help us work our problems out, but it didn't help any. They was gonna make a rule to get the children together, like one mother durin the day would take em out and teach em how to pick the papers up and keep the place clean. But it didn't work, and each day Underhill had a man come around and sweep the stairwells. The people, they just didn't care; they had no responsibility. You'd think when people moved in, when they saw how other people kept clean, they would go back and try to keep their place clean. But they wouldn't.

I think you should have rules that all the stairways will be kept clean. If they could track it down and prove who is throwin trash around or destroys a tree, they ought to fine these people. I think after so many, the people ought to be asked to move, to find some kind of an area that's all blacktop, a place where they don't like trees or shrubbery or grass. If people like these things and you have another family that don't care, those two type people can't mix. If somebody keeps their house dirty, the Health Department or the management should have some kind of policy where they could come in and clean the place and exterminate it, and then charge it to the people that are doin it. I think the association that owns the place has to take the responsibility.

If they screened the families where the family would accept help and suggestions, it would probably work to mix em in this kind of housin. In my opinion, it would be a good thing. But you take one good family, and one bad family that don't even try, and it won't work. Like cases of women that has four or five kids and no husband, if they want help, you can help em. But if they don't, I don't think there's anything you can do. I personally wouldn't even want to tackle it.

I'd rather move into a section of my own type of people right off the bat and not have to worry with em. If people wants help and are willin to accept it and talk to you, you can help em. But if you say somethin to one of em, and they do somethin to destroy your property, or call the police, or spit at you, what are you goin to do? You're only human and you're gonna find someplace else to move.

The ones that don't want your help, I don't think should be livin with people that wants to give em help. If they're comin like from a slum area, they ought to keep these kind of people in a place to theirself and not mix in with other people. Archie said he'd rather for em to live here and maybe learn by people like us. But you can't teach these people anything.

And you can't put em in a section by themselves. It's proven out that if you do that the whole section is gonna drop. Maybe they ought to have a place where they have meetins they can go to, where they'll learn that this person'll help you and you listen to this person to try to make things better. But some people just won't accept it; they think you're nosin in their business, tryin to tell em what to do. And they'll say, "This is the way I wanna live." I guess there's no place for em to go; you can't just say, "You gotta get out." They're liable to move into another place and you haven't solved anything.

We've tried, and even Mrs. Harris has tried, to talk to the little kids. She'd say, "Why don't you children try to keep this place lookin cleaner than this?" And they'd stand and say, "Why, I didn't do this; I didn't do it." She'd say, "Well, whether you did or not, it wouldn't hurt you to pick the paper up and keep it clean."

All the complainin that went on in that stairway, and there're still cans of soft drink and beer layin around half full. You come along, you knock it down, and the beer's runnin all over the place. The place smells like beer, and as much trouble as we had with that stairway, it was still the same way when we left. I mean that's just one item. Now how do you take a place as a whole, when you can't even solve one little problem?

We always thought that we would sell the house and move into an apartment, but maybe it was a good think this flood happened. Now we really see what apartment life is like. Even we had it in our mind to buy one of these condominiums, this turned our heads against it. I personally don't want to live like that.

When I was livin up there in Underhill, fellow employees workin with me had it in their mind that it was strictly for colored people. They knew I was there under HUD and no rent, but they didn't think any white person should be in there atall. When you moved in there, they just thought you was there under welfare or you was too lazy to work or out for a handout. They used to kid me about it. They wasn't serious, but if you kid about somethin like that, it's on your mind that the whole section's like that.

For some reason or another, people thinks that all welfare cases are black. I don't know why. The people that I work with now, they're mostly farmers. There's only two or three of us that actually need the job; the rest of em are there for the benefits. They think everybody should work for a livin; they don't think anybody should need help. It's just their general idea. They never got out and seen it and lived with it, and seen that it is white and black and not just black.

I noticed in Underhill the last pamphlet that we got, the majority of the people was white. They was pretty close to half and half, but in the summertime you'd ride through and you might see one, two white people sittin on the steps. At the same time, you might see 200 blacks sittin on the steps. I don't know why this was, but it seemed like the colored people just wanted to sit on the steps. They had an air conditioned apartment, yet it seemed like the whole neighborhood wanted to sit on the porch. You'd ride through there and you'd think this is an all black section. But actually it wasn't.

You'd very seldom see the white children, only a few of em playin with the black. You'd only see a few whites altogether. I don't know whether they kept em in the house to themselves or what. My boy and a couple of white boys, they didn't care; they'd mix right in with em. But there had to be more white people there; they must of kept their children hid or somethin.

There wasn't any difference from what I seen between a white and a black. They got along real good; they was friendly and if they could help you, they would. One white boy that didn't live in our section, if I had to pick out who was the worst one, he would be the one. He was white, but he would get right out in the middle of the street and just say words that you wouldn't even think would come out of a man's mouth. He didn't care whether a child was standin there or not. It was to his wife, mostly. He would slap her and pull her out of the car. You could hear this all the way up to here. I mean you just don't do those things.

People might be people all over, but we just wasn't prepared for that type. We was in a small village before where there was a small church, and we wasn't used to that type of people, that type of language, and their carryin on. If somethin come up in our neighborhood, we'd sit down and talk about it. We didn't have cussin, carryin on, hootin, hollerin, and complainin.

We couldn't wait to get out. I kept sayin, "I can't wait till we get this house sold so we can buy another one and move out." See we lived out in the country so long, it just seemed like we was crammed up in an apartment. I was used to gettin out and mowin grass. And Sally missed her flowers and hangin her clothes out. To us, it was just like livin in a different world.

There's no way to express how we felt when we left Underhill. Sally was so happy, she actually cried because she was glad to get out to livin again. For me, it was like rentin a motel room; that's what it boils down to. The whole year that I was in Underhill was no more than livin in a motel room, just a place to keep the rain off your head. It was just strange to me, like I was in a different world; it was a nightmare. But bein in my own house now, it's like livin again.

COMMENT

There is no escaping the coercive character of the American welfare state and the loss of self respect it entails. For the Corbins, this loss of self respect is too high a price to pay, although they recognize how essential this help is during their time of need. The Corbins are now living in a new home not very far from Columbia, in an area unlikely to be affected by floods. Their teenage son misses the recreational opportunities of Columbia, but Joe and Sally are happy to be out of the project.

For them, as well as most other residents in the stairwell, it is the involuntary aspects of the welfare state which most thoroughly endanger their self confidence and self esteem. The sense of not having chosen one's neighbors, of not having selected one's type of housing, and of not being able to determine one's pattern of expenditures poses a serious threat to the desire to be in control of one's life and responsible for one's own conduct. For the Corbins, this experience was acute but temporary. For many others in the stairwell, however, the coerciveness of the welfare state is much more pervasive and debilitating. In seeking to help the poor, we also seek to regulate their conduct along lines that are not necessarily of their own choosing. We provide them with housing, but we also impose a population mix on their neighborhood life. We provide food stamps, but they are not negotiable for alternative expenditures that may seem more desirable from the recipients' point of view. We include a plethora of goods and services (such as the air conditioning and recreational facilities at Underhill) that may be well-intended but are not necessarily the things the poor would spend their own money on. Such amenities therefore do not carry with them a sense of responsibility for their effective management. In regulating people's expenditures, we may help them avoid painful mistakes, but we also disallow them the discretion we associate with full adulthood.

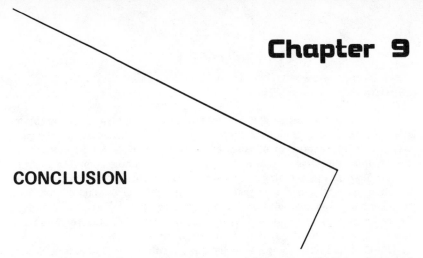

Chapter 9

CONCLUSION

Most of the families in Stairwell 7 are gone, some of them victims of their own problems and others frustrated by the inability of the welfare state to be helpful. Their narratives are a painful and dramatic illustration of the marginal position they occupy in American life. These are people who stand at the periphery of our society, neither totally destitute or nonfunctional, nor clearly able to handle their own problems. In failing to find a secure place in the urban economy, they become casualties of a fragmented welfare state that was not designed to meet their needs.

There are large numbers of such people who are rootless, uncertain, and not quite able to claim full membership in the mainstream of society. They have left the protective environments provided by their ethnic and regional groups in order to seek new opportunities and a better way of life. The private community support systems of family, friends, and neighborhood are no longer available to facilitate mutual help and aid. Complex and overlapping government bureaucracies created largely to assist the very poor do not offer an effective substitute. Indeed, they tend to delimit self-help and contribute to a breakdown of traditional ways of handling human distress.

A number of these families have ethnic or regional cultural practices that bring them into conflict with people of differing backgrounds. Some of them exhibit irritating behavior, and others have brought with them serious racial prejudices. But in this respect, they are not too different from many better off, self-supporting families from the same geographical or cultural groups.

The stories they tell reveal patterns of conflict, frustration, family disruption, and upward and downward mobility. These difficulties are often unknown or ignored by the middle class caretakers, social workers, teachers, public officials, and others who are primarily responsible for assisting them. The pressures inherent in such situations take their toll when friction, hostility, and insufficiency create unbearable tensions and failure.

THE WELFARE STATE

EVOLUTION

The residents of Underhill are caught up in the complexity and frustration that characterize the long history of government involvement in social welfare. While people of all socioeconomic groups derive benefits from the welfare state, the system evolved primarily to handle complete destitution. It grew out of a series of disjointed, incremental decisions that went beyond the tradition of the English Poor Laws, which viewed relief as a local responsibility. The system does not meet the needs of the people of Underhill because they move in and out of economic and social crises and tend to be just above the legal definition of poverty.

The U.S. had little compassion for the poor until the Settlement House movement of the early twentieth century shifted responsibility for poverty away from the individual onto the social and economic conditions of society. Reformers concerned with the poor sought minimum wage laws, elimination of health hazards, and protective legislation for women, children, the aged, and blind. But poverty persisted even through the affluent 1920s, and the poor continued to be dependent on public and voluntary agencies.

America's belief in individualism and the work ethic was dramatically challenged in the 1930s, when millions of people lost their jobs and the economy was threatened with collapse. Individuals were unemployed because of societal rather than personal problems, and it became apparent that government had to become more involved in economic and social areas. New Deal politics and Keynesian economics saved the situation by developing programs aimed at achieving economic security through unemployment insurance, minimum wage laws, farm subsidies, loans to industry, and aid to home builders. The Social Security system was established in order to provide social insurance for the time when wage income was reduced or stopped, but was not intended to cope with the permanent kind of poverty that afflicts many groups in our society.

World War II provided a stimulus to full employment, and by the 1950s, government was operating on the assumption that rapid economic growth would stimulate full employment. But poverty was not eliminated, and the civil rights and group power movements of the 1960s brought the problems of the poor to the surface once again. The social policy interventions of this period substantially reduced the number of poor by changing public assistance from a low paying, restrictive effort to one that provided improved benefits to most single parent families in need and to other families with incapacitated or unemployed fathers.

At the same time, government sought to create and strengthen interest groups to speak for and involve those who were previously underrepresented, so they could gain more of society's rewards. The claims of these groups were often enforced by a new militancy and backed by threats of disorder. They attacked government programs as insufficient, pointing to the lack of improvement in the quality of schooling, minimal gains in the levels of welfare payments and services, deterioration of neighborhoods, inadequate housing, and limited access to health care. The consequence was that programs to placate the poor and defuse the possibility of civil disruption became part of the doctrine of the welfare state.

Inequality in American life is still widely regarded as an urgent issue, and people accept the view that government has a responsibility to affirm and sustain social values. As a result, Congress taxes certain classes of people more heavily than others and, for reasons of equity or social purpose, has created a welfare state that provides transfers of monies and services to those who are thought to need and deserve it.

This movement toward redistribution of wealth happened gradually, and has not been a subject of conscious public policy debate. Today, however, it is much discussed in the political arena when seeking to answer the question of how much the government shall spend and for whom. One of the difficulties is that pressures in the political market to increase services are not necessarily matched by the ability to pay for them. Moreover, the ensuing tax conflict has led to a struggle between those who advocate the redistribution of wealth and those who fear it will slow down economic growth. At the heart of the problem is the notion that government has to intervene because the market is an undemocratic instrument which does not take care of the disadvantaged.

As government has recognized and responded to the social needs of the nation, it has created powerful social expectations that it has not always been able to meet. Responses to problems have often led to new definitions of the problems and to suggestions for greater government actions. The definition of the poverty line has drifted upward as society has become more affluent. The tragedy is that families such as those in Underhill are often just beyond eligibility for public assistance, a situation that contributes to their marginality and sense of isolation. To a great extent, their condition is defined by the ongoing debate on the propriety of redistributing income as a matter of social policy.

FRAGMENTATION

The involvement of government in human affairs has accelerated considerably since the advent of the Great Society. Hundreds of relatively autonomous agencies are involved in a largely uncoordinated helping process. Policy making tends to be widely decentralized although heavily bureaucratized. The specialization of various helping agencies has resulted in the growth of new and inefficient bureaucracies; mechanisms for the delivery of services have become more complex. The welfare state is an imperfect network of multiple relationships at the local, state, and federal levels.

There are no adequate congressional or administrative mechanisms for reviewing the patchwork of government policies and programs in terms of national needs. We do not have adequate data or criteria for making judgments on legislation and administration. The chairmen of legislative committees are often power holders hidden from public scrutiny who allow the growth of administrative agencies with little restriction. This is part of the price that is paid for the wide dispersion of political power in our checks and balances system.

But it is more than a bureaucratic problem of red tape, inefficiency, unresponsiveness, and resistance to change. As government programs grow and become more complex, government agencies are called on to provide resources for agencies at state and local levels. These institutions then develop contractual relationships for the operation of public housing projects, schools, and other services. This leads to developments like Underhill, where resources and services are channelled through a private development corporation. Thus we find responsibility for aiding residents of the project in the hands of developers who, although well-meaning, sometimes thwart or distort the intent of the primary agency.

Welfare state experiments, such as low and moderate income housing programs, rely largely on the resourcefulness of the poor or the enthusiasm of people like Archie Conover. There is a limited pool of people who are willing to have their families live in working class circumstances even though they have the potential to earn middle class incomes. They tend to be ex-ministers or others who derive personal satisfaction from this kind of work. They have the ability to get along with people, to care deeply about them, and to intervene in the systems that provide services. But the problem of finding and coordinating the various public and private programs is a challenge almost beyond comprehension.

The job calls for political and negotiating skills, an ability to organize and encourage community participation, and the willingness to be an advocate for the residents. At the same time, project management skills that involve maintenance, rent collection, and relationships with owners and higher management are also required. But while HUD guidelines call for them to become involved, such people are offered little guidance, training, or assistance. Even the few managers, like Archie, who are highly motivated and possess some human and social skills find it enormously difficult to function under such conditions.

The welfare state calls on the poor and their caretakers to deal with a variety of unwieldy and complicated organizations. The system is designed largely for the destitute or permanent poor, but as already noted, there is also a large, heterogeneous population who frequently pass back and forth across the established poverty lines. These are individuals who live in a condition of recurring crises rather than one of stable indigency. The result is a very uneven delivery of services and funds, the appearance and existence of unfairness, and the discrediting of the welfare state itself.

This is pointed up with some clarity when Wally is put in jail after his emotional outburst. May has no money or food in the house and turns to the welfare system for assistance. She is told they cannot handle her request for a week or more, and Archie has to intervene in order to get emergency help for the family.

Ada Harris is also upset about the inequities of a system that provides support to people whom she perceives as poor, dirty, and unworthy, while she and her husband are denied urgently needed aid. She finds that the health and social work systems are unable to provide adequate care for low income senior citizens who are ill. Despite the efforts of Archie and others to link the Harrises to organizations designed to help such people, the complexity of their problems and the fact that aid has to come from so many different sources makes this an almost impossible task.

A related and perplexing issue is the question of whether federal or local government is best equipped to handle social needs. Some believe that only the federal government has the necessary power and resources to carry out these responsibilities efficiently and equitably. Others feel it is impossible for the federal government to plan for the needs of different local communities, that only local government is close enough to the people to handle the provision of goods and people-oriented services. The Washington bureaucracies are seen as narrow interest groups incapable of cooperating in the formulation of plans or of subordinating their own interests.

There may not be that much difference between federal and local bureaucracies, and when local organizations are unhelpful or inadequate, the client is adversely affected. The welfare system in Howard County was only marginally effective in providing assistance to the residents of Underhill. The welfare agencies were not given enough resources to carry out their mission, and those which they had available often did not meet the needs of their clients.

People like Clara and Verna, while widely divergent in their personal histories and experiences, find the welfare system of Howard County unable to meet the immediacy of their needs. As a handicapped person with two sons in jail, Verna requires considerable psychological counseling to help her function under extraordinarily difficult circumstances. But the county social worker facing the pressure of a huge case load fails to provide adequate assistance. Fortunately, the ever resourceful Archie is able to connect Verna with a private agency. Clara's occasional ventures into the public welfare system are met with rejection and humiliation, and she observes that sometimes social workers "can make you feel pretty bad, like you're beggin or somethin."

It is apparent that welfare programs are often diffuse, uneven and lacking in compassion, and the problems of those they serve are magnified and distorted by a multiplicity of agencies and rules. In order to survive, the poor are required to develop innovative and often deceptive ways of circumventing inflexible government bureaucracies. They are faced with intolerable situations that challenge the legitimacy of the fragmented welfare state.

COERCION

The American welfare state is largely characterized by its coerciveness and the loss of personal control and self respect this engenders. In its efforts to see to it that only the deserving poor receive benefits, a variety of harsh and discretionary measures are taken to keep the number of people who are eligible to a minimum. For those already receiving assistance, the goal is to ensure that they spend their money well, thereby depriving them of the discretion to choose among alternative expenditures. The belief that the poor find welfare more attractive than work undergirds the coercive nature of this system.

The unemployed and underemployed looking for public welfare, food stamps, and other kinds of assistance find that social workers are frequently not there to aid them but to fend them off in order to keep costs down and maintain control for their agencies. New procedures are not efficient; rather, they generate more work for intake personnel so that fewer applicants can be processed and served. Benefits are distributed on an arbitrary basis and not vested in law; securing them often depends on abject compliance with bureaucratic rules and regulations that exercise enormous influence over their recipients' lives.

As rising costs threaten to bankrupt local and state governments, many place ceilings on welfare payments and make across-the-board reductions. Harsh measures including publishing the names of those receiving aid, sterilization of unwed mothers, and harrassment by investigators have been introduced. Some states have adopted residency laws and revised standards so that applicants do not become eligible for a longer period of time. Hundreds of millions of dollars are spent administering programs intended to discourage the poor from gaining benefits. This is the situation of a number of Underhill residents who, despite the critical nature of their needs, stand at the margin of welfare eligibility.

The moral aspects of the welfare state are based on the belief that the poor must be both helped and watched. Among widely held perceptions of the poor is the view that they are apathetic, profligate, and satisfied with their dependency. Underlying such views are important ideological differences on the work ethic, with many Americans seeing welfare as a means of giving money to lazy people for not working. The work requirement for welfare recipients stems from the resentment of taxpayers who feel that giving the poor financial support without coercion to work results in their selecting welfare rather than jobs.

The view that the poor should be required to work is based not only on the values of the Puritan ethic, but on the belief that they are responsible for their situation rather than the victims of it. This value consensus among most Americans has had a powerful effect on the political process, and seriously constrains efforts to reform the welfare system. As a consequence of the continuing welfare problem, the optimism and benevolent anti-poverty efforts of the 1960s have changed dramatically to cynicism and coercion regarding the welfare poor.

But there is no evidence in these case studies of any absence of character on the part of the poor. Rather, it is the poor themselves who are most victimized by the involuntary aspects of the welfare state. In the well-intentioned desire to guarantee that benefits are used wisely, government agencies deprive the poor and near-poor of the opportunity to choose among alternative expenditures. This reduces their incentive for selective frugality and their capacity to accumulate capital. It also lends credence to the view that the poor are demanding and dissolute, while at the same time apathetic about bettering themselves.

The efforts of the welfare state to influence and control the behavior of its beneficiaries reach into the lives of the residents of the stairwell. All of them have been provided with better housing, but their neighbors are chosen for them. This is particularly unpleasant for Ada Harris, who is forced to leave the project because of her objections to the noise and to the unclean and threatening habits of others. The inability to select one's neighbors, type of housing, and life style also afflicts the Corbins, who eagerly escape from Underhill.

The coerciveness of the welfare state is equally pervasive and destructive of individuality and integrity of others in similar circumstances. They are provided with a wide variety of goods and services, including air conditioning, recreation, and beautiful surroundings, but these may not be the way the poor would decide to invest their own resources. Indeed, a number of stairwell residents would like to have freezers and dishwashers, but this is not possible under regulations imposed by the caretakers.

Some of the families are given food stamps, but this limits the kind and proportion of expenditures they might make if they were given cash instead. In regulating the benefits they receive and the way in which they can be used, we are inhibiting the capacity of the poor to be fully responsible and mature.. Thus the coerciveness of the welfare state makes it extremely difficult to develop the motivation needed to overcome the stifling conditions of dependency.

CORRUPTION

The fragmentation, coerciveness, and contradictions of the welfare state often lead to programs, rules, and regulations that make it corruptible. This is evidenced by increased bureaucratic expansion and profit making at the expense of delivering services to the poor.

Large grants aimed at providing decent housing for all Americans go to profiteers and speculators. Urban renewal and redevelopment programs actually worsen the housing conditions of the poor and near-poor by destroying their homes and neighborhoods. Public schools reinforce the low status of many children and do not change the failure and dropout rates of those at the bottom. While the social services sector is expanding dramatically, its growth is accompanied by an increase in delinquency, mental illness, and other pathologies.

As public assistance programs grow, so do their hierarchical structures and regulations. Thus the welfare system has become a center of disaffection and debate. There are inconsistencies, gaps, and difficulties that prevent millions of people from getting protection. Many of those who receive welfare still live in poverty, and categorical aid misses large numbers of the poor. Combining social services with the distribution of income grants is complex, costly, and demeaning to recipients. The individual usually has to liquidate the few assets he may have and submit to careful scrutiny of income and personal conduct in order to remain in a program. Standards vary widely among the states, the system undermines family stability, and there is little incentive to earn income.

It is difficult to determine just standards for the distribution of funds, goods, and services to the poor and near-poor. Those who are slightly better off but who share a particular need are frequently excluded from benefits, and social insurance programs leave substantial gaps in eligibility and coverage. The bureaucracy decides which hungry old person or which blind person will benefit, and many fall through the chinks of an unfair system.

Programs like Medicaid and the food stamp system are incredibly complicated and require large administrative bureaucracies at the federal, state, and local levels. Such bureaucracies are burdened by confusing regulations and administrative procedures and have been victimized by mismanagement, fraud, and abuse. Their very complexity often leads to administrative breakdowns.

The people of Underhill experience the oppressiveness of the bureaucratic appartus in ways that underscore the corruptibility of the welfare state. In order to survive, they are forced to engage in questionable and sometimes illegal behavior. Rules must be bent to accommodate basic needs, and the uneven application of these rules leads to the belief that they are inequitable and unfair.

Apartments are rented to nuclear families, and relatives and friends are not supposed to move in. But Verna is permitted to have a boyfriend live in her apartment because Archie decides that she needs companionship. Verna's neighbors are uncomfortable about this, and some of them seek to avoid the situation by pretending it doesn't exist.

Ceilings on income create difficulties, and additional monies become a problem or are concealed. Verna's very small earnings at the Sheltered Workshop are discovered and deducted from her welfare check, so she decides to leave her job. May does not go to work until after her recertification takes place in order to avoid a rent increase. Others in the project lie about their salaries and second jobs so their expanded earnings are not used as a basis for higher rentals. The acceptance of government responsibility to manage the financial affairs of such families inevitably involves it in the charge that government fails because what it attempts is impossible.

The rules and regulations imposed on the residents of Stairwell 7 also reveal the corruptibility of the welfare state. Many of the rules are violated, which creates tensions because of the fear of being found out. Thus the improved services and housing are undercut by the imposition of social standards the residents do not like and cannot accept.

THE NEAR-POOR

BETTER TIMES

Although welfare programs make benefits available to some of the near-poor in areas such as food stamps, subsidized housing, and health care, many programs are tantalizingly close but inaccessible for those at the margins of poverty. The situation is compounded by the fact that our society does not have enough jobs for everyone who wants to work. Millions of people at the lower levels of the labor market are unemployed and under-employed because of the combination of economic slowdown and inflation.

This is the situation facing many individuals in Underhill, people who have been self-supporting and thus independent of the more obvious parts of the welfare state in the past. In order to cope with their present circumstances, they romanticize "better times," when they lived near family and friends and were freer to make their own choices. Most of them regard welfare as a temporary status, to be endured but not identified with. As they seek to escape from the terrifying clutches of a system that functions through a "Catch 22" bureaucracy, they hark back to better times so much that they often withdraw and do not make the best of the present.

The people described in this book not only remember better times, but most of them look to a better life in the years ahead. Their lives tend to be based on the assumption that their setbacks are temporary and that things will improve in the future. Whether this is illusion or reality, they have a need to identify with a better world, a world which has been lost but which can be reclaimed.

Wally Bonnoli recalls a childhood in which he is happily surrounded by friends and relatives in an all-Italian town. His self esteem is grounded in the values of group identify and family loyalty; through this recollection, he is able to sustain a view of himself as a cut above his neighbors. Wally also looks forward to better times when he can have his own home, a good job, and pride in his self-sufficiency.

Aunt Matty's better times are associated with nostalgia for her childhood in what she perceives as the wholesome, racially segregated environment of the hill-country. She and the Turnfinders are so dominated by recollections of their regional subculture that they make almost no effort to adapt to their present circumstances in an integrated housing project. Aunt Matty looks forward to the time when she can go home and live on a farm, and Elmer wants a "little house out where they're real far apart." The family sees better times as a personal independence and freedom that is steeped in their own distinctive cultural norms.

Joe Corbin reminisces about the better times he experienced living in a small town where people approached one another in a spirit of neighborliness. In pointing up his desire to be with his "own type of people," Joe looks forward to the time when he can be on his own and regain his self respect. For him and his family, life in Underhill is stifling and humiliating, and they eagerly seek to escape from the welfare apparatus.

Ada's memory of better times is tied almost completely to the world in which she and Clarence lived before his retirement and illness. In recalling the time when Washington was "a lovely place," she reflects on growing up in "nice neighborhoods where everybody spoke and everybody became friendly." Her dream of a better future is related to living in a private house rather than an apartment in a publicly assisted project.

Clara also wants her own place and thinks back to a happy childhood in which "there was always plenty to eat and a nice home." Her recollection of better times is associated with a "strictly all black upbringin" now tied to her search for racial identification and pride. Although she and her children benefit from a number of welfare state programs, they want to be self-supporting. Their experiences and those of many others living in Underhill suggest that welfare is a temporary situation, a view that challenges the widely held belief that we are raising a generation of welfare families.

THE EVASION OF COMMUNITY

A heightened positive remembrance of better times and their coercive placement among neighbors they do not choose leaves welfare recipients profoundly ambivalent about their commitment to local community life. Verbal declarations about the desirability of participation, the equality of racial and ethnic groups, and the need for collective effort are quickly forthcoming. But the welfare population, at least among the near-poor, is a very hesitant group. People participate largely when they are pressed to do so, and some drop out, others choose not to become involved, and all engage in a process of mutual discouragement. The same people, unaware of their welfare status, might make for better neighbors.

The attempt in Underhill to encourage interdependence and a sense of community was largely unsuccessful. Archie attempted to build a community almost instantaneously, and learned that it is a very complex process not given to immediate solutions. In a sense, he sought to accelerate the ecological processes of human interrelationships. This would be difficult under any circumstances, but with a welfare population including diverse people with many problems it became an impossible task.

Despite the idealism of a well motivated developer, the concept of a place for all people was too simplistic. The quest for community is a complex, ongoing process that requires involvement and participation over a considerable period of time. It cannot be accomplished immediately, especially where planning limits the options available to people.

"Community" connotes more than a territory with a physical boundary delineating an urban subarea. The term is used interchangeably with words such as neighborhood, district, section, locality, and society, and often reflects an attitude rather than a place. A community is a spatial configuration as well as a setting for social, psychological, economic, and political interactions.

In the New Towns movements of Great Britain and other countries, the values of the developers served as the basis for creating a community environment. They sought to improve the lives of poor people by moving them to garden cities, where it was thought they would happily work and play in their encapsulated communities. This approach stemmed from the belief that the village or small town was a place where close personal ties among family and friends gave social, economic, and psychological support to the individual.

August Comte and other pioneer sociologists also had a positive perception of community. They viewed it as man's natural hatitat and deplored its breakdown. But the founding father of the theory of community may well be Ferdinand Tönnies, who created a framework for the study of community and society. In community (gemeinschaft), human relationships are seen as intimate, enduring, and based on an understanding of everyone's place in society. Status is ascriptive (based on who you are) rather than achieved (based on what you have done). Roles are clear and specific, people stay where they are and tend not to be socially or physically mobile. The community is relatively homogenous, so that intimate contact and loyalties to place and people can be maintained; the family and the church are seen as the moral custodians of the community with clear, internalized codes and injunctions affecting social relationships and continuity.

Society (gesellschaft) refers to the large scale, impersonal, and contractual ties whose emergence was deplored by nineteenth century and later sociologists. They were concerned with the breakdown of community life that stemmed from the upheavals of industrialization, and viewed the competition, conflict, and alienation of the city as tragic aspects of contemporary society.

Tönnies saw social change as a continuum between gemeinschaft and gesellschaft. On the one hand are kinship, neighborhood, and friendship, which are the basis of virtue and morality; on the other hand is capitalism, which represents the loss of community. The dichotomy between community and society is at the heart of a great deal of the conflict between tradition and modernism, between the old order and the new one brought about by the industrial and democratic revolutions.

Some analysts see the gemeinschaft-gesellschaft continuum as an over-simplification, believing that ways of life do not necessarily coincide with settlement patterns. Since the totality of relations may not be found in a particular locality, we may not be talking about the eclipse of a community or local system but, rather, about changing processes and institutions that affect human relationships.

There are differing perceptions about what constitutes a community in contemporary society. Some see urbanization as the extension of patterns typical of the city and as representing a peculiar kind of community formation rather than destruction. Others view suburbia as signifying the end of community with its personal loyalties, because it weakens national, regional, community, and family ties, impairing the primary group and the self-concept of the individual.

In this study, we are concerned not only with the immediate social environment of Underhill families, but also with the network of actual social relationships they maintain, regardless of whether these are confined to the local area or extend beyond its boundaries. There may be a built-in transiency in places like Underhill that works against community. All of the residents maintain primary group contact with friends and relatives outside the project. They also want their own homes and see their stay in Underhill as temporary. Even Verna, who is totally dependent on the welfare system, says she would like to have a house of her own so the kids can have a backyard and a basement in which to entertain their friends.

The residents of Underhill are not very involved in voluntary institutions, despite Archie's insistence in the screening process that they become active in the Tenants Council and "do things around here." May and Clara are among the more committed people who seek to build a better life for themselves and their neighbors through community participation. When they first move to Underhill, the Tenants Council becomes a vehicle for their self-expression and dedication to community self-help.

May organizes a project to create a play area for younger children, a rummage sale to raise funds for a Christmas party, and a fight against yearly recertification of income that could lead to higher rentals. Because the residents have common problems, May sees the need for collective efforts and for unity. At the same time, she recognizes the short term nature of residence in the project, a factor that adds to the difficulty of developing a sense of community.

Clara also feels the need for a strong Tenants Council, and becomes involved in organizing a library in the project office. But after a hard day at work, she has too little time and energy to see the program through.

Despite her belief in the value of community participation, she finds that others don't want the Tenants Council or the manager "tellin residents what to do." Most prefer to make their own decisions and be left alone.

In order to get an apartment, the families in Underhill are required to make a verbal pledge to join in the development of community programs. But most of them feel ambivalent about living in a publicly assisted project and have minimal ties to local community life. Their welfare status contributes to feelings of anomie and sometimes to hostility toward the common effort they are called on to make. There are many obstacles to trust that reduce their capacity to engage in self-help, and third parties, including social workers and housing managers, are called on to deal with their problems, disputes, and needs.

Programs like 236 housing and their support systems make the economic and social conditions of poor and near-poor people like those living in Underhill quite visible. Food stamps, medical cards, and so forth add to the embarrassment they face and inhibit the possibility of developing a more genuine community. It is the omnipresence of the institutions of the welfare state that undermines the potential for real neighborliness and community cohesion.

THE PROTECTIVE ENVIRONMENT

Whether or not there is a culture of poverty is far less important than whether or not American society includes some alternatives which allow the poor to live among one another with some fairly acceptable level of self esteem and potential for mutual assistance. In the past, the protective ethnic or racial community has been the major group within which people have maintained self respect without first achieving financial success. Demographic changes, reinforced by current welfare programs, seem to endanger this protective community, at least among the near-poor. The visibility and categorical character of the welfare state also make it especially difficult for the kinds of people living in Underhill to relate positively to each other and to maintain their self regard.

The agricultural revolution and its automated technology contributed to major economic and demographic changes, driving large numbers of the poor and near-poor into the cities. Entering labor markets where many of them faced prejudice and discrimination combined with a lack of skills and education needed for many jobs, they had little alternative but to turn to the welfare state for assistance.

Massive migration and natural increase have concentrated almost three quarters of the national population in metropolitan areas. The poor and minorities dominate the declining central cities, while the new suburban communities are largely middle and upper income white. Social and economic differences between the core areas and the suburbs have increased as the trend toward placing manufacturing and commercial employment in suburbia goes on. But more and more low income families are moving out of the central cities to suburban areas like Columbia, and new immigrants are also settling in places believed to offer greater opportunities.

As industrialization and urbanization have magnified social problems, the role of the federal government in meeting human needs has also grown. High unemployment and inflation have contributed to a scarcity of jobs in the lower levels of the labor market, with those that are available tending to be insecure and low paying. Unemployed and underemployed individuals who have left the supportive environments of family and friends are forced to turn to government agencies for food stamps, income maintenance, and other forms of welfare. These interventions used to be handled, if at all, by private parties or individual families. But as conditions in society change, pressure is mounting for the government to do more and more.

The community has protected many individuals from the threatening world beyond. It is a place where people tend to have a sense of belonging and safety, often bolstered by social cohesion and identification made meaningful by the structures, values, and habits with which people order their lives. Communities create a framework for interpersonal and group affinity, often along racial, religious, ethnic and socioeconomic lines.

Family and friendship ties develop in communities in order to provide a supportive, protective social environment. The widow, the orphan, the jobless, the sick, and the lonely are aided and nurtured by private community and familial welfare systems. Many of these activities have been institutionalized in a wide variety of movements and structures that emerged in response to the stresses of urban living. Residences and self-help clubs were established by labor organizations for working men and women. The social work movement led to the creation of settlement houses and centers for neighborhood services and community action. And fraternal societies were organized with memberships predicated on village or city of origin and on cultural or religious identification.

Patterns of association among individuals are strongly influenced by the social context in which they occur. Certain segments of the population lose their sure-footedness when they are uprooted and dispersed, and so seek to regain their emotional security in their own primary groups. For example, some low income blacks in Underhill prefer to sit on the front steps talking to one another rather than go to the theater or a concert at the lake. For such people, survival needs and ingroup identification can be more important than middle class entertainment.

Joe Corbin and his family face a similar problem as they are thrust into the welfare environment of Underhill. They are oppressed not only by the different and unpleasant life styles of their neighbors, but by the ridicule and scorn they are subjected to by their friends outside the project. Joe's coworkers see welfare assistance as signifying laziness, profligacy, and character deficiency. In identifying welfare with a kind of moral corruption, they misunderstand and misinterpret the crisis situation that forces the Corbins to accept temporary aid.

For Wally Bonnoli, life in the welfare milieu threatens his need to be self-sufficient as well as his claim to respectability. His residence in Underhill is a constant and visible reminder that he and his family are not making it and that they require welfare assistance. These circumstances challenge the values he learned in his independent, hard-working, ethnic family, and contribute to his frequent episodes of conflict and violence.

All those living in Stairwell 7 have lost the sheltered environments of their ethnic, racial, and regional groups. They are cut off from the daily support and comfort usually provided by family, friends, and neighbors. As they become involved with a complex and often demeaning welfare state bureaucracy, many of them develop negative self-perceptions that contribute to their isolation and inability to live together harmoniously. This is a particularly serious situation for poor and near-poor people like those who live in Underhill, individuals whose marginal position denies them both full access to the benefits of the welfare state and a secure place in the economy.

PEOPLE, PLANNING AND CHOICES

One of the major instruments of the welfare state is the planning process, which brings together social scientists and planners seeking to improve the quality of life for all Americans. During the last century, planners and reformers have focused on the physical environment as a decisive influence in shaping human behavior. The expectation was that improved physical environments would contribute both to a better way of life for, and to changes in the behavior patterns of, the poor and the culturally disadvantaged. This concept of physical environmental determinism is tied to the belief that the middle class is an appropriate model and that the poor will benefit from upward mobility.

The planners and developers of Columbia have been conducting such an experiment by providing better physical facilities as a setting for human interaction and individual growth. But these prove inadequate for successfully bringing together people of diverse incomes, races, health conditions, ages, and life styles.

The situation is exemplified by Clara's description of her family's move to Columbia from the rough Baltimore ghetto: "This is a city, you know, and where you have a city, you have people and you have problems. So all I did for my kids was struggle and work hard and move em to a better environment. Things that I thought I was gettin em away from, they still exist right here."

New towns do have the advantage of more efficient and attractive physical plants that generally improve the quality of life for their residents. But far less can be expected when it comes to improving the delivery of welfare services. Where planning means the coercive management of community life, it may be especially counterproductive.

It is unrealistic to expect that new towns and new physical environments by themselves can transform the lives of people with serious problems. In Columbia, the modern open space school doesn't assure youngsters a good education, the beautiful Interfaith Center doesn't contribute to a sense of religious identification and commitment, and the new medical facility doesn't provide adequate health care for those who can't afford it. Instead, handsome teen centers become ethnic territories; lovely parks and lakes emerge as locations for racial confrontation and violence. Attractive projects like Underhill become tension ridden and unpleasant.

The planning process in Columbia and Underhill is grounded in the belief that racial and socioeconomic heterogeneity enriches the lives of the people, promotes tolerance of social and cultural differences, broadens the educational experiences of children, and encourages exposure to alternative ways of life. This social philosophy of the developers of Columbia stimulated their efforts to bring into the town a high proportion of middle class blacks and more limited numbers of low income people.

Mixing heterogeneous people frequently results in some conflict; indeed, conflict between neighbors is very common even in affluent and relatively homogeneous areas. But in places like Underhill, it is virtually inevitable because the project lacks basic amenities, offers little aural and visual privacy, and is set in a community planned almost entirely for affluent people. All of this adds to the hypertension from which many of the residents suffer, making it difficult for them to adjust.

While physical planning has been accepted for more than half a century and economic planning since the 1930s, social planning has only been recognized recently. Many planners working in antipoverty and Model Cities programs found themselves involved in programs geared to the development of human resources. In seeking basic changes in the delivery of services, they attempted to use rational methods to identify goals and to establish targets and priorities. Social planning was thought to involve a more comprehensive process than traditional welfare programs, which were implemented without the benefits of rational planning and a full understanding of the consequences of intervention.

Social planners and their allies called for the development of governmental institutions that would bring the knowledge of the social sciences and economics to bear on broad social programs. They felt that bringing social scientists into the inner councils of the national administration would foster systematic approaches to social programming because it would create social accounting processes to define and assess progress toward long range goals.

Critics of the trend toward rationality in planning said we lacked the theoretical ability to describe or predict our social problems, nor did we have the societal consensus or civic power to deal with them. They felt that citizens had to be protected from administrative abuses, the biases of planners, and the condescension of caretakers. This was a concerted challenge to the belief of the 1960s that we could plan and develop institutional arrangements to produce whatever social circumstances we desired.

In time, a number of contrary perceptions arose—the ideas that nothing works, that large organizations seek only to serve their own interests, and that social interventions are not helpful. Confidence in the government's ability to achieve its declared objectives waned, while the inadequacy of social knowledge and economic analyses became apparent. The failure of a number of social experiments led to a loss of faith in the social sciences and to re-examination of old premises.

A major concern is that the planned use of our resources to achieve social objectives carries with it the danger of additional government controls over individual behavior. A resident of another stairwell expressed the problem this way: "I think Archie Conover is trying to play God. Once in awhile you get someone with that kind of power over people's lives, and sooner or later it's gonna mess em up. They're gonna get to that point where they're thinking, 'Oh, wow, man; I am it.' I don't like the idea of Columbia because I don't like the idea of having everything planned out for me. I don't like some guy up in a padded office deciding what I'm gonna do. They ought to leave people alone and let em go about things in their own way."

The question is whether we can create conditions in which individual choices are maximized or whether central planning requires adherence to some kind of blueprint. It seems evident that government planning ultimately results in a centralized process in which key decisions emerge in the form of governmental edicts. Thus we end up with inflexible bureaucracies in which the planner's idea of what constitutes the good society is imposed on the individual. Although we cannot afford to invest our resources on a haphazard, inefficient basis, there must be limitations on the further extension of government power and influence over the individual.

The complex programs of the federal bureaucracy limit its ability to deliver intended services, a situation which suggests that simplicity should be the key to any new social initiatives. Hence, the most manageable approach to future social policy may well be the consolidation of a number of existing programs into a single form of public assistance delivered to the poor in cash. Through flat money grants or some version of the negative income tax, which is uncoercive and not very visible, a given level of income would be the right of every American. Eligibility for income guarantees would be based solely on a means test and applied through uniform national standards, perhaps with regional cost of living adjustments. Those who work but do not earn enough to meet the minimums would have their earnings supplemented and would be allowed to keep enough of their earnings after taxes and expenses to provide an incentive to work.

President Carter is considering a promising but expensive welfare reform proposal that calls for a guaranteed minimum annual income to all Americans earning below an established national poverty level. The plan replaces the current food stamp, Supplemental Security Income, and Aid to Families with Dependent Children programs. To avoid the problem of paying people who don't work, Carter is leaning toward a complex system that would remove the employable poor from the welfare population. Only ten or twelve percent of present welfare recipients can work; most of the rest are children, mothers with young children, the aged, and the disabled. The suggestion is that able-bodied adults should be trained for jobs or paid unemployment compensation, with those who cannot work qualifying for a single program of cash assistance.

This approach is opposed by those who argue that restrictive, regulated forms of assistance are needed to prevent the poor from squandering public aid on nonessentials such as whiskey, cigarettes, and entertainment. However, experimental programs conducted by HEW in recent years indicate that most poor people spend cash assistance on basic needs. Moreover, cash assistance programs would be easier to control than the current social welfare labyrinth.

Others argue for consolidating and building on existing programs because they fear the imposition of a uniform national payment would cause millions of families and elderly Americans to lose such noncash benefits as food stamps and housing subsidies. The answer may be the creation of a unitary system that integrates cash and in-kind assistance at a high enough level so that families who benefit from multiple programs do not lose from a single cash payment.

It seems clear, however, that numerous social programs cannot be eliminated because they have become part of the expectations of the American people. Social Security, unemployment insurance, welfare for the disabled and blind, health insurance, and other public investments are here to stay. Moreover, certain kinds of services, such as counseling for problem families, would probably not be available if government didn't provide them.

We live in a society in which individuals are subordinated by organizations, both public and private. Paternalism on the part of the state as well as private organizations stifles individual initiative and innovation, while institutions become so bureaucratized that only the organization man can survive. Thus we are victimized by mechanistic concepts in a technological society where individuals are seen more and more as structural units to be built into a planned system.

Our democratic society is faced with great strains because government has become a costly, large, and complex mechanism. While government has developed social institutions to help provide minimum standards for human health and decency, the constant dilemma in our desire to help persons in need is that we don't want to reduce individual initiative and self-reliance. We have to face up to the issue of how much government intevention is necessary to achieve gains not attainable through voluntary efforts. At the same time, we must be concerned with undue government interference with the personal and economic freedom of the individual. We must strive for a society in which people can best meet their own requirements, while providing public and private mechanisms to meet human needs that would otherwise be unmet.

The power of men to remake themselves and society must coexist with knowledge of the limits of our individual and social resources. This involves agreement on what constitutes inequity, a recognition of priorities, and a sense of fairness in the distribution of benefits. The challenge is to make the decisions that are essential without being authoritarian.

Our goal should be both upgrading opportunity for those whose potential is unrealized and assisting those who must be helped. At the same time, our institutions should encourage maximum individual freedom and the minimum possible amount of government interference in the lives of people. We need a caring government that meets basic human needs but emphasizes individual freedom of choice to the greatest extent possible.

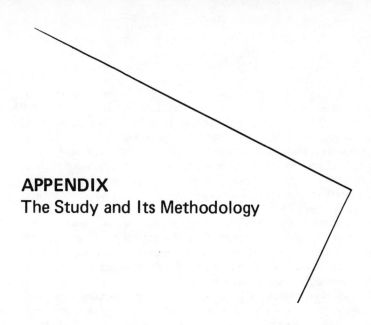

APPENDIX
The Study and Its Methodology

The Underhill project was identified during an earlier analysis I made of comparative conditions in new towns around the world. It represented an ideal laboratory for gathering data on people who have been uprooted from sheltered environments and who face serious social and economic problems. The inadequate efforts of the welfare state to assist them point to serious limitations in public policy.

The study of such people goes beyond analysis of hierarchical differences between categories to a research methodology that examines individual, subjective perceptions of the environment. The narratives are tape-recorded and told in the words of the residents. The background of each family is traced to ascertain where they came from, how they lived previously, what brought them to Underhill, how they adjusted, what problems they face, and which of their needs are unmet.

These case studies combine the traditional approaches used in the social sciences, including questionnaires, interviews, biographies, and participant observation. In addition to securing basic biographical and census data, a very comprehensive schedule was applied to each of the respondents. The items dealt with family and friendship patterns in the stairwell, the project, the town, and the larger society. Contacts with the institutions of the welfare state were also examined.

The questions asked helped us understand factors influencing the quality of life of the residents and relating to such matters as health care, work, community facilities, education, religion, age differences, recreation, shopping, transportation, and housing. The extent to which management was helpful or not helpful was probed, as were the usefulness of public and private social service agencies and the tenants organization.

Special attention was paid to racial and socioeconomic factors that can create tensions and are often cumulative. Sixty percent of Underhill families earn $6,000 a year or less, as compared with 59 percent in the 236 program nationally. But 47 percent of Underhill families are black, a much higher proportion than the 22 percent in the entire 236 program. Moreover, the proportion of black children in Underhill increases as ages go up, reaching 77 percent among teenagers.

It may be that the mix of people in Underhill is too heavily lower socioeconomic and black. However, these data should not be interpreted to suggest that racial and socioeconomic mixing are undesirable, but rather to point up that the mixing of different kinds of people, many with serious difficulties, is being done under very poor conditions.

The research was conducted in a number of visits to Columbia from 1972 to 1974, with most of the interviews taking place in the summer of 1973, when I lived in the project. After considerable analysis of Underhill, the residents of Stairwell 7 were selected for in-depth study as the most representative group in the project. Follow-up interviews, conducted in 1975 and 1976, determined what had happened to the residents of the stairwell.

Numerous interviews were held with officials of the Columbia Association, Howard Research and Development Corporation (the town developers), County Human Relations Commission, Community Action Agency, Commission for the Aging, National Institute of Housing Management, Department of Housing and Urban Development, U.S. Civil Rights Commission, County Department of Social Services, Family Service Agency, County Police Department, County Schools, the media, and representatives of other public and private caretaking institutions.

In order to gain the cooperation of the residents, the sanction of the Tenants Council was sought for the interviewing process. The leadership of the Council discussed the research project in general terms, and then wrote to all the tenants in order to introduce me and ask for their cooperation. This facilitated the entire process and, I believe, minimized the distortion of data sometimes caused by the presence of an investigator. Very little resistance was encountered, and the one person who refused to be interviewed subsequently agreed when payment was offered. None of the others was offered money in advance, but those whose stories appear in the book were given money months after the interviews were completed.

Sociologists usually live in the communities they study, even if only for a short time. They share the experiences and emotions of the people in whom they are interested, and this sometimes affects their presumed detachment. Despite attempts to describe, explain, and make generalizations that are justified by the data, the validity of their findings ultimately rests on their own judgments. But as Gans (1963) has indicated, participant-observation enables the researcher to get close to the realities of social life, and this more than overcomes its other deficiencies.

All of the case histories are presented as they were related and edited, with no substantial changes in substance or content. However, some of the biographical data and names of the residents have been altered, as have the names of the nearby small towns from which some of them came.

The intensive studies of the lives of these families give us a great deal of the flavor and detail not available in more traditional research efforts. The empirical data come alive as their experiences are told, whereas abstract studies often neglect the more human factors involved. In telling their stories, my wish has been to reveal more of the history and problems of such marginal people. Hopefully this will contribute to a greater understanding of their needs and offer useful insights for making policy decisions that impact on our increasingly mobile society.

REFERENCES

AARON, Henry (1972) "Financing welfare reform and income distribution." Paper presented at *Welfare: A National Policy,* A Symposium at the University of California at Los Angeles, September 29.

ALEXANDER, Tom (1972) "The social engineers retreat under fire." *Fortune,* October.

BANFIELD, Edward C. (1970) *The Unheavenly City: The Nature and Future of Our Urban Crisis.* Boston: Little, Brown.

BELL, Colin and NEWBY, Howard (1972) *Community Studies.* New York: Praeger.

BELL, Daniel (1974) "The public household: on 'fiscal sociology' and the liberal society." *Public Interest* 37 (Fall).

——— (1973) *The Coming of Post-Industrial Society.* New York: Basic Books.

BERGER, Peter L. and NEUHAUS, Richard John (1977) *To Empower People.* Washington, D.C.: American Enterprise Institute for Public Policy Research.

BLAU, Peter M. (1969) "Structure of social associations," in Walter L. Wallace, ed., *Sociological Theory.* Chicago: Aldine.

BLOOMBERG, Warner and SCHMANDT, Henry J. [eds.] (1968) *Power, Poverty and Urban Policy.* Beverly Hills, Calif.: Sage.

CAPOCCIA, Victor A. (1973) "Social welfare planning and the new federalism: the Allied Services Act." *J. of the Amer. Institute of Planners* 39, 4 (July).

Changing Issues for National Growth [Third Biennial Report on National Growth and Development] (1976) Washington, D.C.: USGPO.

CLOWARD, Richard A. and PIVEN, Frances Fox (1977) "The acquiescence of social work." *Society* 14, 2 (January/February).

COHEN, Nathan E. (1972) "The family assistance plan: an autopsy." Paper presented at *Welfare: A National Policy,* A Symposium at the University of California at Los Angeles, September 29.

DAVIDOFF, Paul (1975) "Working toward redistributive justice." *J. of the Amer. Institute of Planners* 41, 5 (September).

DAVIDSON, Roger H. (1977) "Those Carter reforms." Los Angeles *Times,* January 16.

DOBZHANSKY, Theodosius (1964) *Heredity and the Nature of Man.* New York: Harcourt, Brace and World.

ETZIONI, Amitai (1976) "Old people and public policy." *Soc. Policy* 7, 3 (November/December).

FRIED, Marc (1963) "Grieving for a lost home," in Leonard J. Duhl, ed., *The Urban Condition.* New York: Basic Books.

FRIEDEN, Bernard J. and MORRIS, Robert [eds.] (1968) *Urban Planning and Social Policy.* New York: Basic Books.

FRIEDMAN, Milton (1977) "Containing spending." *Society* 14, 3 (March/April).

GAFFERT, Gary (1973) "The future of economic inequality and the planning of urban services." *J. of the Amer. Institute of Planners* 39, 3 (May).

GANS, Herbert J. (1963) "Effects of the move from city to suburb," in Leonard J. Duhl, ed., *The Urban Condition.* New York: Basic Books.

——— (1952) "Urbanism and suburbanism as ways of life," in A. M. Rose, ed., *Human Behaviour and Social Processes*. London: Routledge.

GINZBERG, Eli and SOLOW, Robert M. (1974) "Some lessons of the 1960s." *Pub. Interest* 34 (Winter).

——— (1974) "An introduction to this special issue." *Pub. Interest* 34 (Winter).

GLAZER, Nathan (1971) "The limits of social policy." *Commentary* 52, 3 (September).

——— (1967) "Housing problems and housing policies." *Pub. Interest* 7.

GRODZINS, Morton (1968) "The federal system," in *Goals for Americans*. New York: Prentice-Hall.

HAVEMANN, Joel (1977) "The latest stab at welfare reform." Los Angeles *Times*, February 27.

HOLLINGSHEAD, A. B. and ROGLER, L. H. (1963) "Attitudes toward slums and public housing in Puerto Rico," in Leonard J. Duhl, ed., *The Urban Condition*. New York: Basic Books.

KILLINGSWORTH, Charles C. (1972) "Employment as an alternative to welfare." Paper presented at *Welfare: A National Policy*, A Symposium at the University of California at Los Angeles, September 29.

KRISTOL, Irving (1974) "Taxes, Poverty and Equality." *Pub. Interest* 37 (Fall).

LEVANDER, Val (1973) Ellicott City, Md. *Times*, January 18—March 1.

LEVITAN, Sar A. and TAGGART, Robert (1976) *The Promise of Greatness: The Social Programs of the Last Decade and Their Major Achievements*. Cambridge, Mass.: Harvard Univ. Press.

LEWIS, Oscar (1965) *La Vida*. New York: Random House.

LIEBMAN, Lance (1974) "Social intervention in a democracy." *Pub. Interest* 34 (Winter).

LONG, Norton E. (1977) "A Marshall Plan for cities." *Pub. Interest* 46 (Winter).

MARMOR, Theodore R. and REIN, Martin (1972) "Flimflam flop in welfare." *Society* 9, 8 (June).

MARTINDALE, Don (1964) "The formation and destruction of communities," in G. K. Zollschan and W. Hirsch, eds., *Explorations in Social Change*. London: Routledge.

MILLER, S. M. (1971) "Sharing the burden of change," in Louise Knapp, ed., *The White Majority*. New York: Random House.

——— and BLOOMBERG, Warner, Jr. (1968) "Shall the poor always be impoverished?" in Warner Bloomberg, Jr. and Henry J. Schmandt, eds., *Power, Poverty and Urban Policy*. Beverly Hills, Calif.: Sage.

MILLER, S. M. and RATNER, Ronnie Steinberg (1972) "The American resignation: the new assault on equality." *Soc. Policy* (May/June).

MINAR, D. W. and GREER, S. (1968) *The Concept of Community*. Chicago: Aldine.

MONDALE, Walter F. (1968) "Reporting on the social state of the union." *Transaction* (June).

MOYNIHAN, Daniel J. (1965) *The Negro Family: The Case for National Action*. Washington, D.C.: U.S. Department of Labor, Office of Policy Planning and Research.

NATHAN, Richard P. (1977) "Modernize the system, don't wholly discard it." Los Angeles *Times*, February 27.

National Academy of Sciences (1972) *Freedom of Choice in Housing* (Report of the Social Science Panel). Washington, D.C.

NISBET, R. (1966) *The Sociological Tradition*. London: Heinemann.

"Nixon, the Great Society, and the future of social policy" [A Symposium] (1973) *Commentary* 55 (May).

PARSONS, T. (1966) *Societies*. Englewood Cliffs, N.J.: Prentice-Hall.

PERLOFF, Harvey S. (1963) "Social planning in the metropolis," in Leonard J. Duhl, ed., *The Urban Condition*. New York: Basic Books.

PIVEN, Frances Fox and CLOWARD, Richard A. (1971) *Regulating the Poor: The Functions of Public Relief.* New York: Pantheon.

PLOTNICK, Robert D. and SKIDMORE, Felicity (1975) *Progress Against Poverty: Review of the 1964-1974 Decade.* New York: Academic Press.

President's Committee on Urban Housing ["The Kaiser Committee"] (1968) "A Decent Home." Washington, D.C.: USGPO.

Presidential Commission on Income Maintenance Programs (1969) *Poverty and Plenty: The American Paradox.* Washington, D.C.: USGPO.

RAINWATER, Lee (1969) "The American underclass," *Trans-action* 6, 4 (February).

RAWLS, John (1971) *A Theory of Justice.* Cambridge, Mass.: Belknap.

ROUSE, James W. (1973) Address to the Association for New Community Social Planning. Columbia, Md., May.

——— (1966) Address to the National Association of Mutual Savings Banks. Philadelphia, Pa., May 17.

SANDBERG, Neil C. (1973) "The realities of integration in new and old towns," in Harvey S. Perloff and Neil C. Sandberg, eds., *New Towns: Why—And For Whom?* New York: Praeger.

SCHULTZ, Charles L. et al. (1972) *Setting National Priorities: The 1973 Budget.* Washington, D.C.: Brookings.

SCOTT, Mel (1969) *American City Planning.* Berkeley: Univ. of California Press.

SHILS, Edward (1972) *The Intellectuals and the Powers and Other Essays.* Chicago: Univ. of Chicago Press.

STEIN, Bruno (1972) "Poverty and the present welfare system." Paper presented at *Welfare: A National Policy,* A Symposium at the University of California at Los Angeles, September 29.

STEIN, Maurice (1964) *The Eclipse of Community.* New York: Harper and Row.

STEINER, Gilbert Y. (1974) "Reform follows reality: the growth of welfare." Pub. Interest 34 (Winter).

SUTTLES, Gerald D. (1969) "Anatomy of a slum." *Trans-action* 6, 4 (February).

SUTTON, Gordon F. (1968) "Policy implications of some non-economic dimensions of urban poverty," in Warner Bloomberg, Jr. and Henry J. Schmandt, eds., *Power, Poverty and Urban Policy.* Beverly Hills, Calif.: Sage.

TÖNNIES, Ferdinand (1957) *Gemeinschaft and Gesellschaft* (Community and Society). New York: Harper Torchbook.

"U.S. Courts Order Scattered Projects." (1974) *Trends in Housing* 18, 5 (September/October).

U.S. Department of Housing and Urban Development (1971) *Management of HUD: Insured Multi-Family Projects under Section 221(d)3 and Section 236.* Washington, D.C.: USGPO.

WALLACE, Walter L. [ed.] (1969) *Sociological Theory.* Chicago: Aldine.

WEINBERG, Nathan (1977) "Advancing Equality." *Society* 14, 3 (March/April).

WESTERGAARD, J. H. (1972) "Sociology: the myth of classlessness," in R. Blackburn, ed., *Ideology in Social Science.* New York: Fontana.

WILBER, Charles K. and JAMESON, Kenneth P. (1977) "Beyond pragmatism in the American economy." *Society* 14, 3 (March/April).

WILDAVSKY, Aaron (1973) "Government and the people." *Commentary* 56, 2 (August).

WILSON, James Q. and RACHAL, Patricia (1977) "Can the government regulate itself?" *Pub. Interest* 46 (Winter).

WRIGHT, Sonia R. and WRIGHT, James D. (1975) "Income maintenance and work behavior." *Soc. Policy* 6, 2 (September/October).

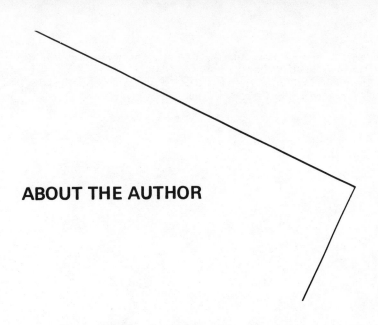

ABOUT THE AUTHOR

NEIL C. SANDBERG has been a practitioner in the field of human relations for more than twenty-five years, lecturing and writing extensively on ethnic, cultural and intergroup problems in a plural society. Dr. Sandberg is professor of sociology at Loyola Marymount University in Los Angeles and Western Regional Director of The American Jewish Committee, where he also serves as advisor on community relations to a number of government, private and religious institutions. He is author of *Ethnic Identity and Assimilation: The Polish-American Community* (1974) and coeditor of *New Towns: Why—And For Whom?* (1973).